Conceived Presences

A *volume in the series*

Massachusetts Studies
in Early Modern Culture

Edited by Arthur F. Kinney

Conceived Presences

Literary Genealogy
in Renaissance
England

RAPHAEL FALCO

UNIVERSITY OF MASSACHUSETTS PRESS

AMHERST

LC 94–14812
ISBN 0–87023–935–X
Designed by Susan Bishop
Set in Linotron Garamond No. 3 by Keystone Typesetting, Inc.
Printed and bound by Braun-Brumfield, Inc.

Library of Congress Cataloging-in-Publication Data
Falco, Raphael, 1952–
Conceived presences : literary genealogy in Renaissance England /
Raphael Falco.
p.   cm.—(Massachusetts studies in early modern culture)
Includes bibliographical references (p.) and index.
ISBN 0–87023–935–X (alk. paper)
1. English poetry—Early modern, 1500–1700—History and criticism.
2. Nationalism and literature—England—History—16th century.
3. Nationalism and literature—England—History—17th century.
4. Influence (Literary, artistic, etc.) 5. Authority in literature.
6. Renaissance—England. I. Title. II. Series.
PR545.N27F35   1994
821'.309—dc20   94–14812
                                                                        CIP
British Library Cataloguing in Publication data are available.

An earlier version of Chapter 1 appeared in *Studies in Philology* 89, no. 1 (1992),
© 1992 by the University of North Carolina Press; an earlier version of Chapter
2 appeared in *Modern Philology* 91, no. 1 (1993), published by the University of
Chicago Press, © 1993 by the University of Chicago, all rights reserved. Both
are used by permission.

For my mother and father

This conceived presence of antient and the true presence of moderne masters will do us more good, if we do constantly beleeve, that the estimation of these present and following times dependeth on the judgement of those whom we make choice of for the reforming of our works.

 —Franciscus Junius, *The Painting of the Ancients,* 1638

CONTENTS

ACKNOWLEDGMENTS

B ecause this is a book about genealogy I am particularly self-conscious about the list of mentors, friends, and colleagues whose names follow in a brief catalogue. While I am grateful to all of them for the improvements their suggestions fostered in the text, it goes without saying that they are not responsible for any infelicities in the final version.

My gratitude to Anthony Low is profound and probably inexpressible. I began this project as a dissertation under his direction, and his erudition continues to serve as a model.

I am grateful to Daniel Javitch and Ernest Gilman, both of whom read the manuscript at various stages of completion. Professor Javitch and I spent many a thunderous half hour on the IRT, discussing the Renaissance at the top of our lungs. His help has been of particular significance since I began to think about genealogy, genre, and literary transmission in the sixteenth century.

I am grateful to many people who encouraged me at different stages of the project, including Roger Deakins, Blanford Parker, Harold Bloom, Kenneth Daley, Devorah Silberstein, Emily Rothman, Richard Harrier, Elizabeth Mazzola, Rosanna Camerlingo, Deniz Şengel, Pamela Boker, Lyell Asher, Steven Shankman, and Daniel Epstein.

I am grateful to Arthur F. Kinney, my editor at the University of Massachusetts Press, for his consideration and his firm support during the march toward publication. In addition, I am indebted to two anonymous readers for the Press for their meticulous comments, and to Anne Lake Prescott, a later reader, whose recommendations I have also had the chance to include.

This study was supported by a Lane Cooper Fellowship and by a New York University Penfield Award.

Chapter 1 appeared as an article in *Studies in Philology* (Winter 1991); chapter 2 appeared in *Modern Philology* (Summer 1993). I am grateful to those journals for permission to reprint.

Special thanks go to Susan Braudy, who about ten years ago suggested—or commanded—that I go to graduate school.

The dedication acknowledges my deepest and longest debt. Besides my parents, my sister Jody and her husband, Jeffrey Steinman, have supported my work with enthusiasm.

David J. Rothman's friendship and brilliant force have sustained me.

And Ani makes it all worthwhile.

Introduction

He was a kind of nothing, titleless,
Till he had forged himself a name o' th' fire
Of burning Rome.
　　　　　　　—*Coriolanus,* V. i

In the *Genealogia Deorum Gentilium,* Boccaccio shrewdly con-cludes his chapter on the origin of poetry with a catalogue of genealogical choices, refusing to pledge himself to any particular one. In a way, he endorses genealogical rummaging, protesting that scholars are at variance ("discordantes") and that there is a dearth of evidence in classical authors:

Apparet tamen ex temporibus descriptis, si Leontio credendum sit, apud Grecos prius quam apud Hebreos, et si Veneto, apud Caldeos prius nunc quam apud Grecos comparuisse poesim. Si vero Paolo fidem prestare velimus, sequetur Moysem primo quam Babilonios aut Grecos eiusdem fuisse magistrum. Ego autem quanumcunque Aristotiles [*sic*] dicat, ratione forsan superiori tractus, poetas primos fuisse theologos, existi-mans eos Grecos intellexisse . . . non credam huius poesis sublimes effectus . . . sed nec in Museo, seu Lyno, vel Orpheo quantumcunque vetustissimis poetis (nisi, ut arbitrantur aliqui, Musaeus et Moyses unus et idem sint) primo infusos . . . cum legamus Moysem, hoc percitum, ut reor, desiderio, Pentatheuci partem maximam non soluto stilo, sed heroyco scripsisse carmine, Spiritu Sancto dictante.

It appears, however, from descriptions at the time, if Leontius is to be believed, that poetry came into existence among the Greeks before the Hebrews, and if we believe the Venetian [Paolino], then among the Chaldeans before the Greeks. If we put our faith in Paul, it follows that Moses before the Babylonians or the Greeks themselves was the first master. But, to be sure, Aristotle says, perhaps for the reasons above, that poets—meaning the Greeks—were the first theologians. Never-

I

theless, I will not believe that the lofty effect of this poetry . . . is poured first into Musaeus or Linus or Orpheus, however ancient (unless, as some maintain, Musaeus and Moses were one and the same) . . . For we read that Moses, aroused by what I judge to be [poetic] longing, wrote the major part of the Pentateuch, not in prose but in heroic verse, dictated by the Holy Ghost.[1]

The possible amalgamation of Moses and Musaeus, the appearance of the Holy Ghost as a kind of muse, and the portrait of Moses as an epic poet all demonstrate the flexibility of genealogical truth. Along with this flexibility, moreover, comes the cagey application of certain self-serving norms, both for Boccaccio and for later objectors and defenders. In this case, without losing the verse form of Homer, Boccaccio simply merges a pagan poet and a Hebrew theologian, reminding us of his earlier assertion that the pagan poets were the "primos theologizantes." Too rigorous to deny its Homeric origin, he merely grafts poetry onto the family tree of the precursors of Christianity.

The practice of merging disparate traditions becomes the hallmark of literary genealogy in the Renaissance. Particularly in Elizabethan England, where both linguistic difference and the paucity of national poets conspired against the natural formation of a poetic lineage, authors resorted to making audacious connections between present and past literatures. During the sixteenth century, they began to forge the poetic genealogy that has lasted to this day. Like us, they were fully aware of the double meaning of *forging,* and their success involved the suppression of their legitimate lingual genealogy in an effort to attach themselves to the Continental tradition. Although Chaucer, Gower, and sometimes Lydgate turn up as distant precursors, for the most part the authors of the English Renaissance, like Boccaccio, forged their poetic lineage by merging and amalgamating alien traditions.

Some time ago Herbert Weisinger made the persuasive observation that "even if we nowadays have discovered that the Renaissance was not altogether what it thought it was, the fact that it did think of itself as a Renaissance is an objective criterion of the

1. Giovanni Boccaccio, *Genealogie Deorum Gentilium Libri,* 2 vols., ed. Vincenzo Romano (Bari: Gius. Laterza & Figli, 1951), 2:704–5. All translations are mine except where otherwise noted.

Renaissance."[2] This statement has undeniable significance for the study of literary genealogy, especially in England, where the Elizabethans' consciousness of themselves as distinct from all previous English writers is manifestly an "objective criterion" of literary genealogy. In his *English Reformation Literature*, a comprehensive study of the Tudor roots of later English poetry, John N. King acknowledges the Elizabethan posture of difference:

assessment of the statements of Sir Philip Sidney, George Puttenham, and their Elizabethan contemporaries, who decry the decadence of their English predecessors, reveals that these critics are united by a new disdain for medieval literature and native vernacular tradition. Their scorn derives from the imported standards of Continental literature which, by the 1580s, had supplanted the native English tradition.[3]

King argues persuasively that there is less discontinuity between early Tudor and Elizabethan literature than the Elizabethans would have us think. He emphasizes that modern critics "inherit the stylistic criteria" (p. 12) of Sidney, Puttenham, and others of the period and that an accurate reassessment of "mid-Tudor" literary tastes reveals much interest in medieval writings. King's point is well taken, and his evidence of mid-century interest is voluminous. Indeed, from the standpoint of descriptive literary history, the omission of the Tudor origins of Elizabethan verse—and of Elizabethan literary genealogy—reflects a distortion (or forgery) as old as the English Renaissance itself.

---

2. Herbert Weisinger, "Self-Awareness of the Renaissance as a Criterion of the Renaissance," *Papers of the Michigan Academy of Science, Arts, and Letters* 39 (1943), p. 567; Weisinger summarizes, "[t]he assertion of difference is in this case a substantiation of difference, and those who deny the existence of the Renaissance must be prepared to deny its self-consciousness" (p. 567). We can substitute the words "Elizabethan literary genealogy" for "Renaissance" to approximate the importance of the "conceived presence" in the invention and subsequent transmission of poetic descent in England. See also Weisinger's "The Renaissance Theory of the Reaction against the Middle Ages as a Cause of the Renaissance," *Speculum* 20 (1945), pp. 461–67.

3. John N. King, *English Reformation Literature: The Tudor Origins of the Protestant Tradition* (Princeton: Princeton University Press, 1982), p. 11. See also p. 12: "One cannot deny that late sixteenth-century authors believed that they were participating in the rebirth of English literature. Late Elizabethan disdain for earlier Tudor literature, like the modern lack of sympathy, springs from a retrospective application of imported standards of Italianate criticism to older native traditions"; and p. 210: "By the end of the sixteenth century, the verse of Tudor courtiers had diverged from its homely origins."

But the distortion that King recognizes is part and parcel of what I would like to call the "conceived presence" of antecedents in late sixteenth-century literary genealogy. The "new disdain for medieval literature and native vernacular tradition" that we find in Sidney and his contemporaries might be seen as a stepping-stone to the formation of a new literary genealogy on the Continental model. (It is worth recalling, for example, that Castiglione's word *sprezzatura,* which has always been seen as a crux in the attitude of Elizabethan courtiers, is derived from the Italian verb *sprezzare,* to disdain.) From a disdainful attitude toward their vernacular predecessors, Elizabethan poets moved effortlessly to compare themselves with the famous literary originators of Italy, such as Petrarch and even Ariosto. The break with the English past was the initial step in the forging of a literary family tree, and it is not insignificant that even in this early posture—before any positive step had been taken to name an Elizabethan genealogical original—the practice of genealogical distortion was already evident. Certainly, as Lee Patterson recently reminded us, we should be wary of regarding the Renaissance version of literary history as genuine or comprehensive: "[t]hat . . . claims to original forms of thought are themselves central to Renaissance self-definition—that they arose within the Renaissance and served it as part of its own cultural *prise de conscience*—should encourage literary historians to view them with skepticism."[4] Even as skeptics, however, we are constrained to acknowledge the mythic force of the conceived presences that we have inherited, and, as much as possible, to calibrate the extent to which the myth of literary descent has transformed itself into literary history.

Rather than to provide a descriptive literary history, my aim is to trace genealogical distortions through a series of imaginings or tropes of literary succession. An anonymous reader of my manuscript characterized the project as "a serial fable on the psychogenesis of poetic self-authoring and self-authorizing in the English Renaissance," and, with the stipulation that we acknowledge the importance of collective or national descent to every self-authorizing author, I would not quarrel with the characterization.

---

4. Lee Patterson, "On the Margin: Postmodernism, Ironic History, and Medieval Studies," *Speculum* 65 (1990), p. 93.

The readings that follow seek to isolate the "conceived presences" of literary genealogy in the English Renaissance and to demonstrate how these presences—or inventions or distortions or forged family trees—come to constitute the poetic identities of Spenser, Jonson, Milton, and, in a different form, Sidney. Of course, except in rare cases, we do not encounter poets in the act of rejecting a specific lineage of literary predecessors by name (such as the Lydgate-Barclay-Skelton line, the Sidney-Greville line, or even the Spenser-Drayton line). Rather, an examination of the "serial fable" of literary succession repeatedly confirms the value, particularly for English Renaissance poets, of a posture of rejecting prior literary lineages. The "new disdain" permits the arbitrary suppression of those forebears who fail to satisfy the stylistic, linguistic, or generic tastes of the period. Thus vernacular English poets manage to pose as descendants of ancient Latin or Greek poets who are exceedingly remote in language, religion, political orientation, morality—in short, in every possible way *except* genre and selected stylistic conventions. The English poetic genealogy that has endured was formed when a foundation of conceived presences was grafted onto the flowering branches of Elizabethan literary culture.

Yet, conceived presences notwithstanding, the concept of literary genealogy remains a bit elusive, insofar as texts do not, except in the most figurative manner, beget other texts. To a certain extent, all literary genealogy is invented, running from myths of the poets' descent from Jupiter or Apollo to assertions, like Philip Sidney's, that the ancient mythological poets might be called the fathers of learning itself.[5] The differences among supposed origins provide a largely unexplored map of the motives of Renaissance writers as well as highlight the effect of those motives on the way we continue to read the texts of particular traditions. This is especially evident in the consideration of English literature, because the forging of genealogy contributed so manifestly to the sudden appearance of a literary tradition in England in the late

---

5. *An Apology for Poetry*, ed. Geoffrey Shepherd (London: Thomas Nelson and Sons, 1965), esp. p. 96: suggesting that only Orpheus or Linus could claim to be "fathers in learning" to Musaeus, Homer, or Hesiod, Sidney asserts that "not only in time they [Orpheus and Linus] had this priority (although in itself antiquity be venerable) but went before them, as causes to draw with their charming sweetness the wild untamed wits to an admiration of knowledge."

sixteenth century. The sociological impulse to establish a pedigree, so much a part of Elizabethan courtly life, bears an important relation to the need among Elizabethan writers to justify their literary practices. Just as courtiers strove to establish the ancient roots of their line, poets in this period began to put together a literary family tree.

At times, in analyses of literary origins, the difference between bogus and bona fide genealogy all but disappears. In contrast, that difference is the raison d'être for advocates of heraldic tradition. The science of genealogy all but came into being as an aggressive means of debunking dubious genealogical assertions in the pursuit of genuine pedigrees. Sir Anthony Wagner, currently Clarenceux Herald, concludes that "[m]odern scientific genealogy originated in the sixteenth and following centuries mainly in the criticism of pedigrees designed to establish rights of property and nobility."[6] One gets the impression that before the sixteenth century all genealogy had a tendency to be a bit bogus. "To a genealogist," Sir Anthony goes on, "history is a tournament of combining or competing families, whose subtle interplay and manoeuvres, never wholly to be understood, we can only begin to grasp by first analysing and clarifying their genealogies. All history is full of myth. Men see in it what they need to see and distort truth to support themselves."[7]

Under Queen Elizabeth, the "tournament" of families was a matter of daily competition for royal patronage. That Elizabeth encouraged the representation of this familial competition in actual tilts is not coincidental. Rather, it emphasizes the palpable struggle for recognition at her court. For instance, Sir Philip Sidney's famous disappointment when Leicester produced an heir, resulting in his self-lampooning emblem, ~~SPERAVI~~, only underscores the mercenary candor and frank competitiveness of Eliz-

6. Sir Anthony Wagner, *Pedigree and Progress: Essays in the Genealogical Interpretation of History* (London: Phillimore, 1975), p. i. At the publication of his book Sir Anthony was Garter King of Arms, the highest English herald.

7. Wagner, *Pedigree and Progress*, p. 7. Unlikely as it may seem, we can almost hear Foucault in this quite conservative passage. See his essay "Nietzsche, Genealogy, History," in *Language, Counter-Memory, Practice: Selected Essays and Interviews*, ed. Donald F. Bouchard, trans. Donald F. Bouchard and Sherry Simon (Ithaca, N.Y.: Cornell University Press, 1977), pp. 139–64. See also Denis Donoghue, "Attitudes Toward History: A Preface to *The Sense of the Past*," *Salmagundi* 68–69 (1985–86), pp. 107–24, esp. p. 112.

abethan genealogy.[8] In the Heralds' Visitations of the latter part of the sixteenth century, which, according to the *OED,* were periodic visits to a district "to examine and enrol arms and pedigrees," the number of gentry "created" nearly doubled. The Heralds' opportunities encouraged a fanatical urgency to produce historical proof of ancestry. Genealogies became sophisticated works of putative historical connections, to some extent reminiscent of extended literary allusion. Familial blazons ran to quarterings in the hundreds as threatened aristocrats vied with parvenu squires for royal preferment. According to Lawrence Stone, "the rise of new men was disguised by forged genealogies and the grant of titles of honor."

In a period of such extraordinary social mobility, forgery and falsification were, perhaps, inevitable; more to the point, however, this very special kind of historicizing fiction turned out to be a swift route to preferment. Stone continues:

One of the most striking features of the age was a pride of ancestry which now reached new heights of fantasy and elaboration. Though it soon became a fad, a craze, a quasi-intellectual hobby for the idle rich, its prime purpose was social integration, the welding of a homogeneous group of seemingly respectable lineage from a crazy patchwork of the most diverse, and sometimes dubious, origins. Genuine genealogy was cultivated by the older gentry to reassure themselves of their innate superiority over the upstarts; bogus genealogy was cultivated by the new gentry in an effort to clothe their social nakedness, and by the old gentry in the internal jockeying for position in the ancestral pecking order. A lengthy pedigree was a useful weapon in the Tudor battle for status.[9]

8. There is a contemporary account of Sidney's behavior in Camden's *Remaines* (1605), where Camden maintains that Sidney used the motto at a tilt-day exhibition. See Katherine Duncan-Jones, *Sir Philip Sidney: Courtier Poet* (New Haven: Yale University Press, 1991), p. 194: "Camden had been a close observer and admirer of Sidney's ever since they had lodged together at the Deanery at Christ Church, and his account of Sidney's tiltyard motto is likely to be correct. It is given confirmation by Whetstone's reference to Sidney's using the motto *Spero* ('I hope'), which would make the 'dashed hopes' motto especially telling. . . . His hopes were doubly negatived in the motto, by being put in the past tense, and by being visibly dashed through, in a line similar to those used on 'tilting cheques' to indicate the number of staves that had been broken."

9. Lawrence Stone, *The Crisis of the Aristocracy* (Oxford: Clarendon Press, 1965), p. 23. On the subject of heraldic blazons, see also Wagner, *Pedigree and Progress,* p. 45: " the pompous effigies with their many quartered shields reflect at once the love of funeral pomp, of which Professor Lawrence Stone has reminded us, and the assertion of ancestry to which a traditional but partly parvenu society attached importance. The successive

The fledgling Tudor court faced enormous difficulties in funding an idle aristocracy. Part of the rationale for the frantic production of pedigrees was to avoid contaminating the gentry with merchants. Among other changes, the erosion of a *consensus gentium* regarding the inalienability of land fostered new resolve among the squire-archy (the rank of the Sidney family) to cement their rights to preferment in genealogical proofs.

In any case, the mania for genealogy became fairly common-place. It eventually prompted James I to remark about a particu-larly excessive courtier, "I did na ken Adam's name was Lumley" (Stone, p. 24). But Lumley was in good company. In the sixteenth century, the Tudor heralds, as Stone attests, "were kept busy contriving vast rolls tracing the ancestry of the nobility back to the Norman conquerors, to the Romans, to the Trojans" (p. 23). Some went as far back as the Hebrew Bible, and Queen Elizabeth's genealogy was traced to the Garden of Eden. By the middle of the seventeenth century this sort of wildly improbable genealogizing had become prevalent enough to be worthy of Samuel Butler's satire in *Hudibras:*

> Nor does it follow, 'cause a herald
> Can make a gentleman, scarce a year old,
> To be descended of a race,
> Of ancient kings, in a small space;
> That we should all opinions hold
> Authentic, that we can make old.[10]

The skepticism behind this passage is easily transferred to literary genealogy, where, though there are no Heralds' Visitations, we nevertheless find rather extensive attempts to prove ancient lin-eage. In fact, during the Elizabethan period, English literary gene-alogy was itself "scarce a year old," and its authority depended on the promulgation of a myth of descent from the most ancient fonts of poetry. Again, by Butler's time this notion of origins could be mocked and undermined: " 'Tis not antiquity, nor author,/That makes Truth Truth," Sir Hudibras asserts a few lines before the passage quoted above. Butler was already jaded, however, by the

---

cycles of heraldic visitation between 1530 and 1688 both illustrate and fit into this picture."

10. Samuel Butler, *Hudibras, with Dr. Grey's Annotations* (London, 1819), Part II, canto iii, lines 669–74. I am grateful to David J. Rothman for this reference.

century-old literary history he inherited.[11] A hundred years earlier the formulation of the legacy he so cavalierly denounces required the explicit connection between antiquity and truth. Forged genealogy was the means of establishing such a connection.

The forging of genealogy had, of course, a sacred precedent. The New Testament opens with an extensive, and extremely tenuous, lineage of Jesus Christ. The heading on the first page of Matthew in the Geneva Bible is "The genealogie and birth of Jesus Christ," and an annotation explains that the first chapter shows "[t]hat Jesus is that Messias, the Saviour promised to the Fathers." As in all English Bibles, 1:1 announces itself as "The Booke of the generation of Jesus Christ, the sonne of David, the sonne of Abraham." From a genealogical perspective, it is very bold to claim that Jesus of Nazareth is a direct descendant of King David, the "pedigree of Davids flocke," as in the Geneva Bible annotation. Not only was David, as actual royalty, Jesus' social superior, but also the number of generations between David and Jesus was too large to sort out with any pretense to accuracy.

So all the generations from Abraham to David, *are* fourteene generations. And from David untill they were caried away into Babylon, fourteene generations: & after they were caried away into Babylon until Christ, fourteene generations.[12]

One has to take this particular genealogy literally on faith. And, in point of fact, the accuracy of Matthew's twenty-eight-generation descent from David is confirmed beyond all doubt by the miracles and the Resurrection. So it would be wrong to suggest that Renaissance readers considered Jesus' genealogy to be of dubious provenance. To the contrary, his genealogy is important precisely because readers believed in its plausibility and in its truth.[13]

---

11. Dryden states the case clearly, accepting the fact of an English literary family tree: "Milton was the poetical son of Spenser, and Mr. Waller of Fairfax; for we have our lineal descents and clans as well as other families." See "Prefaces to Fables Ancient and Modern," in George Watson, ed., *Of Dramatic Poesy and Other Essays,* 2 vols. (London: J. M. Dent, Everyman's Library, 1962), 2:270.

12. Matt. 1:17. All quotations in this section are from the Geneva Bible (The Annotated New Testament, 1602 Edition), ed. Gerald T. Sheppard (New York: The Pilgrim Press, 1989).

13. The Old Testament, or Hebrew Bible, also contains genealogies that would have been impressive to Renaissance readers. As Anne Lake Prescott pointed out to me, there are several sixteenth-century references to David's passage from the "sheephook to the

The authority of the Biblical model would have served aspiring noblemen well. That royal blood ran, unheralded for years, in the veins of the lowly carpenter carried a message of genealogical hope—as well as a hope of salvation—to the pedigree-conscious. In fact, references to the royal genealogy of Jesus turn up regularly in contemporary treatises on heraldry. John Ferne, for instance, in *The Blazon of Gentrie* characterizes "our Saviour and King Jesus Christ": "a Gentleman of bloud, according to his humanitie, Emperour of heaven and earth, according to his deitie, even as his holy Hereald, (the Evangelistes) have out of their infallible recordes testified the same."[14] Ferne's assertion that the Evangelists kept "infallible recordes" indicates the power of the genealogical model in Matthew. He goes on to emphasize the common roots of kings, using Solomon, significantly, as an example: "the wisest of all men, and he a Gentleman, nay he a king, could say: I also a mortall man, like to all other, receiving the matter of my creation from the same forge, that the first man received his . . . and behold, yet was there never king otherwise borne" (p. 28). Just as Solomon receives the "matter" of his creation from the "same forge" as Adam, all subsequent Gentlemen are forged of the same matter as Solomon. But this is not precisely an egalitarian argument. To the contrary, those not of noble birth who aspire to pedigrees are tempered in their pursuit by the fundamental equality of the "matter" that constitutes human beings. But their objective is nonetheless hierarchical. To be "created" is, moreover, both to come into existence through God and to be given a coat of arms by a herald, as in being created a knight. Ferne's loose association of the forge (in which arms themselves would be fashioned), the nobility of all men, and the act of creating a gentleman like Solomon calls attention to the herald's importance in the formation of an ideal society. But Ferne was not even a genuine herald. He was an amateur—a mere writer—propounding a theory of heraldry that urged meritorious conduct as a criterion equal or superior to birth in the determination of a gentleman.

Ferne's thesis and others like it made it possible to choose one's

---

scepter." See Anne Lake Prescott, "Evil Tongues at the Court of Saul: The Renaissance David as a Slandered Courtier," *Journal of Medieval and Renaissance Studies* 21 (1991), pp. 163–86.

14. John Ferne, *The Blazon of Gentrie* (London, 1586), p. 3.

ancestors. Descent could be seen as an association of moral attributes quite apart from blood. And the typical elitism of blood
lineage could be shifted to other areas, such as prudence, learning,
and—as we see in many *artes poeticae*—poetical skill. This shift in
the meaning of lineage has far-reaching implications in the Renaissance and afterward, justifying, as we might expect, everything
from poetic laurels to revolution. Whereas, in the social arena,
getting caught choosing one's ancestors brought condemnation—
the notorious scorn accorded to "mushroom gentlemen"—in the
context of poetry and learning, choosing one's precursors was all
but mandatory.[15] Particularly in England, where the literary past
yielded no natural lines of descent to the Elizabethans, the careful
selection (and identification) of a poetic genealogy gave an imprimatur not merely to the individual poet, but to the fledgling
literary culture as well.

Werner Sollors makes a useful distinction on the subject of
descent relations. Though discussing the origins of American national identity, his observations seem to me to apply equally well
to the choices and constraints shaping the literary culture of Renaissance England. He distinguishes, for example, between "contractual and hereditary, self-made and ancestral," terming these
polarities *consent* and *descent:*

Descent relations are those defined by anthropologists as relations of
"substance" (by blood or nature); consent relations describe those of
"law" or "marriage." Descent language emphasizes our positions as heirs,
our hereditary qualities, liabilities, and entitlements; consent language
stresses our abilities as mature free agents and "architects of our fates" to
choose our spouses, our destinies, and our political systems.[16]

It is not so surprising, perhaps, that an ideal of consent, of choice
in law and marriage and even destiny, should illuminate the study
of the genealogies of poetic history during and since the Renaissance. The difference between contractual and consensual relations
with predecessors and, on the other hand, hereditary relations is,

15. "Mushroom gentlemen" was a contemporary term applied to upstarts in the
gentry. See J. F. R. Day, "Venal Heralds and Mushroom Gentlemen: Seventeenth Century Character Books and the Sale of Honor" (Ph.D. dissertation, Duke University,
1985).

16. Werner Sollors, *Beyond Ethnicity: Consent and Descent in American Culture* (New
York: Oxford University Press, 1986), p. 6.

in essence, tantamount to the difference between bogus and bona fide genealogy. Poets are not the hereditary offspring of earlier poets, or earlier poems, except when they claim—by allusion or allusory evasion—to be descendants. Such claims, tacit or explicit, arguably represent choices, and, therefore, we might better characterize the genealogical relations of poets in the language of consent, contract, and even a kind of conspiracy. We might say that it is not poetic fathers but poetic *fathers-in-law* that govern the poetry of later generations.

In the Renaissance, as people have always pointed out with varying degrees of approbation and disapprobation, the humanists received both praise and privilege chiefly for their efforts toward the recovery, resuscitation, rebirth, revival, restoration—in short, the rescue of the antique past from the blind maw of the Middle Ages. People have expressed varying degrees of credulity, too, about the value of these "rescues." But it is impossible to deny in the rhetoric of these rescuing efforts a recurrent lament for the discontinuity between epochs. From Petrarch to Erasmus, from Thomas More to Ben Jonson, poets and humanists rescue their literary forebears from across the abyss in order to present themselves as progeny. The rescue, therefore, has a double purpose. It is as much the reason *for* genealogical connectedness as the result *of* it. Until poets are no longer humanists per se, their family trees remain largely consensual: as rescuers of ancient texts, they conspire with their own *auctores* to establish—to *forge,* in both senses of the word—their hereditary lines.

"Modernity exists," Paul de Man suggests, analyzing Nietzsche, "in the form of a desire to wipe out whatever came earlier, in the hope of reaching at last a point that could be called a true present, a point of origin that marks a new departure."[17] This particular version of modernity took several forms in England, including Tudor efforts to return to the primitive church and Sidney's repudiation of rustic dialect. But sixteenth-century English poetry owed its development in large part to the humanist movement, to the obsessive repair and reconstruction of the shredded classical past. It is impossible to read English poetry without bearing in mind the humanist aspirations of the English poet,

17. Paul de Man, *Blindness and Insight* (Minneapolis: University of Minnesota Press, 1983), p. 148.

aspirations that embrace the philosophical syncretism of the movement in addition to the dedication to the physical rescue of lost texts. I would argue that, until Milton, although there may be humanists who are not poets, there is no great English poet who is not a humanist in the conventional sense of the term. Therefore, as long as the rescue of the past remains a feasible posture, poetic genealogy remains a flexible condition. As long as the past, and thus "tradition," continues to be under formulation, genealogy can never represent a constraint.

While I do not think we can so easily apply Harold Bloom's agonistic model to poets and poetic theorists before Milton, I am nevertheless indebted to Bloom's powerful arguments concerning the belatedness felt by all modern poets since the Renaissance, what he terms the "tyranny of time."[18] But the stigma of descendency, as I demonstrate, does not take hold until after poets have established a supposedly genuine lineage. Rather than the binding or inevitable continuity supposedly inherited by later poets, Renaissance poets have a tangible discontinuity to contend with, the lost languages and moribund arts that are, in Luther's words, "in an imperfect manner, recovered from fragments of old books rescued from the worms and dust."[19]

Forging a literary genealogy presented considerable problems in England. Not only was the language remote from the classical languages, but also Chaucer, the salient English precursor, was distant in time and alien in diction.[20] Thomas Greene suggests the roots of English anxiety:

The focus of England's sense of disjuncture lay most visibly in its embarrassment over its rude vernacular. . . . The embarrassment of the English with their language should be read, I think, synecdochically, as an

18. See Harold Bloom, *Agon: Toward a Theory of Revisionism* (New York: Oxford University Press, 1982) and also *The Anxiety of Influence* (New York: Oxford University Press, 1973).

19. From Luther's "Letter to the Aldermen of All the Cities of Germany in Behalf of Christian Schools"; cited by Herbert Weisinger, "The Renaissance Theory of the Reaction against the Middle Ages," p. 463.

20. Even Dryden believed, wrongly, that Chaucer's verse did not scan, though he found "the rude sweetness of a Scotch tune in it, which is natural and pleasing, though not perfect." Ironically he has contempt for Thomas Speght, who, in his second edition of Chaucer's works (1602), suggested that scansion might be possible. See John Dryden, "Preface to Fables Ancient and Modern," in George Watson, ed., *Of Dramatic Poesy*, 2:281.

oblique lament over a broader cultural poverty. Not only the language was inadequate; the nation as a whole was seen as suffering from a kind of privation which translations from antiquity or even from the continental vernaculars could only underscore.[21]

The Elizabethans dispel, or distract attention from, their embarrassment chiefly in the praise of their newly elected poetic lineage. But their embarrassment continues to represent a measure of their anxiety about the parvenu status of English poets in the literary pantheon.

It is important, in counterpoint, to remember that the embarrassment regarding the "rude vernacular" was not shared by everyone. Under Henry VIII, for instance, the defense of the English Bible required the assertion that the vernacular was a suitable language to bear the word of God. In *Obedience of a Christian Man,* William Tyndale not only regards English as suitable, but insists that it is superior to Latin because of its closeness to both Greek and Hebrew:

The sermons which thou readest in the Acts of the apostles, and all that the apostles preached, were no doubt preached in the mother tongue. Why then might they not be written in the mother tongue? As, if one of us preach a good sermon, why may it not be written? Saint Jerom also translated the bible into his mother tongue: why may not we also? They will say it cannot be translated into our tongue, *it is so rude.* It is not so rude as they are false liars. For the Greek tongue agreeth more with the English than with the Latin. And the properties of the Hebrew tongue agreeth a thousand times more with the English than with the Latin. (Italics mine)[22]

Tyndale's assertions regarding the distance of English from Latin, though proffered in the good cause of praising the vernacular, would have been problematic for Elizabethan poets who hoped to

21. Thomas Greene, *The Light in Troy: Imitation and Discovery in Renaissance Poetry* (New Haven: Yale University Press, 1982), p. 33.

22. *The Work of William Tyndale,* ed. G. E. Duffield, (Appleford, England: The Sutton Courtenay Press, 1964), p. 326. Commenting on this passage, the *Cambridge History of the Bible* observes that "[i]f this makes too little of that forcing of Hebraisms into English which proved successful only because the Bible became so familiar, it remains true that Tyndale made of the spoken English of his day a fit vehicle for the communication of Holy Scripture and determined the fundamental character of most of the subsequent versions." See *The Cambridge History of the Bible: The West from the Reformation to the Present Day,* ed. S. L. Greenslade, (Cambridge: Cambridge University Press, 1963), p. 145.

forge a genealogical link to Virgil and his Continental heirs. Nevertheless, it is noteworthy that as early as 1528 we find a well-developed argument against the myth of a rude vernacular. Even if such an argument would have been antipathetic in detail to the later Elizabethans, it was useful in its objective of setting English beside the holy languages.

In their eagerness to support the English Bible and to outflank popery, the Protestant reformers enthusiastically embraced their national poets. For example, John Bale's remarkable bibliography, *Illustrium maioris Britannae scriptorum summarium* (1548), contains a comprehensive list of English authors from the legendary origins of the nation to the present day. In fact, John N. King suggests that "[b]y arranging authors in chronological order into five '*centuriae*' or groupings of one hundred, Bale imposes on the text a correspondence between the development of English literature and the pattern of the seven historical ages expounded in *Image*, a work that he wrote as he completed *Summarium*" (pp. 66–67). The impulse to connect English literary production with a larger pattern of cosmological destiny adumbrates attempts later in the century to link English poets to divine sources such as the Evangelists, or to mythological precursors such as Orpheus and Amphion.[23] The search for English "antiquities," such as John Leland's *The Laboryouse Journey & Serche for Englandes Antiquitees* (edited by Bale, 1549), testifies to an early interest in the homegrown roots of national tradition. But the English poetic past was disparaged by Sidney and others as "rustic," and Bale and Leland are the forefathers of Bodley and Cotton and Bishop Percy, not of imaginative

---

23. David Quint (*Origin and Originality in Renaissance Literature: Versions of the Source* [New Haven: Yale University Press, 1983]) maintains that the awakening of historical consciousness in the Renaissance fueled the search for origins:

> [T]he positing of authorizing origins acquired urgency in a culture which had gained a new historical awareness. On the one hand, there was a kind of epistemological anxiety, heightened by nostalgia, in the task of depicting a source which sanctioned what were otherwise "counterfeit," purely man-made fictions. On the other hand, Renaissance culture valorized the human creativity which it had newly come to recognize, and it could only define the individuality of the creator in historical terms. (P. x)

Quint's study is provocative on the allegory of the source in Renaissance texts. But I tend to disagree that "historical terms," in a strict sense, are the only terms by which Renaissance authors could define themselves. Indeed, it seems at times that Renaissance authors use genealogy precisely to circumvent historical definition.

genealogists. Even in our own day Bale's obsessively complete compilations—which incidentally make Francis Meres's *Palladis Tamia* look a paltry thing—would be categorized as antiquarianism rather than as the kind of literary history that brought to light demonstrable links between authors of different epochs. That the proof of demonstrable links depends on reading genealogy backwards—tracing influence of one kind or another—should alert us to the dubious historical status of poetic descent. That authors themselves identify their precursors through imitation, forging (or, at least, proposing) a family tree in every line they write, emphasizes the importance of conceived presences in the critical appraisal of literary genealogy.

It would be more scientific to eschew historical frauds like the one perpetrated by Sidney, Puttenham, and their contemporaries. Suppressing the English literary past in favor of an Italianate model, with classical ancestors thrown in for good measure, is comparable to fabricating a coat of arms that reaches back to Adam. But the suppression of the vernacular past is, in Weisinger's terms, an "objective criterion" of English Renaissance genealogy. It stands to reason, therefore, that the literary genealogy having the greatest effect on our reading of Renaissance texts will be derived, not from the historically complete national descent that we find in Bale, but, rather, from the conceived genealogy that we trace in poets expressly concerned about their relation to the literature of the past.

The pitfall of conceived genealogies is that we lose in great gouges the genuine vernacular predecessors of the English Renaissance. In the *Defence,* Sidney seems aware of the loss when he complains "that poesy . . . should only find in our time a hard welcome in England. . . . For heretofore poets have in England also flourished, and, which is to be noted, even in those times when the trumpet of Mars did sound loudest" (*Apology,* p. 131). But Sidney's opinion of those past poets does little to endear them to the *mysomousoi* (poet-haters). In a well-known passage, he neglects to praise the *Canterbury Tales* and banishes Chaucer to dim antiquity: "Chaucer undoubtedly did excellently in his *Troilus and Criseyde,* of whom I know not whether to marvel more, either that he in that misty time could see so clearly, or that we in this clear age walk so stumblingly after him. Yet had he great wants, fit to be forgiven in so reverent antiquity" (p. 133). The tone of Sidney's "undoubtedly" is enough to sow doubt in any reader. In addition, the polarization of a "misty time" in the past and a "clear age" of the present, despite Sidney's flattering appraisal of Chaucer's precocity, emphasizes (or, perhaps, helps to create) the gulf between the two eras.

By the time Sidney wrote, however, there was already a precedent for excising the native vernacular tradition. Even in John Skelton's *Garlande or Chapelet of Laurell*, which was written very early in the sixteenth century, we find a suppression of fifteenth-century poets. Chaucer and Gower are the only poets who speak in the poem, and "Mayster Gower" urges Skelton to take up where he and Chaucer left off one hundred years earlier:

> "Brother Skelton, your endevorment
> So have ye done, that meretoryously
> Ye have deservyd to have an enplement
> In our collage above the sterry sky,
> Because that ye encrease and amplyfy
> The brutid Britons of Brutus Albion,
> That welny was loste when that we were gone."[24]

Gower's "collage above the sterry sky" is a humanist's genealogical pantheon, including in its ranks Orpheus, Amphion, Quintilian, Theocritus, Hesiod, Homer, Cicero, Sallust, Ovid, Lucan, Virgil, and Livy. Skelton's poem should dispel the mistaken impression, given at times by Elizabethan intellectuals, that the arrival of continental humanism in England more or less coincides with the first blooming of the literary family tree in the last quarter of the century. The *Garlande* is, moreover, a rough prototype of later genealogical compendiums in which the very definition of a national tradition is expanded to include Latin and Greek writers. It is ironic that the genealogical expansion provides the means to suppress such homegrown poets as, for example, Dunbar and Douglas.[25]

24. John Skelton, *The Complete English Poems*, ed. John Scattergood (New Haven and London: Yale University Press, 1983), p. 323.
25. We find an exception to the usual omissions in Francis Thynne, whose *Animadversions* includes a poem, "Upon the Picture of Chaucer":
> What *Pallas* citie owes the heauenly mind
> Of prudent *Socrates*, wise Greeces glorie;

Chaucer, and sometimes Gower, are solitary figures anchoring poetic descent in England. Their survival was permitted by law under Henry VIII, whose Act 34, meant to prohibit books printed in English like Tyndale's translations, specifically exempts Chaucer and Gower.[26] This exemption may indicate that the two fourteenth-century poets were considered toothless old men, no threat to henrician policy. In his 1532 edition of *Chaucers Workes*, William Thynne, "chefe clerke" of Henry VIII's kitchen, presents Chaucer as a curiosity:

For though it had been in Demosthenes or Homerus tymes / whan all lernyng and excellency of sciences florisshed amonges the Grekes / or in the season *tha*t Cicero prince of eloquence amonges latyns lyued / yet it had been a thyng right rare & strau*n*ge, and worthy perpetuall laude /

What fame *Arpinas* spreadingly doth find
By *Tullies* eloquence and oratorie;
What lasting praise sharpe-witted Italie
By *Tasso's* and by *Petrarkes* penne obtained;
What fame *Bartas* vnto proud France hath gained,
By seuen daies world Poetically strained:

What high renowne is purchas'd vnto Spaine,
Which fresh *Dianaes* verses do distill;
What praise our neighbor Scotland doth retaine,
By *Gawine Douglas,* in his *Virgill* quill;
Or other motions by sweet Poets skill,
The same, and more, faire England challenge may,
By that rare wit and art thou doest display,
In verse, which doth *Apolloes* muse bewray.
  Then *Chaucer* liue, for still thy verse shall liue,
  T'unborne Poets, which life and light will give.

Because the poem appears in an edition of Chaucer, the reference to Gawain Douglas does not seem inappropriate. But Douglas is an unusual figure to appear amid the more familiar names of the late sixteenth century, poets such as Tasso, Petrarch, and Du Bartas. (See Francis Thynne, *Animadversions uppon the Annotations and Corrections of some Imperfections of Impressiones of Chaucers Workes* [1598], ed. F. J. Furnivall [London: Kegan Paul, Trench, Trübner and Co., 1875], pp. cvi–cvii.) Given Thynne's attempt at genealogical accuracy, perhaps it is also worth noting that he was created Lancaster Herald in 1602.

26. See Thynne's *Animadversions,* p. xiv: "Provided allso that all bokes in Englishe printed before the yere of our Lorde a thousande fyve hundred and fourtie intytled the Kinge*s* Hieghnes proclamac*i*ons, injunctions, translac*i*ons of the Pater noster, the Ave Maria and the Crede, the psalters, prymers, prayer[s], statutes and lawes of the Realme, Cronycles, *Canterburye tales, Chaucers bokes,* Gowers bokes, and stories of mennes lieves, shall not be comprehended in the prohibic*i*on of this acte, ooneless the Kinge*s* saide Majestie shall hereafter make speciall proclamac*i*on for the condempnac*i*on and reproving of the same or any of them."

that any clerke by lernyng or wytte coulde than haue framed a tonge, before so rude and imperfite / to suche a swete ornature & composycion / lykely if he had lyued in these dayes / being good letters so restored and reuyude as they be / if he were nat empeched by the enuy of suche as may tollerate nothyng / whiche to vnderstonde their capacite doth nat extende / to haue brought it vnto a full and fynall perfection. (Thynne's *Animadversions,* p. xxiv)

Chaucer is commendable, according to Thynne, because he has "framed" a "rude and imperfite" language into sweet composition. Even among the ancients, he maintains, such a feat would have been praised. More significantly, if Chaucer had lived in the sixteenth century, when "good letters" had been "restored and reuyude," he would have brought the language to its final perfection. Thus Chaucer himself is rescued from the rude medieval past, while the spires of ancient culture and sixteenth-century revival communicate across the chasm of the English Middle Ages.[27]

Although Chaucer was considered a legitimate poetic precursor, there were only two editions of his work between William Thynne's second edition in 1542 and Speght's in 1598.[28] We can surmise that interest in Chaucer, except for antiquarian purposes, was spotty, and that the Elizabethans, largely by their own design, inherited a paucity of useful native antecedents. Nevertheless, in an astonishingly short period of time at the end of the century the Elizabethan poets established themselves, and their national literature, as plausible contenders with the most renowned Italian authors from Petrarch to Ariosto. By the end of Elizabeth's reign, English poetry had attached itself to a tradition reaching back to Virgil, Hesiod, Theocritus, and Homer.

After Gascoigne, Googe, Lyly, Ascham, and other first-generation Elizabethan intellectuals had broken the ground, it remained for the next generation to plant the seed and to nurture the family tree, all within a few years. This would seem, even in retrospect, an impossible task, but we need only consider our own present idea of sixteenth-century literary genealogy to realize how successfully they accomplished it. Led by Spenser and the other elegists who

27. See Alice Miskimin, *The Renaissance Chaucer* (New Haven: Yale University Press, 1975); and King, *English Reformation Literature,* passim.
28. Francis Thynne suggests there might have been three editions, but the editors find only two, one in 1550 and the other, by John Stowe, in 1561 (*Animadversions,* pp. 5–6).

wrote in the years following Philip Sidney's untimely death, the later Elizabethan poets managed to erect, in Sidney, a homegrown vernacular precursor from whom the national literature could descend. Simply, they invented a pedigree for English poetry. Sidney's presence as a poetic antecedent furnished the start of a lineage on which poets from Spenser to Jonson were able to depend. And even if Jonson himself was suspicious of Sidney's precursor status, he recognized that the presence of a genealogical original helped to establish the much-desired continuity between English vernacular poetry and the classical poetic past.

Like the work of earlier Renaissance authors, English poetry of the period contains a certain anxiety regarding its lack of a true literary past. At times we almost detect in the poetry a guilty impulse to own up to the forged pedigree of the national literature—or, if it is not guilt exactly, then perhaps what we sense is a patent fatigue accompanying the continued effort to rescue the past, to reassemble it, and, in the act of reassembly, to fashion a contemporary lineage in imitation of it.[29] In treating the question of literary genealogy as if it were largely a national issue, there is a tendency to overlook the individual struggles of Elizabethan poets with the formidable reputation of their Greek, Latin, or Continental predecessors. Spenser clearly struggled with Ovid and Ariosto; Jonson with Horace and Juvenal; Daniel with Lucan. The personal component of their struggle cannot be denied, nor, for that matter, can their success be questioned. But, once again, we must remind ourselves that our appreciation of their difficulties is the product of a post-Renaissance (or Miltonic) literary sensibility. Recognition of a personal struggle with the classical poets was precisely the objective of Spenser, Daniel, Jonson, and many others: their anxiety was that, as vernacular English writers, they would be unable to patch together a Latinate literary heritage—that, in all likelihood, their attempts would only emphasize the gulf. It is a measure of their success that, rather than seeing the genealogical gulf, we now consider their personal struggles as proof of continuity with the classical past. The irony would have pleased the Elizabethans.

---

29. One manifestation of the fatigue might be the absence of a full-fledged imitation of the *Georgics,* though of course there were compelling reasons at the time to avoid a poem in praise of work. See Anthony Low, *The Georgic Revolution* (Princeton: Princeton University Press, 1985).

I would call our view "Miltonic" because, in contrast to his predecessors, Milton betrays little anxiety regarding continuity. He accepts both the past as intact and his descent as legitimate. Our present sense of literary history reflects Milton's genealogical confidence. Rather than doubting the existence of a literary past, we, like Milton, tend to seek vulnerabilities in the demonic grip of our putatively legitimate forebears. W. J. Bate identifies John Dryden as "the first great European (not merely English) example of a major writer who is taking it for granted that the very existence of a past creates the necessity for difference."[30] But, in a way, this is too gullible a conclusion, and Dryden is too comfortable a candidate for the office he himself noticed and named. Rather, I am inclined to suggest that Milton is the first major (English) poet to take the past for granted. Milton's great boldness is the utter denial of discontinuity. Although we tend to see him as a culminating and baroque figure, the closing bracket of the English Renaissance, it is perhaps worthwhile to consider him as first in the line of poets who simply do not need the recovery of the past to establish their genealogical status.

SIR THOMAS ELYOT

Dante insisted that in the Romance countries even vernacular poetry contained an indissoluble lingual tie to ancient Latin poetry, and Italian poets in particular could boast a close descent. But Dante's assertion did not hold true for the English language, and the poets of Renaissance England were able to claim no scientific connection to the classical authors. Consequently, in hopes of remedying both the linguistic and the temporal disjuncture, Tudor authors sought to graft English onto the Mediterranean languages, especially Italian, by importing and adopting the literary conventions of the true descendants of Latin (and, to some extent, Greek). Ignoring etymological reality, they set out to show that the essence of poetry could be transferred from ancient Latinate tongues to modern Saxon ones. They found some precedent for this, predictably, in the poetic origin myths of Continental theorists such as Boccaccio, whose extended treatment of the subject in the *Ge-*

---

30. W. J. Bate, *The Burden of the Past and the English Poet* (Cambridge, Massachusetts: Harvard University Press, 1970), p. 31.

nealogia provided a model for centuries after it was written. If poetic divinity could transcend language and form to arrive in Italy in, say, the fourteenth century, then perhaps "Poesie" itself could travel across large barriers, even lingual ones. Indeed, the English project to demonstrate this transcendent quality of poetry, which we often find anatomized in defenses of the period, was an astonishing success. We now read the poetry of Sidney, Spenser, Drayton, Shakespeare, Daniel, and the rest, as thoroughly English products—as, in fact, the foundations of literature in our language. It requires a certain force of will to recognize the hybrid peculiarity of Renaissance English poetry and to notice its adoptive parentage.

Richard Helgerson, in his study of the first generation of Elizabethan writers, astutely recognizes the inevitable genealogical condition of an upstart literature: "Though we have learned to appreciate 'the anxiety of influence,' 'the burden of the past' which weighs heavily on writers who must follow a Spenser, a Shakespeare, or a Milton, we have achieved no comparable appreciation for the anxiety of those who work without such models, in an atmosphere of doubt as to whether literature can or should be made in their time or in their language."[31] This anxiety resounds throughout the period. It inspires a flurry of translations and imitations of Continental authors as diverse as Castiglione, Ariosto, Tasso, Du Bartas, and Du Bellay.[32] Simultaneously, however, these Continental gleanings cause great anxiety in England, as we see especially in Roger Ascham's notorious attack on Italian books and manners.[33] Partly, this anxiety reflects the earliest stages in the

31. Richard Helgerson, *The Elizabethan Prodigals* (University of California Press, 1976), p. 5. See also Helgerson's *Self-Crowned Laureates: Spenser, Jonson, Milton and the Literary System* (University of California Press, 1983), especially the discussion of Spenser, p. 68: "England had no poet. . . . Italy and France had theirs, as did Greece and Rome before them. Why not England?"

32. Sir Thomas Hoby, *The Book of the Courtier* (1561); Sir John Harington, *Orlando Furioso* (1591); Edward Fairfax, *Godfrey of Bulloigne, or The Recoverie of Jerusalem* (1600); Joshua Sylvester, *Bartas His Devine Weekes & Workes* (1605; completed 1608). Spenser translated Du Bellay's *Les Antiquitez de Rome* in the *Complaints* (1591).

33. Roger Ascham, *The Scholemaster* (1563–68), ed. Edward Arber (Boston, 1898). See, for example, p. 161: "These be the inchantementes of *Circes*, brought out of *Italie*, to marre mens maners in England; much, by example of ill life, but more by preceptes of fonde bookes, of late translated out of *Italian* into English, sold in euery shop in London, commended by honest titles the so[o]ner to corrupt honest maners"; or, p. 165: "And yet

debate over the ancients and moderns. But there is also the sore subject of who should be awarded, ex post facto, the fatherhood of English poetry, the Greek and Latin authors or their Italian Renaissance imitators. There is no resolution to this debate, and in the end the Elizabethans find it most satisfying and convenient to avoid the issue by the remarkable device of conflating these origins into a fabricated English precursor, Sir Philip Sidney.

But the Sidney solution, if we can so term it, could not have succeeded without the establishment in England of a broad foundation of humanist values. A mere fifty years earlier it was necessary to persuade the English upper classes that poetry belonged in the commonwealth at all. Thomas Elyot's *The Boke Named the Governor* (1531), though primarily a handbook of conduct for young nobles, nevertheless contains one of the earliest defenses of humanism in England, most notably the defense of music and dancing as venerable, holy, and heroic pursuits. According to John M. Major, the *Governor* includes "the first formal defense of poetry in modern English literature," but the defense he refers to is a pale thing in comparison with later efforts.[34] It is true that Elyot asserts the divine origins of poetry, citing the Latin "*Vates,* which word signifieth as much as prophets."[35] He never discusses English poetry, however, and never actually mentions the writing of poetry as a legitimate pursuit. In truth, it is rather sad to realize how assiduously he is obliged to defend even the mere reading of poetry

---

ten *Morte Arthures* do not the tenth part so much harme, as one of these bookes, made in *Italie,* and translated in England"; and so forth. Despite Ascham's warnings, however, Italian books and Italian courtly ideals survived and thrived.

34. John M. Major, *Sir Thomas Elyot and Renaissance Humanism* (Lincoln: University of Nebraska Press, 1964), p. 267. As Major points out, in *The Defense of Good Women* "Elyot is also the author of an attack on poetry" (p. 267). The attack takes a platonic approach, banishing poets from the commonwealth, and Major accounts for the difference between the *Governor* and the later text with curious ambiguity: "If ever there were proof of Elyot's almost instinctive deference to the authority of Plato, it is here in this fantastic split attitude of his toward poetry, in which he invokes the philosopher's name first in order to vindicate poetry and then to condemn it" (p. 268). I disagree with Major, or at least with Major's assumption that Elyot attacks and defends the same entity. It seems to me that in the *Governor* he defends ancient texts as worthwhile pedagogical tools—in essence, he reiterates the humanist project for an English audience. In *The Defense of Good Women,* however, he attacks poets themselves as useless to a modern civic system, and, in this respect, is more the precursor of Gosson than of Sidney.

35. Thomas Elyot, *The Book Named the Governor* (1531), ed. S. E. Lehmberg (New York: Dutton, 1962), p. 47.

among the gentry: "But since we be now occupied in the defense of poets, it shall not be incongruent to our matter to show what profit may be taken by diligent reading of ancient poets, contrary to the false opinion, that now reigneth, of them that suppose that in the works of poets is contained nothing but bawdry (such is their foul word of reproach) and unprofitable leasing" (p. 47). Elyot follows this statement with a defense of specific poets, particularly Terence, Ovid, Catullus, and Martial. He confines his explicit defense to comedies, no doubt surmising that these pose the most obvious threat to seriousness. After quoting a few passages that forcefully condemn vice, he draws the conclusion that "good and wise matter may be picked out of these poets" (p. 49).[36]

Elyot's defense of poetry really begins with his defense of pedagogy. With a slight distortion of the Horatian dictum regarding the profit and delight of poetry, he emphasizes the delightful aspects of poetry as an incentive to young students. He suggests that sound pedagogy would require that a child be taught the ancient poets in tandem with ancient languages, "a much pleasant lesson and also profitable" (p. 29). The trick, of course, is for him to show how delight is itself profitable. If a child delights in hunting, Elyot explains in his justification of the *Aeneid,* then he would take great pleasure in reading Virgil's fable of Aristeus, or of the hunting parties of Dido and Aeneas. Similarly, if a child enjoys wrestling, running, and physical exercise, then there are Euryalus and the funeral games; if he prefers "hearing minstrels," then he would appreciate Jopas in Carthage and (with a plug for Homer) blind Demodokos at Alkinoos's court. He notes that it would be impossible for children to read all the great books, but desires "that they have, in every of the said books, so much instruction that they may take thereby some profit" (p. 33). Elyot knows his audience and argues accordingly: the nobles surrounding Henry VIII were notoriously recalcitrant about book learning; they hunted, fought, and caroused as befitted feudal lordlings.

---

36. After having translated the passages from Terence, Plautus, and Ovid, Elyot also points out that he could "recite" a great number of similar sentences from other "wanton" poets, "who in the Latin do express them incomparably with more grace and delectation to the reader than our English tongue may yet express" (p. 49). This observation is a long way from a defense of the English vernacular, or, for that matter, from a defense of vernacular poetry at all.

Elyot appeals directly to their interests, and, moreover, concludes that the study of poetry will make better men of action. "The child's courage," he insists, "inflamed by frequent reading of noble poets, daily more and more desireth to have experience of those things that they so vehemently do commend in them that they write of" (p. 33). Not only does he promise appropriate delectations in poetry, but he also predicts that the reading of noble poets will produce valorous noblemen and therefore profit the commonwealth.

This kind of reading has obvious drawbacks. If poetry is persuasive enough to prompt action, then, depending on the author they happen to be reading, impressionable young nobles could be moved toward virtuous *or* reprehensible deeds. One need not look far, especially among the pagan poets (or the Italians), to find examples of equivocal moral or ethical value. Moreover, poetry's detractors could eventually argue that it is precisely because poetry is delightful that it is so dangerous. As Stephen Gosson puts it some years later, "The Harpies haue Virgins faces, and vultures Talentes."[37] For the time being, however, Elyot is satisfied to justify poetry as a useful tool in fashioning a gentleman, a soldier, and a prince. He is less worried about the content of poetry's persuasion than about its acceptance as a conduit of noble values. Like many defenders in the early part of the century, both in England and abroad, he unproblematically associates poetry with rhetoric. He takes the utilitarian view, still extant in some measure as late as Tasso's *Discorsi,* that poetry produces better citizens and is therefore most usefully subsumed under political or moral philosophy.

We see this utilitarianism most clearly in Elyot's defense of music a few pages earlier. It is noteworthy that, in addition to David and Alexander, Elyot cites Achilles as a prime example of the salubrious effects of singing and harp playing. People of the period probably thought of Achilles as a historical figure without stopping too long to consider the distinction between history

---

37. Stephen Gosson, *The Schoole of Abuse* (1579), in Arthur F. Kinney, *Markets of Bawdrie: The Dramatic Criticism of Stephen Gosson* (Salzburg, Austria: Institut für Englische Sprache und Literatur Universität Salzburg, 1974), p. 77. All further references are to this edition. I have silently added the consonants indicated by diacritical marks in the text.

and poetry. (They were not utterly wild in their assumptions, of course, since Agamemnon and others turn out to be genuine figures, if we believe the Linear B tablets.) Nevertheless, Elyot is begging the question by using Achilles as an example, since Achilles is, on some level, a Homeric "fiction" and Elyot has not yet proved that poetry belongs in the curriculum. He begins with the observation that "[t]he most noble and valiant princes of Greece oftentimes, to recreate their spirits and in augmenting their courage, embraced instruments musical" (*Governor*, p. 21). The underlying reason for this music appreciation by Greek aristocrats is, apparently, to temper their warlike urges. Elyot explains that after the confrontation with Agamemnon, the inflamed Achilles, playing the harp Chiron the Centaur taught him, "was therewith assuaged of his fury and reduced to his first state of reason" (p. 21). This is a slight rewriting of the *Iliad,* but more than that it establishes a parallel between Chiron and Achilles and the humanist tutor and his student. This pupil-teacher relationship is seen in other classical poetry, such as Pindar. Chiron is the archetypal teacher of civilized graces and tutor of heroes. Elyot's example is a kind of genealogical proof of the value of the pedagogical relationship among prospective heroes and princes. He opens the section with the assertion that "[t]he discretion of a tutor consisteth in temperance" (p. 20). Perhaps thinking of Plato's *Charmides,* Elyot seems bent on presenting the humanist agenda as a direct descendant of famous tutor-student collaborations.

Moreover, he contends that the appropriate use of music, resulting from a tutor's discretion, also teaches discretion to the student (or warrior). This argument will find its way into almost all future defenses of poetry, whether the defenders see poetry as an instrumental craft or as an architectonic science. According to Renaissance ethics, *discretio* is a kind of support for prudence, which Elyot himself calls "the first moral virtue" (p. 78), devoting a significant section of the *Governor* to the analysis of its eight branches. It is noteworthy, therefore, that he identifies music as a technology that induces discretion, and, by extension, prudent behavior. Elyot maintains that Achilles, to calm himself after the quarrel with Agamemnon, "had sung the gests and acts martial of the ancient prince of Greece, as Hercules, Perseus, Perithous, Theseus, and his cousin Jason" (p. 21). Further, as Elyot assures his readers, a little

harp-strumming does not weaken the will or dissipate the necessary rage of the soldier: in fact, Achilles "so tempered himself in
the entertainment and answering the messengers that came to him
from the residue of the Greeks, that they, reputing all that his
fierce demeanour to be (as it were) a divine majesty, never em-
braided him with any inordinate wrath or fury" (p. 21). This
assertion, of course, is pure humanist propaganda. Achilles is
excessively wrathful by any account. Regardless of whether we
accept Helen North's thesis that a Greek epic hero can never be
sophron, to make Achilles a model of temperance is, I would suggest, an almost laughable distortion.[38] But, again, Elyot knows
his audience: if his noble readers have perused the *Iliad* at all,
which may be doubtful in the early part of the century, then they
would likely admire Achilles' restraint (in not killing Agamemnon
straightaway). They might well identify his behavior as a kind of
feudal loyalty, his withdrawal from the national army representing
an assertion of feudal rights.

While music is of some importance, however, Elyot's chief
argument concerns dancing. In the fifteenth and early sixteenth
centuries, dancing had been outlawed at village fetes and quarter-
day celebrations, perhaps in part because dancing inflamed the
young people and resulted in too many pregnancies among unmar-
ried women. Elyot never mentions this particular problem, but he
is nonetheless at pains to show the moral advantages of dancing.
He maintains that dancing provides an "introduction" to prudence: "this my little enterprise is to declare an induction or mean,
how children of gentle nature or disposition may be trained into
the way of virtue with a pleasant facility" (p. 78). In other words,
he is applying the Horatian poetic formula to dancing. Training in
dancing will serve as the *dulce* by which to acquire "an excellent
utility," both a healthy body from the physical exercise and a
prudent moral character.

Elyot's argument for dancing in many ways echoes by anticipation the typical justification for poetry later in the century. He

---

38. Helen North, *Sophrosyne: Self-Knowledge and Self-Restraint in Greek Literature* (Ithaca, N.Y.: Cornell University Press, 1966), p. 2: "the choice of exemplars makes it clear
that sophrosyne is not a 'heroic' virtue, since the greatest fighting men of the Homeric
epic, Achilles and Ajax, are the very ones who most notoriously lack this quality." In
general, *sophrosyne* is associated with moderation and means "the saving of prudence."

begins his *apologia* with an elaborate genealogical analysis of the origins of dancing, precisely the kind of analysis Boccaccio applies to poetry. Indeed, Elyot seems to use dancing as a substitute for poetry, and very possibly he had in mind Renaissance neoplatonic theories equating poetry with dancing as a means to get souls and bodies in tune.[39] He notes that in the ancient temple of Apollo "no solemnity was done without dancing," as if dancing were the equivalent of Christian hymns. And his own interpretation of the "interpreters of Plato" suggests that the imitation of nature has comparable value in the ideal forms of dancing and of poetry, a kind of *ut poesis saltatio:*

The interpreters of Plato do think that the wonderful and incomprehensible order of the celestial bodies, I mean stars and planets, and their motions harmonical, gave to them that intensity and by the deep search of reason behold their courses, in the sundry diversities of number and time, a form of imitation of a semblable motion, which they called dancing or saltation; wherefore the more near they approached to that temperance and subtle modulation of the said superior bodies, the more perfect and commendable in their dancing, which is most like to the truth of any opinion that I have hitherto found. (P. 73)

Elyot's mention of temperance and modulation is shrewdly contrary to the typical prejudice that dancing causes wantonness of emotion. The motions of the celestial bodies are imitated by "sundry diversities of number and time," and, like poetry, this kind of dance requires a "deep search of reason." The imitation of the stars and planets has a civilizing force, introducing, through motion, a rational economy of body, mind, and soul.

Elyot begins his defense of dance with a familiar ploy, the divine genealogy. From the first he emphasizes dancing's physical appeal to a gentry enamored of rough-and-tumble sport: "The poets do feign that when Saturn, which devoured divers his children, and semblably would have done with Jupiter, Rhea the mother of Jupiter devised that *Curetes* (which were men of arms in that country) should dance in armour, playing with their swords and shields, in such form as by that new and pleasant device they

---

39. See D. P. Walker, *The Ancient Theology: Studies in Christian Platonism from the Fifteenth to the Eighteenth Century* (Ithaca, N.Y.: Cornell University Press, 1972), esp. pp. 22–41, on "Orpheus the Theologian."

should assuage the melancholy of Saturn" (p. 71). This is an excellent conflation: the "men at arms" are set to dancing in order to hide the infants' cries with their own clashing of arms and to save the rightful god of the universe. The obligatory comparison to the Tudor court is here, as well as the utilitarian origin of dancing. Elyot hastily continues, after citing Rhea's similar success in Phrygia, by connecting the pagan origin to a Biblical episode:

[W]hich fable [of Saturn and Jupiter] hath a resemblance to the history of the Bible in the First Book of Kings, where it is remembered that Saul, . . . declining from the laws and precepts of God, was possessed of an evil spirit which oftentimes tormented and vexed him, and other remedy found he none but that David . . . being at that time a proper child and playing sweetly on a harp, with his pleasant and perfect harmony reduced his mind into his pristine estate. (P. 72)

The story of Saul and David is a strange counterpart to that of Rhea and Saturn, though Saturn's melancholy and Saul's evil spirit might be compared. That aside, however, the juxtaposition of the stories (which are both contained in one long sentence) seems intended to prove that dancing *and* musical song (poetry) are acceptable forms descended from divine sources.[40] Elyot recognizes his digression into "the efficiency of music" and promises forthwith "to return to speak of dancing." It is instructive, however, to note that the pagan genealogy cannot proceed without an infusion, in this case digressive, of tandem proto-Christian development. If this is not precisely bogus genealogy, since Elyot admits the difference between music and dancing, then it is a kind of para-genealogy whose very awkwardness helps us to identify Elyot's normative tack.

Anticipating the most prevalent literary debates of the later part of the century, Elyot concludes with a discussion of genres. He names the four kinds of dance in ancient times, *Eumelia, Cordax, Enopliae,* and *Hormus.* As we might expect, these kinds correspond essentially to tragedy, comedy, martial exploits, and love, each of which is characterized by its own principles of decorum. In itself,

---

40. See Walker, *The Ancient Theology,* p. 24: "Music, in that it harmonized the dissonances in the soul produced by its conjunction with the body, could be used as a preparation for philosophic or religious contemplation . . . or, combined with magic rites, as a means to religious ecstasy." Walker cites the "theurgic method of singing the Orphic Hymns that Ficino and Giovanni Pico discovered" (p. 24).

such explicit generic classification is virtually unheard of in England at this time. Further, in a strategy that will often be repeated, most notably perhaps by George Puttenham, Elyot draws a direct parallel between mimetic representation and noble behavior at court. The first book of the *Governor* is essentially a disquisition on the fit application of such representation—both dancing and, by inference, poetry. As such, the treatise presages all subsequent English defenses of poetry, stage plays, and music. That alone is of interest. Moreover, there is Elyot's constant use of dubious genealogies to establish a persuasive justification for importing ancient foreign culture and grafting it onto English habits. While it is not clear how influential Elyot's *Governor* was later in the century, we should nevertheless recognize its primacy among defenses. Later generations of writers might well have found in Elyot's book both a set of models and a methodology.

THE PARENT OF POETRY AND POETRY AS PARENTAGE: JOHN RAINOLDS AND STEPHEN GOSSON

In 1572 John Rainolds delivered an oration at Oxford entitled *Oratio in laudem artis poeticae.*[41] It constitutes one of the first systematic defenses of poetry in England, though, of course, Rainolds delivered it in Latin and virtually nobody heard it or read the text. Performed as an academic exercise, the short treatise is somewhat overblown, packed with a deliberate copiousness of classical allusions. Nevertheless, the *Oratio* dutifully echoes Boccaccio and begins to explore the uses of Aristotle's *Poetics.* As if recalling Elyot, for instance, Rainolds claims that "The *Poetics* of Aristotle hands over the uncultivated minds of children to be formed by the imita-

---

41. J. W. Binns has recently made a strong case that Henry Dethick is the author of this work; he suggests that Dethick's *Oratio in laudem poeseos* was found among Rainolds's papers and mistakenly printed as one of his Oxford lectures. See J. W. Binns, *Intellectual Culture in Elizabethan England: The Latin Writings of the Ages* (University of Leeds, England: Francis Cairns Ltd., 1990), pp. 444–47, 146–48. I have been unable to examine Dethick's work, and since, according to Binns, his text differs from the text ascribed to Rainolds in the edition I used, I have continued to refer to the author as John Rainolds. It seems unlikely, in any case, that a reascription of authorship would significantly affect my argument.

tion of immortal deeds" ("*Aristotelis* poetica puerorum rudes animos ad rerum immortalium imitationem informari tradit").[42] Poetry is "that famous Persuasion" ("illa Suada") that moves its readers in the directions to which they are otherwise reluctant to go, "the sensitive to danger, the slothful to battles, and the cowardly to encounter death courageously" ("molles ad pericula, socordes ad praelia, timidos ad mortem animose oppetendam," p. 38). William Ringler claims, about Rainolds and Philip Sidney, that "both authors regard poetry in much the same light, as being in essence a form of persuasion" (p. 32).

There is a distinction in Rainolds's argument between persuasion and rhetoric, insofar as poetry can be persuasive without assuming rhetoric's insubstantial trappings. According to Rainolds's genealogy, poetry precedes and begets rhetoric, which, for its part, inevitably borrows from poetry:

Iam unde tandem Rhetorica numeros? A semetipsa? nihil minus. Unde igitur? A poetis sumptos fatetur ipsius *Ciceronis* orator. Ex quo efficitur, ut quicquid virium, suavitatis, nervorum, venustatis habet ars dicendi (habet enim plurimum) id totum in ejus rivulos e Poetarum fontibus transfusum & derivatum esse videatur. (P. 50)

Now where, may I ask, does Rhetoric get its rhythms? From itself? Not at all. Where then? Cicero's Orator himself admits a debt to the poet. Whereby it is conceived that whatever of strength, sweetness, vigor, and charm the art of eloquence has (and it has much indeed), is all seen to be derived and poured into its channels from the fonts of the Poets.

Rainolds has a very low opinion of rhetoric, which he clearly distinguishes from poetic persuasion. He considers that rhetoric, "utterly devoid of sagacity, full of empty talk . . . shines forth deceptively" ("inanissima prudentiae, loquacitatis plenissima . . . fallaciter enitescit," p. 48). He likens it to a harlot's curling irons and claims that rhetoric resembles the trees that grow beside the Dead Sea, "which exhibit great beauty to the sight, but if one plucks their fruit, he finds it full of embers and ashes" ("quae magnam aspectu prae se ferunt pulchritudinem, earum fructus si quis decerpat, favilla & cinere plenos reperiret," p. 48). This is

---

42. John Rainolds, *Oratio in laudem artis poeticae* (ca. 1572), ed. William Ringler (Princeton: Princeton University Press, 1940), p. 38.

fairly precocious criticism of rhetoric in England, and its harshness adumbrates such puritanical diatribes as Phillip Stubbes's *The Anatomie of Abuses* (1583).[43]

Further, Rainolds's sharp division of poetry and rhetoric, while relying on the accepted hierarchy of nature and art, reiterates the commonplace platonic notion that the poet is gifted with a divine afflatus. For Rainolds, as for other earlier theorists who tend to ignore Plato's ambivalence regarding the *furor poeticus,* this natural inspiration reflects the poet's superior status. Moreover, this ostensible divinity has, at least for Rainolds, a genealogical aspect:

Quis est enim omnium, qui se tanta stultia tam insigniter infatuarit, aut in tantam insaniam tam furenter proruperit, ut cum intueatur animo coelum ipsum, splendidissimum praepotentis Dei domicilium, poetices quasi parentum extisse, non incredibiliter suspiciat & obstupescat? (P. 34)

Who is there truly that makes such a fool of himself, or breaks out so furiously in madness, that when he gazes with his soul upon heaven, that most brilliant dwelling place of all-powerful God, will not look upwards and be incredibly astounded to see stand forth the parent, as it were, of poetry.

Though later in his career Rainolds will write a stinging critique of stage plays, in the *Oratio* he demonstrates an exemplary faith in the supremely high origins of the poetic urge.[44] As is common in authors who subscribe to the divine myth, Rainolds cites the texts of the early Hebrews to establish the sacred genealogy of poetic forms. As Israel Barroway put it some time ago, "it was generally agreed that the primacy of Hebrew prosody and Hebrew poetry in general was temporal as well as qualitative."[45] In Rainolds's ver-

43. *The Anatomie of Abuses* (New York: Garland Publishing, 1973). Among the abuses that Stubbes attacks, there is "the horrible vice of pestiferous dauncing," music, bear-baiting, and hawking and hunting.

44. If Henry Dethick in fact wrote the *Oratio,* as Binns maintains, then the contrast of Rainolds's later work is not relevant.

45. Israel Barroway, "The Bible as Poetry in the English Renaissance: An Introduction," *JEGP* 32 (1933), p. 477. Barroway notes that the chief sources for the belief in the metricality of Biblical Hebrew are Josephus and Philo. He cites a number of English treatises that discuss the hexameters of, for instance, Jeremiah, Solomon, and David. See also Barroway's subsequent essays on the subject: " 'The Lyre of David': A Further Study in Renaissance Interpretation of Biblical Form," *ELH* 8 (1941), pp. 119–42; "The Accentual Theory of Hebrew Prosody: A Further Study in Renaissance Interpretation of Biblical Form," *ELH* 17 (1950), pp. 115–35.

sion, as in Boccaccio's, metrical language comes into being as a kind of decorum:

Nam illi prisci patres, homines sapientia & virtute florentissimi, quibus Dei Opt. Max. sermones accipere contigit, ab ultimis seculis ista studia colverunt. Suas nimirum cogitationes, non ea pervulgata, & detrita, & dissoluta qua quilibet uteretur oratione, consignare, sed alia exquisita, & astricta, & numerosa, & vinculis illigata, praeclarum existimarunt. (P. 40)

For the early fathers, men of the highest repute in knowledge and virtue, to whom it befell to receive the words of Almighty God, cultivated this study [of poetry] from earliest times. They undoubtedly judged it excellent to record their thoughts not in common, hackneyed, and enervated speech, but, rather, in speech carefully worked out, concise, rhythmical and bound together [by the rules of prosody].[46]

This is an eloquently illegitimate scenario. As is well known, Hebrew poetry is not metrical, and Josephus's claims for its metricality result from his anachronistic comparison of Hebrew to Greek. Rainolds probably did not have any Hebrew. His adaptation of the origins of prosody is, to some extent, already a commonplace. That he relies on genealogy to defend the English poet is, however, notable, especially since the *Oratio* comes some time before even the poets themselves (professionals, in particular) had begun to agitate for special status and general commendation.

In fact, Rainolds concludes his oration with a characterization of poetry that will become familiar in later years, a catalogue of hero-rulers and their bards (or publicists):

Testis est Alexander *Magnus,* qui tanti fecit *Homeri* Poemata, ut fortunatum *Achillem* duceret, cui tantus virtutis praeco contigisset. Testis *Octavius Augustus,* qui cum Poetas omnes impense coluit, tum inprimis *Virgilium* honore summo decoravit. . . . Testis est *Scipio Africanus,* qui suas victorias *Ennii* buccina decantari voluit, eumque adeo in *Scipionum* sepulchris in Marmore constituit. (Pp. 56–58)

As witness there is Alexander the Great, who made so much of Homer's poem that he considered Achilles fortunate in having such a herald of his bravery; and there is Octavius Augustus, who eagerly cultivated all Poets, and honored Virgil first and foremost. . . . And there is Scipio

---

46. See the translation by Walter Allen, Jr., in Ringler's edition, p. 41. Allen translates "dissoluta" as "unmetrical."

Africanus, who so much wanted his victories to be sung by Ennius's horn that he fixed Ennius in marble on the tomb of the Scipios.

This is a veiled plea for the patronage of poets. It anticipates, almost literally, the language used by Sidney's first elegists to establish their own value, both to Sidney's family name and to poetic tradition. Sidney was often compared to Alexander, and his elegists cast themselves as the Homer Alexander never had.

Rainolds continues, as a matter of fact, in a vein redolent of the ways of courtly solicitations. He catalogues the manner in which princes went to great lengths to protect poets in the past. (The most famous example is again Alexander, who, when he destroyed Thebes, spared only the descendants of Pindar.)[47] Implying more than simply protection or even patronage, however, Rainolds's catalogue suggests an elite sort of utility in great poetry while playing on the inevitable yearning for fame among ambitious nobles.

Within two decades this use of poetry will start to change. As Sidney's earliest elegists are succeeded in the 1590s by poets with more literary ambitions, the Alexanders and the Scipios are replaced by the immortalized lover of the English version of the Petrarchan sonnet. This gradual transformation does not occur, however, without some resistance. As the herald of great deeds, poetry was not only a potential advertiser of the nobility but also a vehicle for moral expression. As such, it had an instrumental utility, something that so-called trifling stage plays and idle verses did not have. As Edwin H. Miller has suggested, many writers sought to prove the newly debased condition of literature. Literary criticism, such as it was, suffered as a result.

The increasing body of critical writings toward the end of the sixteenth century underscored the indictments of moralists and humanists. This is understandable, since English critics were children of an age given to moralistic evaluation and for the most part were unoriginal expounders of secondhand platitudes and generalities borrowed from foreign and classical writers. Literature they appraised in the light of what it was supposed to be—and to do—according to the sterile precedents they quoted at length. . . . In short, English criticism consisted of intellec-

47. Rainolds, *Oratio,* p. 58: "*Alexander* . . . cum vniuersas *Thebas* euerteret, solius *Pindari* poeteris pepercit."

tualizations, or moralizations, unrelated to the emotional and aesthetic qualities of literature.[48]

The polarization of "the emotional and aesthetic qualities of literature" and its intellectual or moral counterparts is singularly instructive. It reminds us that, for all intents and purposes, there is no such thing as aesthetics in Renaissance criticism, especially not in England, unless we can speak of a kind of athletic aesthetics. The literary arguments are only half serious. In reality, the very stringent competition for advancement in the courtly milieu is played out in the battle of what Miller calls "sterile precedents." And it is not so much the precedents as the battle itself that is important.

Because the constraints of primogeniture produced an enormous surplus of second sons who were unemployable, and who consequently glutted the avenues of patronage, it is not surprising to find the debates about poetry attached to ongoing debates about the value of action over contemplation. Ostensibly, these debates focus on the value of poetry as the bearer of philosophical truth, but in reality they are concerned to show the value of poetry as action. One reason for this concern, of course, is that action—or potential action, as in the case of armed gentry—wins reward from Elizabeth. Daniel Javitch has suggested that "[i]n a milieu like the court, where avenues of advancement for outsiders were so limited and arbitrary, sophisticated poetic performance, compatible as it was to courtly style and taste, could indeed be seen as a means to secure preferment there."[49] Another reason is that, in the climate of Puritan antitheatrical diatribe, poetry is viewed as immoral insofar as it is useless. "Artistic fictions," Russell Fraser contends in *The War against Poetry,* "are condemned on moral grounds; the critical objection is, however, to their utility."[50] The humanists, though in themselves products of a luxury class, wished to be seen as practical scientists and philosophers. Fraser cites Bacon especially, who, though a derider of poetry, in his practicality paradoxically characterizes the humanist defenders of poetry: "The human-

48. Edwin Haviland Miller, *The Professional Writer in Elizabethan England* (Cambridge, Mass.: Harvard University Press, 1959), pp. 67–68.

49. Daniel Javitch, "The Impure Motives of Elizabethan Poetry," *Genre* 15 (1982), pp. 227–28.

50. Russell Fraser, *The War against Poetry* (Princeton: Princeton University Press, 1970), p. 4.

ist, like Sidney or like the Italian critics from whom he takes his cue, belongs in this company [of practical men]. The association is unexpected; it is, however, demonstrable. The humanist justifies poetry as it is an ethical discipline. Poetry is useful. In each case, utility, very amply construed, is the master motive informing the judgment of poetry and the theatre" (p. 5).

Utility, or the lack thereof, is the generating theme of Stephen Gosson's *The Schoole of Abuse* (1579). Though not a very rigorous theorist by any means, Gosson is still known chiefly because Sidney's *Defence of Poesie* is a response to his *Abuse*. (Sidney never mentions Gosson by name, however, and never acknowledges Gosson's dedication to him of *The Schoole of Abuse*.) Despite its literary shortcomings, Gosson's text is worth examining for its characterization of acceptable poetry in genealogical terms. Although, as Arthur F. Kinney observes, Gosson "cites his authorities to deny [the] efficacy of art," nevertheless his somewhat feudal approach to literature as a fund of utilitarian family trees turns out to be more prescient than one would expect.[51] In fact, though subsequent defenders of poetry automatically dismiss Gosson as puerile and uninformed, their own views of poetry as an instrumental science are not far removed from his.

Still, so far as I can tell, little serious concern attended Gosson's contention that the poet is a "deceitfull Phisition" who "giueth sweete Syroppes to make his poyson goe downe the smoother" (p. 77). One suspects that only Puritan fanatics agreed with him that, as a result of having "robbed *Greece* of Gluttonie, *Italy* of wantonnesse, *Spaine* of pride, *Fraunce* of deceite, and *Dutchland* of quaffing" (p. 91), the poets of the theater brought about the physical decay of English citizens. Nostalgic for the rough and tumble physicality of Old England, the hunting, wrestling, running, and shooting of Elyot's day, Gosson extravagantly blames the irresistible delights of poetry for serving up only pleasure without profit:

But the exercise that is nowe among vs, is banqueting, playing, pipyng, and dauncing, and all suche delightes as may winne us to pleasure, or rocke us in sleepe.

51. Kinney, *Markets of Bawdrie*, p. 28. Kinney notes that "[d]espite Gosson's masterful attempt to order his argument through parallelism, repetition, accretion, and metaphor, *The Schoole of Abuse* must finally be considered his work of apprenticeship" (p. 38).

Oh what a wonderfull change is this? Our wreastling at arms, is turned to wallowyng in Ladies laps; our courage, to cowardice, our running/to ryot, our Bowes into Bolles, and our Dartes to Dishes. (P. 77)

Decay theorists are by no means new in England at this time, and the connection between "bad" poetry or loose speech and odious deeds had already been the subject of harangue. For instance, seven years before Gosson, Roger Ascham insists that "ye shall surelie find that, when apte and good wordes began to bee neglected, and properties of those two tonges [Greek and Latin] to be confounded, than also began ill deedes to spring."[52]

Gosson's complaints chiefly focus on the wrong use of poetry in the present day in contrast with the "right vse of auncient Poetrie." While his approach is broadly tendentious, its emphases are not literary by any stretch of the imagination:

52. Roger Ascham, "Of Imitation," from *The Scholemaster,* in G. Gregory Smith, ed., *Elizabethan Critical Essays,* 2 vols. (Oxford University Press, 1904), 1:6. See also Edmund Hunt, *"Laudatores Temporis Acti," Classical Journal* 40 (1945), pp. 221–33. In both Ascham and Gosson there is something of a modern attempt to be *laudatores temporis acti,* "the dominant Roman habit," according to Hunt, "of expressing chagrin at the social degradation of their own days as compared with the *virtus vetus*" (p. 221). Hunt makes it fairly clear that "the 'decline' theme must have been a familiar topic for discussion in Rome" (p. 222), and he emphasizes that "it became traditional for historians to mention some exact point and cause of decline" (p. 223). He gives examples from Sallust, Polybius, Livy, Tacitus, Florus, and others, all or most of whom would have been known to Elizabethans. What is most interesting, however, is the extent to which Roman authors copy their precursors in the disparagement of the present. "[M]ost of the historians' outcry," Hunt continues, "was merely conventional and showed little speculation on details or on faults peculiar to any given age, much less on adequate reform measures" (p. 225). It is worthwhile to bear the conventionality of these postures in mind in considering the Elizabethan disparagement of poetry, of contemporary eloquence, and of, in Ascham's contumely, "the whole doctrine and all the bookes of phantasticall Anabaptistes and Friers, and of the beastlie Libertines and Monkes" (p. 7). In decrying the present degradation, writers as different as Ascham and Gosson both manage to align themselves with a very tendentious version of genealogical revision. This is not a conscious alignment necessarily, but the result of imitating what we might call "revisionary models." The English writers disparage their contemporaries and revise their precursors by imitating dutifully these Roman authors who do the same things to their contemporaries and precursors.

I have not come across the notion of revisionary models, but see G. W. Pigman III, "Versions of Imitation in the Renaissance," *Renaissance Quarterly* 33 (1980), pp. 1–32. This quite erudite discussion addresses the notion of revision in terms of "transformative" imitation, as in digestive or apian metaphors, and of "eristic" imitation, the open rivalry and intent to defeat earlier models.

The right vse of auncient Poetrie was to haue the notable exploytes of woorthy Captaines, the holesome councels of good fathers, and vertuous liues of predecessors set downe in numbers, and sung to the Instrument at solemne feastes, that the sound of the one might draw the hearers from kissing the cupp too often; the sense of the other put them in minde of things past, and chaulk out the way to do the like. (P. 82)

The passage is, to some extent, a prescription for poetry as genealogy. A poetry that consists of the "vertuous liues of predecessors" would be a family tree of sorts. It does not include a claim for the divine origins of poetry. Rather, a poetry of predecessors would entrench the continuity of human civic conscience. It is further proof, for us, of the instructional use to which Elizabethans put the competition for a literary past. Moreover, Gosson undoubtedly has ulterior motives in describing this early scene of poetry. For example, his asseveration that the sound of poetry once wooed "hearers from kissing the cupp" contains the quaint implication that a right use of the same art in England might cut down on drunkenness, bawdiness, dicing, and all the other rambunctiousness the Puritans deplored. He also contrives to point out to a possibly abstemious audience the high value ancient civilizations placed on alcoholic temperance. Fraser maintains, in fact, that Gosson's preferment was the direct result of his suspiciously tailored polemic.[53]

Nevertheless, Gosson is careful not to recommend that the modern Englishman do as the ancient pagan did. He recognizes the ethical danger in that, and therefore sticks to praise of utility in general. He rather sidesteps the issue of how exactly modern poets should use ancient poetry and he reveals, instead, how ancient poets used their genealogically inspired odes and music as calls to arms. Predictably, Gosson himself follows suit: he cites a sort of genealogical catalogue to support his conclusion that ancient poetry, by recounting past martial exploits, would "chaulk out the way to do the like." As the ancients used exempla so does he: "Af-

---

53. See especially Fraser, *The War against Poetry*, p. 72: "The *School of Abuse*, which is the instrument of Gosson's new fortunes, enjoys a first printing of 3,000 copies, as against the normal run of 500. . . . Presumably the proceeds are already in hand before a single copy is sold." Also p. 73: "[H]is way is smoothed by employment as a tutor in the country, and perhaps as a government agent. At last he is rewarded with a series of ecclesiastical appointments. He ends his days as the incumbent of one of the richest livings in London."

ter this maner were the *Baeotians* [sic] trained from rudeness to ciuilitie, the *Lacedaemonians* instructed by *Tyrteaeus* verse, the *Argiues* by the melody of *Telesilla,* and the *Lesbians* by *Alcaeus* Odes" (p. 82). This is an unusual, strangely unfamiliar genealogy for poetry in the sixteenth century: a more familiar list would include Hesiod and Theocritus, not to mention Homer. Yet it should be considered a genealogy inasmuch as descent is the lesson, if not in the pure sense of actual begetting. Indeed, the figurative value of Gosson's genealogy to my analysis, in contrast to its actual value as descriptive literary history, reveals the extent to which the tracing of conceived presences depends on troping. Inauspicious as Gosson may be, his normative distortions of conventional genealogy provide a felicitous instance of the expansion of the notion of genealogy from literal definitions of rank or poetic lineage.

There is no love poet and, significantly, no pastoral poet among Gosson's examples. As far as the sixteenth-century reader could have determined, from Diogenes Laertius or fragments in Hesiod, the poets Gosson mentions were famous especially for inspiring the populace to take up arms. Tyrtaeus was a Spartan general and elegiac poet of the seventh century; he would have been known for his war songs perhaps, though Gosson seems to be referring to Tyrtaeus's *Politeia,* written for the Lacedaemonians. Telesilla was a female poet of the fifth century, famous for arming the Argive women after the defeat of Argos by Cleomenes. Though Herodotus does not refer specifically to Telesilla, he cites the oracle she helped fulfill: " 'But when the female subdues the male and drives him out,/And wins thereby great glory amongst the Argives.' "[54] (One is inclined to contrast the martial Telesilla to the amorous Sappho, about whom Gosson earlier remarks: "*Sappho* was skilfull in Poetrie and sung wel, but she was whorish" [p. 80].) Finally, Alcaeus, a lyric poet of seventh-century Lesbos, is somewhat more problematic: it is unlikely that Gosson would be referring to the fragments of Alcaeus's drinking songs or love lyrics; probably he is alluding to Diogenes Laertius's report on Alcaeus's combative poetry, in which particularly he attacked the tyrant Pittacus for his riotous behavior and political madness.

---

54. Herodotus, *The Histories,* trans. Aubrey de Sélincourt (Harmondsworth, England: Penguin Books, 1987), p. 415.

Gosson continually adheres to a rather narrow notion of poetry as something with which to placate princes. It is noteworthy, moreover, that in recalling how "[p]oetrie and pyping, haue all-waies/been so vnited togither" (p. 82), Gosson follows Elyot's prescription for the utility of music. But by Gosson's time the audience has changed. Feudal barons are comparatively domesti-cated, and it is scarcely necessary to persuade the Elizabethan patrons that Achilles had been a worthy musician and therefore that the schools should teach Homer. To the contrary, Homer was in no danger of neglect. Not for Homer's sake does Gosson mar-shall Elyot's old-fashioned argument aligning music and heroic action, poetry and prudence. Rather, his aim is clearly to encour-age readers to see poetry as a civic tool, like a curfew or a sumptuary law, by showing its connection to music. He acknowledges the restraining properties of poetic song, but he attributes them to mathematics, medicine, and law, which, he claims, are the actual characteristics of ancient poetry.

To this end are instruments vsed in battaile, not to tickle the eare, but to teach euery souldier when to strike and when to stay, when to flye, and when to followe. *Chiron* by singing to his instrument, quencheth *Achiles* [*sic*] fury:/*Terpandrus* with his notes, layeth the tempest, and pacifies the tumult at *Lacedaemon: Homer* with his Musicke cured the sick Souldiers in the *Grecians* campe, and purged euery mans Tent of the Plague. (P. 82)

Drawing largely on Plutarch, Gosson then paraphrases Pythago-ras, his scientific source, who "condemnes them for fooles, that judge Musicke by sounde and eare" (p. 83). The right use of music is to see in it perfect harmony, "the order of the Spheres, the vnfallible motion of the Planets, the just course of the yeere, and varietie of seasons, the concorde of the Elementes and their qualy-ties" (p. 83).[55] And it turns out, Gosson triumphantly announces, that "[t]he politike Lawes in well gouerned common wealthes . . . are excellent maisters too shewe you that this is right Musicke, this perfecte harmony" (p. 83).

So he now expands the earlier catalogue to reveal the civic

55. This view of music is not unusual in the period. See, for example, Sigmund Spaeth, *Milton's Knowledge of Music* (Princeton: Princeton University Library, 1913); and John Hollander, *The Untuning of the Sky* (Princeton: Princeton University Press, 1961; rpt. New York: W. W. Norton, 1970).

motives of Chiron and Terpander and the nearly messianic powers of Homer:

Chiron when hee appeased the wrath of *Achilles* tolde hym the duetie of a good souldier, repeated the vertues of his father *Peleus,* and sung the famous enterprises of noble men. *Terpandrus* when he ended the brabbles at *Lacedaemon,* neither pyped *Rogero* nor *Turkelony,* but reckoning by the commodities of friendship, and fruites of debate, putting them in minde of *Lycurgus* lawes, taughte them too treade a better measure. /When *Homers* musicke droue the pestilence from the *Grecians* camp, there was no such vertue in his penne, nor in his pipe, but if I might bee vmpier, in the sweete harmonie of diuerse natures & wonderful concord of sundry medicines. (P. 83)

Under the microscope the catalogue seems very odd, full of doctors and lawyers—exactly the professions Boccaccio claims that poets supersede in his remarks to the jurists in the *Genealogia.* And the catalogue is reminiscent of Tasso's *Discorsi* insofar as it encourages a view of the poet as legislator. Chiron, the son of Kronos, is a mythological half-beast chiefly famous as an educator: among his renowned pupils we find Asclepius, the god of healing, who, as A. Bartlett Giamatti suggests, embodies in his reassembly of Hippolytus the humanist effort to salvage the shredded texts of the past (which is also a Boccaccian notion). Next, the seventh-century poet Terpander cites Lycurgus, founder of the Spartan constitution, and by singing some legal history restores order to the quarreling tribes (as Chiron pacified tribal squabbling by soothing Achilles). Gosson seems to imply, moreover, that Terpander accomplished his feat forensically, as opposed to Ariosto, of all people, whose hero Ruggiero relies on love songs and magic spells to assuage discord in his legions. Finally, and most puzzling, there is a Homeric legend that the blind poet drove away a plague. But a melodious medical miracle is not enough for Gosson. He insists that neither Homer's pen nor pipe is responsible for the action, but, rather, that "the sweete harmonie of divers natures, and wonderful concorde of sundry medicines" saved the Greek camp.

One deduces from these historical contortions that poetry (or music) is most useful as technology. Poets at their civic best are pillars of the practical arts, and only as such, at least in Gosson's view, can the commonwealth utilize them. It is very clear on which side of the old division between *scientia* and *facultas* we find *The*

Schoole of Abuse. Gosson's only interesting addition to the debate is the notion that the most practical poetry is a kind of genealogy in itself.

THE POET AS GENEALOGIST

Early in his *Defence of Poetry* (1579), which is an explicit response to *The Schoole of Abuse,* Thomas Lodge reverses Gosson's notion of the poet as a "deceitfull phisition": "seing the world in those daies was unperfect, it was necessary that [poets] like good Phisitions should so frame their potions that they might be appliable to the quesie stomaks of their werish patients" (Smith, 1:66). This is naturally a historical argument, meant to recreate the primal scenes of poetry. It is the preface to Lodge's proof that poetry helps humanity, a proof that depends, predictably, on the recognition of poetry as the result of divine inspiration and sacred charity. Lodge offers a remarkably innovative genealogy to support this assertion:

Among the precise Jewes you shall find Poetes. . . . Beroaldus can witness with me that David was a poet, and that his vayne was in imitating (as S. Jerome witnesseth) Horace, Flaccus, and Pindarus; sometimes his verse runneth in Iambus foote, anone he hath recourse to a Saphic vaine. . . . Ask Josephus, and he wil tel you that Esay, Job, and Salamon voutsafed poetical practices, for (if Origen and he fault not) theyre verse was Hexameter and pentameter. Enquire of Cassiodorus, he will say the beginning of Poetrye proceeded from the Scripture. (Smith, 1:71)

The chronology is scrambled in such a way that Christians defend Hebrews, while, astonishingly, David imitates the classical poets, some of whom follow him by more than a thousand years. In addition, the Hebrews and the pagans are accompanied by church fathers. Their hermeneutic authority ostensibly proves not only the origin of poetry (and prosody) among the "precise Jewes" but also testifies to Christian sanction of poets descended from David.

This forged descent, it turns out, is an important aspect of Lodge's *Defence.* His treatise concludes with the following prayer for Elizabeth: "God preserve our peacable Princes, and confound her enemies: God enlarge her wisdom, that like Saba she may seek after a Salamon: God confound the imaginations of her enemies, and perfit his graces in her, that the days of her rule may be

continued in the bonds of peace, that the house of the chosen
Israelites may be mayntened in happiness" (Smith, 1:86). The
genealogy of poetry that began with David comes to its present-
day fruition in England, which, according to Lodge, has become
"the house of the chosen Israelites." The connection between politics and poetic descent is unmistakable. Moreover, it is notable
how useful a forged genealogy can be in defending poets, granting
them a royal lineage as well as a divine origin.

In a less spectacular way, Philip Sidney promotes poetry to the
ranks of the peerage in his *Defence.* In the language of the tilt,
Sidney disparages the philosopher's "wordish description, which
doth neither strike, pierce, nor possess the sight of the soul so
much as that other doth" (p. 107).[56] This is extraordinary language
to describe a verbal image, which, after all, is itself something of a
"wordish description." The violence of striking, piercing, and
possessing seems, if nothing else, faintly inappropriate to the
static arts. In a way, however, Sidney is performing his own Herald's Visitation. He has "created" poetry a knight, thereby permitting the poetic image to bear arms and to engage, successfully of
course, the noble discourses of the philosopher and the historian.
Few Elizabethans would have missed Sidney's correlation between
the indispensable practical value of armigerous gentry in the com-
monweal and that of martially superior poetry.

Yet, despite Sidney's awareness of the political impact of rank,
he is rather naive about the need for literary genealogy in the
England of his day. In Sidney's ideal, as Rosalie Colie has recognized, poetry seeks to subsume philosophy and history as arbiter of
paideia. Colie explains that "again and again Sidney reiterates,
always in generic lists, his belief that the *paideia* is born *as* poetry
and borne *by* poetry. . . . along with Antonio Minturno, Scaliger,

---

56. See also Catherine Barnes, "The Hidden Persuader: The Complex Speaking Voice
of Sidney's *Defence of Poetry, PMLA* 86 (1971), p. 424: Barnes cites this passage to support
her observation that in the *Defence* "[p]oetry, rather predictably, is portrayed in terms of
sexual relations and reproduction." I would like to accept this reading, especially if we
could furnish both a sexual and a martial significance for Sidney's description, but I have
some trouble with the word "strike" in the vein of "sexual relations and reproduction." (I
am aware that the Anglo-Saxon *feocan* is translated "to strike," but I find that too much of
an etymological stretch.) Another link between poetry and sex (or poetry and chivalry)
might be the horse, which in different contexts can serve as a symbol for knights, passion
(often in a comic vein), and poetry (Pegasus and Hippocrene).

William Webbe and a host of others Sidney presents the whole
paideia as poetic topics."[57] This suggests a kind of genealogy, but,
significantly, it is poetry that gives birth to everything else. Thus
poetry is pre-genealogical, and the poet is removed from the task of
recording his family tree, as Gosson would have poets do.

Unfortunately, it is family trees that English literary tradition
needs above all else. Even if it is not precisely poetry as genealogy
that Elizabethans require, nonetheless it is the poet as genealogist
that captures their interest. In direct contrast to Gosson, Sidney's
Defence effectively contends that poetry is more than mere *techne,*
that, both genealogically and heuristically, the poet subsumes the
rhetorician and the practitioner of the practical arts. As O. B.
Hardison explains in a discussion of Sidney's definition of *poesis,*
"[t]he concept of making does not lead [Sidney], as it did Cas-
telvetro, for example, to the concept of poetry as a rational craft, or
techne, but in precisely the opposite direction, to the concept of the
poet as inspired creator."[58] He resists the notion of poetry as genealogy, just as he avoids thinking about the poet as a latter-day
genealogist. For Sidney, as for Boccaccio and Antonio Minturno,
the divine origins of poetry preclude the necessity of practicing a
kind of poetry whose function is to instruct prosaically on the
subject of Gosson's "vertuous predecessors."[59]

Nevertheless, however improbable it may seem, it is Gosson's
point rather than Sidney's that is taken up by later Elizabethan
defenders of poetry. Even Puttenham, who is often adduced as
Sidneian, blithely declares that "the Poets were also from the
beginning the best perswaders and their eloquence the first Rhetoricke of the world" (*Arte,* p. 6). This is a less skeptical view of

57. Colie, *The Resources of Kind: Genre Theory in the Renaissance,* ed. Barbara K. Lewalski
(Berkeley: University of California Press, 1973), p. 20. The ellipsis is of Colie's redaction
of Sidney's "generic lists," which, somewhat significantly, are made up of the genealogical acorns of the humanist orchard: "Musaeus created dithyramb and prophecy, Homer
heroic matter, Hesiod theogony and agriculture, Orpheus and Linus hymns and prophetic poetry, Amphion architecture, Thales, Empedocles and Parmenides philosophy,
Pythagoras and Phocylides ethics, Solon politics, Plato philosophy and dramatic dialogue, Herodotus history."

58. O. B. Hardison, "Two Voices of Sidney's *Apology,*" in Arthur F. Kinney, ed., *Sidney
in Retrospect* (Amherst: University of Massachusetts Press, 1988), p. 50.

59. See A. C. Hamilton, *Sir Philip Sidney: A Study of His Life and Works,* (Cambridge:
Cambridge University Press, 1977), esp. chapter 4.

rhetoric than we find in Rainolds's critique of the empty talk, the cinder-filled fruit of the rhetorician's words. And Puttenham's "first Rhetoricke of the world" seems far from Sidney's expressly architectonic notion of poetry. Yet, to make poetry into a practical art and to invest it with civic potential are precisely what poetry's defenders attempt to do after the death of Sidney.[60] Ironically, Gosson's elaborate subterfuge, the suborning of Homer and others for his antipoetical purposes, becomes the very strategy by which his putative enemies prove the extensive utility of poetry. Indeed, they defend poetry not as poetry, as Sidney obstinately required, but as a particularly deliberative kind of rhetorical persuasion, the province of Gosson's lawyers.[61]

60. See for example Sir John Davies, *Orchestra* (1596), in Robert Krueger, ed., *The Poems of Sir John Davies* (Oxford: Clarendon Press, 1975). Davies praises dancing as an endeavor that is more than practical, or that is practical in a more profound sense. Dancing represents a correspondence with nature, allowing human beings to achieve an ideal concord between the mind and the body in the world. Davies echoes Elyot's neoplatonism, and, like Elyot, defends the genealogy of dancing much as defenders of poetry evoke the noble origins of their art: "I will forthwith his [dancing's] antique Gentry read,/And for I love him, will his Herault be/And blaze his armes, and draw his Pedigree" (st. 27). *Orchestra* concludes with several stanzas in which Davies wishes that he were able to write poetry, and thus praise dancing, with the skill of greater poets. He sketches a familiar genealogy, briefly invoking Homer, Mantuan, Tasso, Spenser, and Daniel. Significantly, he devotes an entire stanza to Sidney:

> Yet *Astrophell* might one for all suffize,
> Whose supple Muse Camelion-like doth change
> Into all formes of excellent devise:
> So might the Swallow, who swift Muse doth range
> Through rare *Ideas,* and inventions strange,
> And ever doth enjoy her joyfull spring,
> And sweeter then the Nightingale doth sing. (St. 130)

61. Resistance to quantitative verse, the use of classical norms of prosody in English, is probably a case in point. For instance, Samuel Daniel, in *A Defence of Rhyme,* directly addresses the question of persuasion when discussing the superiority of measure and accent: "the English verse then hath number, measure, and harmonie in the best proportion of Musicke. . . . And so naturall a melody is it, and so vniversall, as it seems to be generally borne with al the Nations of the world as an hereditary eloquence proper to all mankind. The vniuersalitie argues the generall power of it: for if the Barbarian vse it, then it shewes that it swais th' affection of the Barbarian: if ciuil nations practise it, it proues that it works vpon the harts of ciuil nations: if all, then that it hath a power in nature on all" (Smith, *Elizabethan Critical Essays,* 2:361). See Derek Attridge, *Well-Weigh'd Syllables: Elizabethan Verse in Classical Metres* (London: Cambridge University Press, 1974); John Thompson, *The Founding of English Meter* (New York: Columbia University Press, 1961); and O. B. Hardison, *Prosody and Purpose in the English Renaissance* (Baltimore and London: Johns Hopkins University Press, 1989).

After his death, and in contrast to his own unpublished opinions, Sidney becomes the perfect example of a poet who is also a virtuous civic figure. Ben Jonson begins to see the flaw in this myth, and perhaps he even recognizes the extent to which it contradicts Sidney's own impulses in the *Defence*. Not until Milton, however, does Sidney's ideal of poetry as *paideia* actually entrench itself: "it is Milton," Geoffrey Shepherd points out, "who inherits the doctrine of the *Defence* most unreservedly. In Milton's literary theory and practice, in his range, even in the order of his works, particularly perhaps in *Paradise Regained* with its fastidious dialogues of conscience in an Arcadian wilderness, Sidney would have rejoiced to see his own literary aspirations realised with compelling magniloquence" (*Apology,* p. 87). Indeed, far earlier than *Paradise Regained* we find the "doctrine of the *Apology*" worked out. *Lycidas,* in fact, constitutes Milton's simultaneous challenge of the Sidney myth and his implementation of Sidney's notion of poetry as the subsumption of history and religion.

Obviously this is a crucial realignment in English literary history, but, like Samuel Butler's satire, it can only occur in the presence of an established tradition. The use of Sidney by the Elizabethans has more to do with the insemination of a poetic genealogy than with a rejection of rhetoric. For them, if they read it at all, the *Defence* represents a way to resist the older generation of English intellectuals, in particular the civic humanists for whom poetry was merely an idle pastime of youth.[62] Indeed, one might read the *Defence* as much as a reply to Roger Ascham's notorious prejudices as an answer to Gosson. For instance, in the *Scholemaster* (1570), Ascham hyperbolically proscribes the Italians and Chaucer: "And you that be able to understand no more than ye find in the *Italian* tong, and never went farder than the schole of *Petrarke* and *Ariostus* abroad, or els of *Chaucer* at home, though you have pleasure to wander blindlie still in your foule wrong way, envie not others that seeke, as wise men have before them, the fairest and rightest way" (Smith, 1:33). This passage turns out to be a virtual prescription for Edmund Spenser's work. The chronology is fascinating: Ascham forbids the imitation of Petrarch, Ariosto, and even Chaucer in 1570; within twenty years, however, Spenser

62. See Helgerson, *The Elizabethan Prodigals,* esp. pp. 16–43.

has imitated all three, and especially Ariosto and Chaucer, on a grander scale than Ascham would ever have expected.[63]

It is too much to suggest that Spenser's poetic achievement, not to say his generic audacity, owes everything to Sidney's authority. Still, it is worth remembering that, challenging Ascham while affirming the Reformers' taste, Sidney definitively acknowledges Chaucer's place in the canon. But Sidney notes that Chaucer "had great wants," presumably in form, and he does not recommend the imitation of his ancient dialect. His rejection of the antiquated language has profound genealogical significance, for it is the same complaint he makes about *The Shepheardes Calender,* the only contemporary work he considers: "That same framing of his [Spenser's, or Immerito's] style to an old rustic language I dare not allow, since neither Theocritus in Greek, Virgil in Latin, nor Sannazzaro in Italian did affect it" (p. 133). It is as though Sidney, ostentatiously following E. K.'s footnote, were grafting together Chaucer and Spenser to form an English family tree with branches spreading to Greece, Rome, and modern Italy.

More significantly, the linking of Chaucer and Spenser results from Sidney's focus on the English vernacular. His objection to the obsolete diction of *The Shepheardes Calender* constitutes a back-handed sanction of modern vernacular poetry. Similarly, in the *Arte of English Poesie* (1589), George Puttenham is at pains to demonstrate the worth of the vernacular. Indeed, Puttenham goes so far as to assert its genealogical primacy. Besides the typical conceit that "King *David* also & *Salomon* his sonne and many of the holy Prophets wrate in meeters," we find the striking addition of the use of rhyme to the commonplace assertions about Hebrew metrical poetry:

the Hebrues & Chaldees who were more ancient than the Greekes, did not only use a metricall Poesie, but also with the same a maner of rime. . . . Whereby it appeareth, that our vulgar running Poesie was common to all the nations of the world besides, whom the Latines and Greekes in speciall called barbarous. So it was notwithstanding the first and most ancient Poesie, and the most universall.[64]

63. See John Guillory, *Poetic Authority: Spenser, Milton, and Literary History* (New York: Columbia University Press, 1983), especially chapters 1–3.

64. George Puttenham, *The Arte of English Poesie* (Menston, England: The Scolar Press Limited, 1968), p. 7.

His defense of rhyme seizes the high ground of origins and authority and includes an unusually pointed attack on Latin and Greek elitism. Puttenham's objective seems to be to wrest poetry from the schools and to free the English tradition from the classics.

In the same passage he asserts that it "is proved by certificate of marchants & travellers" that vernacular poetry is used for the "highest and holiest matters" throughout the Americas, even among cannibals: "which proves also that our maner of vulgar Poesie is more ancient then the artificiall of the Greeks and Latines, ours comming by instinct of nature, which was before Art or observation" (p. 7). Puttenham's insistence on priority in time and worth is a substitution for other forms of valorization. Ultimately it represents the genealogical argument we encounter so often in the period. "Instinct of nature" supplants "Art or observation" in the same way that putative bloodlines supplant achievement or contemporary merit. Puttenham's conclusion is a neat reversal of the received opinion on the value of poetry in England: "The naturall Poesie therefore being aided and amended by Art, and not utterly altered or obscured, but some signe left of it, (as the Greekes and Latines have left none) is not lesse to be allowed and commended then theirs" (p. 7). Thus Greek and Latin are deprecated as artificial, while English becomes not vulgar but "natural." The argument for the vernacular as more natural and less "obscured," as well as more ancient and universal, supplies a "scientific" rationale for the fostering of the English tradition. Most interesting is Puttenham's use of a highly dubious genealogical priority to ground this rationale.

More than is the case with any other English critic, forged genealogy is very much in Puttenham's mind. He is, par excellence, a "social" critic. He not only characterizes the poet as a genealogist but also suggests the extent to which all genealogies are poetic fabrications:

[T]o praise the Gods of the Gentiles, for that by authoritie of their own fabulous records they had fathers and mothers, and kinred and allies, and wives and concubines, *the Poetes first commended them by their genealogies and pedigrees,* their marriages and alliances, their notable exploits in the world for the behoofe of mankind, and yet, as I sayd before, none otherwise then the truth of their owne memorials might beare, and in such sort as it might be well avouched by their old written reports,

48

though in every deede they were not from the beginning all historically true, and
many of them verie fictions, and such of them as were true grounded upon
some part of a historie or matter of veritie, the rest altogether figurative
and misticall. (Pp. 21–22; italics mine)

This is all part of one sentence, as if to suggest the continuity in
poetic history from praise to genealogical fiction. And the sentence
is exceptional in my experience of Elizabethan treatises. It calls
attention to the doubtful foundation of all genealogical history and
to the complicity of the poets in promulgating the genealogical
fictions. Perhaps, in analyzing the texts of the period, we should be
warned not to be too credulous about the genealogies we encounter
in the poetry of Puttenham's contemporaries.[65]

We might appropriately conclude this survey with Francis
Meres, a writer who is often called the first English literary critic.
His *Palladis Tamia, Wits Treasury* (1598) is a kind of literary commonplace book, as Smith notes, a compendium of aphoristic reflections on a wide variety of subjects. When Meres discusses
poets, he relies on catalogues literally to join the famous names of
the ancient poetic traditions to the names of contemporary poets:

As the Greeke tongue is made famous and eloquent by Homer, Hesiod,
Euripedes [*sic*], Aeschylus, Sophocles, Pindarus, Phocylides, and Aristophanes; and the Latine tongue by Virgill, Ovid, Horace, Silius Ital-
icus, Lucanus, Lucretius, Ausonius, and Claudianus: so the English
tongue is mightily enriched and gorgeously invested in rare ornaments
and resplendent abiliments by Sir Philip Sydney, Spencer, Daniel, Drayton, Warner, Shakespeare, Marlow, and Chapman. (Smith, 2:315)

Such extended association of "famous and eloquent" classical poets
and their recent English counterparts would have been impossibly
audacious twenty years earlier. Note that Chaucer is absent again
and that Sidney has the place of honor corresponding to Homer and
Virgil, as the first in each list. Even as late as 1575, in *Certayne
Notes of Instruction,* George Gascoigne had hailed Chaucer as his

---

65. For a provocative discussion of the extent to which Puttenham's *Arte of English
Poesie* was, in fact, written as a kind of prescription for Elizabethan poets on how to attain
courtly status by other means than bona fide genealogy, see Daniel Javitch, *Poetry and
Courtliness in Renaissance England* (Princeton: Princeton University Press, 1978); and also,
Louis Adrian Montrose, "Of Gentlemen and Shepherds: The Politics of Elizabethan
Pastoral Form," *ELH* 50 (1983), pp. 415–59.

master and father, a sentiment Spenser extends to mystical proportions.[66] But whereas Gascoigne compared the poetry of his
own time unfavorably with Chaucer's, suggesting a period of decadence between Chaucer and the mid-sixteenth century, Meres ignores the English genealogy entirely, turning from Sidney to the
classical past.[67] Meres implies not only that English poetry is
now as famous as its ancient models but also that English poets
are obviously counterparts and descendants of the ancient bards.
Throughout his discussion the genealogical connection is taken as
a fact, and there can be no doubt that poetry has managed to cross
the barriers of time, language, and religion.

Not surprisingly, Meres proves his jerrybuilt genealogy with
examples drawn from different genres, as if the existence of these
genres in England in itself demonstrates the bona fide lineage of
English poetry. For example, he defends prose as a worthy form of
literary writing: "[A]s Heliodorus writ in prose his sugred invention of that picture of Love in *Theagines and Criclea* . . . so Sir
Philip Sidney writ his immortal poem, *The Countess of Pembroke's
Arcadia* in Prose; and yet our rarest Poet" (Smith, 2:315–16).
Mere's first example is the *Arcadia* and, in his list, Sidney, more so
than Spenser or Chaucer or any other, is the poetic progenitor and
first patriarch of the modern vernacular. He goes on at some length
with his recitation of evidence, linking Homer to Spenser (as well
as Theocritus and Virgil to Spenser), Parthenius Nicaeus to Daniel,
Sophocles and Flaccus to Drayton, Gallus to Warner, Ovid and
Plautus and Seneca to Shakespeare, and so forth with lists of poets
we have all but forgotten. For all the variety of detail, however, the
message remains the same: Meres unblushingly contends that English poets can be profitably compared to the ancients and, therefore, that a coherent English poetic tradition already exists.

Meres admits, however, that this tradition, for all its generic

66. *The Faerie Queene,* in *Spenser: Poetical Works,* ed. J. C. Smith and E. de Sélincourt
(Oxford: Oxford University Press, 1912), 4.2.32–34: Speaking of "Dan Chaucer,"
whose "Famous moniment [Time] hath quite defaste," Spenser asserts that "through
infusion sweete/Of thine own spirit, which doth in me survive,/I follow here the footing
of thy feete." All subsequent references to Spenser are to this edition.

67. Gascoigne considers Chaucer's versification equal to that of the Latinists, main-
taining that, to the contrary, the poems of his own time "may justly be called Rithmes,
and cannot by any right challenge the name of a Verse" (Smith, *Elizabethan Critical
Essays,* 1:50).

accomplishment, has been underway a very short time, that it might very well have begun with the writing of *The Countess of Pembroke's Arcadia*. This is an extraordinary admission of the arriviste nature of English poetry. But Meres's version of the tradition has very familiar lineaments, particularly if, like most Elizabethans, we accept the convenient portrait of Chaucer laboring in that "misty time" with a crude vernacular, and if we expediently suppress the Reformer's Chaucer, Surrey's Wyatt, and Sidney's Surrey.[68] The assertions of the *Palladis Tamia* clearly defy Gascoigne's notion of a decay in English poetry since Chaucer.

Rather than from the *Arcadia* itself, it is from the mythologized figure of Philip Sidney, fabricated in the decade following his early death, that English literary genealogy chiefly descends. There are other genealogies, such as the one that leads backward from Spenser's Colin Clout to Skelton to Chaucer, or, as in the *Mutabilitie Cantos* 7, from Alanus to Chaucer to Spenser. But these other descents are eventually reorganized under Sidney's aegis. Meres's remark about the *Arcadia* is simply evidence of the successful marketing of Sidney's invented status as the first modern precursor of English poetic tradition.

68. In his epitaph "[Of the Death of Sir Thomas Wyatt the Elder]," the Earl of Surrey says of Wyatt that he had "A hand that taught what might be said in rime,/That reft Chaucer the glory of his wit" (see *The Renaissance in England,* ed. Hyder E. Rollins and Herschel Baker [Lexington, Mass.: D.C. Heath and Company, 1954], p. 197, 11. 13–14). The Earl of Surrey is the only English poet Sidney mentions by name in the *Defence* (*Apology,* p. 133); we might add that Drayton, too, singles out Surrey in *England's Heroical Epistles.*

ONE

Instant Artifacts

Vernacular Elegies for Philip Sidney

O lying Spirit!
To say the Friar was dead; Ile now beleeve
Nothing of all his forg'd predictions.
—*Bussy D'Ambois,* V.iii

We tend to take for granted Sir Philip Sidney's place in English poetic tradition. His canonical status after the Elizabethan period is evident in the popularity of the *Arcadia* in the seventeenth century as well as, for instance, in Ben Jonson's praise of Sidney in "To Penshurst." But the origins of Sidney's canonization as a poet have remained largely obscure. This chapter examines those origins where they are most pronounced, in the vernacular elegies for Sidney that proliferated in the decade following his death. Between 1587, when the first volumes of elegies were published by Oxford and Cambridge, and 1595, the date of the *Astrophel* collection, the characterization of Sidney undergoes a significant transformation. Whereas the earliest elegists describe the dead knight almost exclusively as a patron and soldier, the later elegists focus on Sidney as a poet. It is true, of course, that this change of focus occurs in part as a result of the publication of the *Arcadia* in 1590 and *Astrophil and Stella* in 1591. But the publication of Sidney's works does not in itself explain why the later elegists effectively cease to refer to Sidney as a patron, nor why the early elegists, many of whom probably had read the circulated manuscripts, tend to underplay Sidney as a poet. I suspect that this change in emphasis, in addition to marking the origins of the Sidney myth, also indicates a change in the attitudes of Elizabethan poets toward their own literary genealogy.

The Sidney of these later elegies represents a genealogical source for the poets who come behind him. In literary historical terms, Sidney had debatable claims to originary status, even in the young English tradition. Spenser published earlier, and either Wyatt or Surrey would have been reasonable choices for the role of first modern precursor. Nevertheless, Sidney was heralded by his contemporaries as the unchallenged original, and his name came to represent the first firm root of the vernacular family tree in sixteenth-century England. Sidney's poetic status is, at least in part, a conceived presence in Renaissance literary genealogy. As a result, the literary descent that we trace from Sidney defines itself in tropes of contemporary responses to that original conceived presence. But we cannot utterly banish this phenomenon from the realm of descriptive literary history. Certainly we must be skeptical, but just as Sidney himself is transformed into a source once he is named a source, the tropes of literary descent themselves become genealogical history when their presence is confirmed in subsequent generations.

Vernacular funeral elegies were like instant artifacts on the English literary scene. Their advent presumed the existence not only of an established tradition of public mourning but also of a vernacular poetic tradition as generically complex as the traditions of Italian and the learned languages. John Buxton suggests that, in establishing a national literature, the English strove to achieve the vernacular poetic success of the Italians, and he concludes that Spenser was hailed as the first English poet to accomplish this feat: "very soon the anonymous New Poet would be everywhere acclaimed for *The Shepheardes Calender* as the man who promised a new age in English poetry."[1] As it turned out, however, and as Spenser himself determined, it was advisable to fashion another genealogical original from whom he, as New Poet, could descend.

It is impossible to establish a national literature without being able to produce a national literary genealogy. In a practical sense, therefore, Philip Sidney became the first modern precursor in English literary history, *The Shepheardes Calender* notwithstanding. This is not to say that before the circulation of *The Defence of Poesie* or the publication of the *Arcadia* there were no references to earlier poets. To the contrary, Spenser makes much of his debt to and de-

1. John Buxton, *Sir Philip Sidney and the English Renaissance* (1954; reprint, New York: St. Martin's Press, 1965), p. 14.

scent from Chaucer, both in *The Shepheardes Calender* and in *The Faerie Queene*. And in the *Defence* Sidney himself "restores" Chaucer in defiance of Roger Ascham. Nor were Skelton, Wyatt, and Surrey forgotten by the Elizabethans. But Chaucer's language was antiquated and he did not write in the fashionable genres that the Elizabethans were so intent on imitating. Similarly, between Chaucer and the mid-sixteenth century, which is the period of the great poetical anthologies, there is no outstanding poet to whom English authors may turn as a source. In Harold Bloom's terms, there is no Great Other—or, at least, there is no Great Vernacular Other. The Latin authors, especially Virgil, Horace, and Ovid, continue to exert their influence. But in an epoch often characterized by its translations from the classic languages, it is not surprising that a contemporary vernacular poet should be honored. Furthermore, given the close relation under Elizabeth between courtly success and poetic grace, it is almost predictable that Sidney should be chosen as that honored vernacular poet. There were many other courtier-poets, of course, but few had his flair for creating a public persona or his splendid family connections. Fewer still were such well-known radical Protestants or such generous patrons of intellectuals. And none suffered Sidney's untimely death.

Even during his life Sidney was genealogized. Du Bartas, in his *Babylone,* makes Sidney one of the four pillars of England, along with Thomas More, Nicholas Bacon, and Elizabeth.

> Le parler des Anglois a pour fermes piliers
> Tomas More et Bacon, tous deux grands chancelliers,
> Qui, sevrant leur langage et le tirant d'enfance,
> Au sçavoir politique ont conjoint l'eloquence.
> Et le milior Cydné qui, cigne doux-chantant,
> Va les flots orgueilleux de Tamise flatant;
> Ce fleuve, gros d'honneur, emporte sa faconde
> Dans le seine de Thetis, et Thetis par le monde.[2]

> Our *English* tongue, three famous knights sustaine;
> *Moore, Bacon, Sydney:* of which, former twaine,
> (*High Chancellors* of *England*) weaned first

---

2. *The Works of Guillaume de Salluste Sieur Du Bartas,* 3 vols., ed. Urban Tigner Holmes, Jr., John Coriden Lyons, Robert White Linker (Chapel Hill: University of North Carolina Press, 1940), 3:141.

Our infant-phrase (till then but homely nurst)
And childish toyes, and rudenes chacing thence,
To civill knowledge, joyned sweete eloquence.
And world-mournd *Sydney,* warbling to the Theames
His swan-like tunes, so courtes her coy prowd streames
That all with child with fame, his fame they beare
To *Thetis* lap, and *Thetis,* everie where.[3]

Joshua Sylvester's translation, first appearing in 1598, reflects the
enormous impact of Sidney's death: "world-mournd" Sidney replaces Du Bartas's "le milior Cydne."[4] Du Bartas's poem, which
preceded Sidney's death by two years, is a meditation on the
history and establishment of various languages, from Hebrew,
Greek, and Latin to the Continental vernaculars. That Du Bartas
chose Sidney as a pillar of the English tongue is impressive indeed;
and even if his motives were diplomatic, as might have been the
case, his choice nevertheless turned out to be prescient. Moreover,
as we shall see, Du Bartas's amalgamation in Sidney of poetic gifts
and martial prowess (the association with Thetis) anticipates the
prime impulse of Sidney's first elegists.

Sidney died in October 1586. Louis Adrian Montrose suggests
that "[w]ell before his early death, he had already been mythologized by his family, friends, and political allies," but this is a bit of
exaggeration, Du Bartas notwithstanding.[5] The myth of Sidney
inherited by the next generation of Elizabethan courtier-poets is
largely dependent on the public funeral and the efflorescence of
elegiac verse in the late 1580s. Richard A. Lanham, for example,
contends that "[n]othing he did while alive rivals in interest his
romantic death and the outburst of grief it occasioned."[6] The

3. *The Divine Weeks and Works of Guillaume de Saluste Sieur Du Bartas,* trans. Joshua
Sylvester, ed. Susan Snyder, 2 vols. (Oxford: Clarendon Press, 1979), 1:439.

4. Robert Barret also translated the *Babylone;* and both Thomas Nash (*Pierce Penilesse*)
and Henry Peacham (*The compleat gentleman*) mention Du Bartas's four English pillars. See
Anne Lake Prescott, *French Poets and the English Renaissance: Studies in Fame and Transformation* (New Haven and London: Yale University Press, 1978), pp. 189–190, 215–16.

5. Louis Adrian Montrose, "Celebration and Insinuation: Sir Philip Sidney and the
Motives of Elizabethan Courtship," *Renaissance Drama,* n.s., 8 (1977), p. 7. See also Ross
Stolworthy Esplin, "The Emerging Legend of Sir Philip Sidney, 1586–1652" (Ph.D.
diss., University of Utah, 1970).

6. Richard A. Lanham, "Sidney: The Ornament of His Age," *Southern Review* (Australia) 2:4 (1967), p. 319. See also Alan Hager, "The Exemplary Mirage: Fabrication of
Sir Philip Sidney's Biographical Image and the Sidney Reader," *ELH* 48 (1981), pp. 1–
16, esp. p. 3.

editors of a recent facsimile edition of the 1587 *Elegies for Sir Philip Sidney* have pointed out that Sidney "became the subject of mass national mourning, which included a funeral unprecedented for a member of his social rank."[7] And W. L. Renwick, in the Spenser Variorum, underscores the unprecedented circumstance that "the early death of Sir Philip Sidney, the son of a mere knight however highly employed, should produce an outburst of elegy only to be surpassed by that of Prince Henry in the next reign."[8] Further, as Buxton notes, "the two Universities produced volumes of elegies in his memory, mostly written in Latin, but with a few poems in Greek, Hebrew, and Italian." He provides an impressive list of poets and scholars who saw fit to acknowledge Sidney's influential stature in English letters—somewhat prior to the establishment, or even public documentation, of this stature. Nevertheless we find among Sidney's vocal admirers the entire range of Elizabethan literary figures from Spenser, Ralegh, and Bryskett to Drayton, Greville, Barnfield, and less well known writers like John Gifford who, "contributing an elegy called *Lycidas* to the New College volume," canonized Sidney in the pastoral mode he had helped to establish.[9]

There is a great deal of speculation as to whether Sidney was a modern tactician or an outmoded grandstander as governor of Flushing, where he received his fatal wound. According to Buxton in a recent article, there were three different explanations at the time of why he was without his thigh armor:

Sir John Smythe says that Sidney was following a new Continental fashion of dispensing with heavy armour to allow greater mobility. Thomas Moffett says that Sidney was hastening to the rescue of Lord Willoughby de Eresby whom he saw beset by the enemy, and had no time to put on his cuisses. Fulke Greville says that Sidney saw Sir William Pelham riding into action without his thigh armour and, since he disdained to go into action better armed than the Lord Marshal, discarded his own.[10]

7. A. J. Colaianne and W. L. Godshalk, eds., *Elegies for Sir Philip Sidney* (1587) (Delmar, N.Y.: Scholars' Facsimiles and Reprints, 1980), v.

8. *The Works of Edmund Spenser*, A Variorum Edition, 9 vols., ed. Edwin Greenlaw, C. G. Osgood, F. M. Padelford, Ray Heffner (Baltimore: Johns Hopkins University Press, 1932–49), 2:489–90.

9. Buxton, *Sir Philip Sidney*, pp. 173 and 177. For a good introduction to the poets who wrote encomia, see pp. 173–77.

10. John Buxton, "The Mourning for Sidney," *Renaissance Studies* 3 (1989), p. 46.

A modern debate has grown from these possibilities. William Ringler, who echoes Sir John Smythe and sees Sidney as an advanced military man, has claimed that "[h]e went into battle without cuisses, not for the sake of a chivalric gesture, but for the calculated and practical purpose of more efficient fighting."[11] In contrast, Richard McCoy blames the "persistent anachronism" of chivalric glory in the period. He maintains that "[i]n a futile skirmish at Zutphen he sportingly cast off part of his armor and was shot in the thigh. Thus Sidney succumbed to the cult of martial glory and died of his gangrenous wounds."[12] Ringler says there was no such "theatrical gesture," but nonetheless this rather unflattering view has persisted. A. C. Hamilton, who is less vehement than McCoy, ultimately admits that "Sidney's failure to wear leg-armour displays the conspicuous bravery, or bravado, of the Renaissance courtier."[13] Hamilton goes on to link the wound to the famous anecdote in which the bleeding Sidney offers his water bottle to a thirsty, dying comrade. As Fulke Greville puts it:

being thirsty with excess of bleeding, he called for a drink, which was presently brought him; but as he was putting the bottle to his mouth, he saw a poor soldier carried along, who had eaten his last at the same feast, ghastly casting up his eyes at the bottle. Which Sir Philip perceiving, took it from his head, before he drank, and delivered it to the poor man, with these words, "Thy necessity is greater than mine".[14]

This account raises a quintessentially perplexing issue of Sidney's biography, because it is as likely to be true as to be a fiction of Greville's generous imagination. For instance, in pointing out the importance of *maiestas* (roughly "magnanimity") to the concept of chivalry in the sixteenth century, David Loades emphasizes that it would just as likely have been Sidney's impulse to make a flamboyant gesture on the battlefield as it would have been Greville's to interpolate the water-bottle scene. Loades reminds us that the

---

11. W. A. Ringler, "Sir Philip Sidney: The Myth and the Man," in *Sir Philip Sidney: 1586 and the Creation of a Legend,* ed. Jan Van Dorsten, Dominic Baker-Smith, and Arthur F. Kinney (Leiden: E. J. Brill/Leiden University Press, 1986), p. 8.

12. Richard McCoy, *Sir Philip Sidney: Rebellion in Arcadia* (New Brunswick, N.J.: Rutgers University Press, 1979), p. 9.

13. A. C. Hamilton, *Sir Philip Sidney,* p. 5.

14. Fulke Greville, *The Life of the Renowned Sr Philip Sidney* (1652), introduction by Warren W. Wooden (Delmar, N.Y.: Scholars' Facsimiles and Reprints, 1984), pp. 148–49. Hamilton, who also quotes this passage, points out that it is "too well known to be omitted."

Alexander of romance, "when all his army are tormented by thirst, refuses the one small supply of water in a gesture which must surely have provided the model for Sir Philip Sidney at Zutphen."[15] Sidney, himself a writer of romance, would probably have known this story. He might have expected, moreover, that his peers would recognize the austere genealogy of his *maiestas*.[16]

Of course, Sidney's possible awareness of literary models for his behavior does not rule out the prevalence of fabrication in the biographies and elegies. To the contrary, Sidney's erudition allows writers to imply that his every act was an allusion to, almost a typological fulfillment of, heroic moments in the past. Conversely, almost any literary allusion can be applied to Sidney's life. We find a relatively unambitious example of this in *The Manner of Sir Philip Sidney's Death* by George Gifford, a suspended English preacher whom Sidney apparently summoned eight days after being wounded. According to Katherine Duncan-Jones, "Gifford's account, like Greville's, is basically a piece of pious myth-making." She cites in particular "the detail which strikes one as most vivid in *Sidney's Death,* the passage about the hand raised as an affirmation of faith."[17] Duncan-Jones maintains that this detail is lifted from Holinshed's *Chronicles,* that both the old Earl of Essex and Sir Henry Sidney in Worcester raise their hands to God in their final minutes. The similarity between Gifford and Holinshed, however, proves little. Again it is a question of who is doing the imitating, biographer or subject. Duncan-Jones acknowledges the problem and wonders whether "[t]his may have indeed been the way in which Elizabethan noblemen died" (p. 163). Presumably this remark is tongue-in-cheek, but in the same paragraph she admits that "[t]he element of convention may have been as strong in men's behaviour as in accounts of it."

15. David Loades, *The Tudor Court* (Totowa, N.J.: Barnes and Noble Books, 1987), pp. 1–2.

16. George Whetstone begins his elegy for Sidney by associating his early death with that of "Alexander the chiefe of Royal Peeres." In the edition printed by Thomas Cadman, Whetstone includes this marginal note: "King Alexander was poysened by the envie of Antepater beinge but 24 years of age." The association of treachery with Sidney's death is provocative, though it is difficult to know whether to read this statement as a veiled accusation directed at a particular person or political faction. We shall examine Whetstone's elegy more closely below.

17. *Miscellaneous Prose of Sir Philip Sidney,* ed. Katherine Duncan-Jones and Jan Van Dorsten (Oxford: Clarendon Press, 1973), pp. 162–63.

Perhaps we can emphasize the difficulty of separating Elizabethan behavior from accounts of it by speculating on a remarkable
coincidence of Sidney's death. Along with Theocritus's first *Idyll*
and Moschus's "Lament for Bion," Bion's "Lament for Adonis" is
often cited as a model for the Renaissance pastoral elegy, and the
influence of pastoral elegy in creating the Sidney legend has long
been noted.[18] Moreover, Sidney is more than once compared to the
dying Adonis in the Elizabethan elegies, most memorably in Spenser's "Astrophel." Consequently, it is notable that Bion's Adonis
dies of a thigh wound: "Cruel, cruel the wound Adonis bears upon
his thigh" (Lambert's translation). The Nymphs wail in the hills
and Aphrodite, seeing the thigh desperately covered in blood,
begs Adonis to awaken for one last kiss. The poem ends with a
deathbed scene in which the "Loves" (*Erotes*) bathe Adonis's thighs,
fling bow and arrows upon the body, and fan him with their wings.
The coincidence, if that is what it is, cannot easily be ignored.
Sidney's thigh wound is confirmed, of course, by Leicester's letter
to Burghley of September 1586, which describes the bullet hole
"three fingers above the knee."[19] Still, the coincidence leads one to
ask about the suggestibility even of letter writers and whether the
story of the wound, like the tale of the water-bottle incident,
might also be a fiction borrowed from an earlier text.

Paradoxically, such indeterminacy paves a way to the formation
of an English poetic tradition. It permits Sidney's elegists the
historical and genealogical latitude they need to present their
subject as the descendant of great captains, poets, and human-
itarians. The inference is that anything they can allude to in the
course of laying bare (or inventing) Sidney's inmost motivations,
Sidney himself could have anticipated in his reading, riding, and
prayer—even if there is no evidence for this perceptive anticipation. Thus the elegists pretend to attenuate the Sidney myth
while, in point of fact, they are creating it. It is impractical,
however, to try to determine definitively what prompted them.
They were numerous and different in background, some being
scholars and some political connections. Their motives run from

---

18. See, for example, Ellen Zetzel Lambert, *Placing Sorrow: A Study of the Pastoral Elegy
Convention from Theocritus to Milton* (Chapel Hill: University of North Carolina Press,
1976), pp. 143–50, 221ff.

19. See Buxton, "The Mourning for Sidney," p. 46.

the desire to support the Earl of Leicester in his radical Protestantism to the hope of having their names circulated (as poets) among
the nobles.

Many of the elegists knew the Sidneys and even Sir Philip
well—Edmund Spenser, Walter Ralegh, Fulke Greville, George
Whetstone, for example. There were, as well, elegists who knew
the family but were not prominent as members of Sir Philip's
circle. William Gager, editor of the official Oxford volume, comes
to mind. By far the largest group of elegists, however, did not
know Philip Sidney at all; they volunteered or were more or less
contracted to contribute some verse to the three university volumes. As Dominic Baker-Smith has pointed out, "Oxford and
Cambridge produced verse miscellanies for the first time to mark
[Sidney's] death, and thus initiated a tradition of such commemorative volumes."[20] G. W. Pigman III largely concurs: "[b]etween
1551, the year of the first two collections (on Bucer and the
Brandons), and 1587, the year which saw three for Sidney, I am
able to find only one other, in late 1583 or early 1584 for Sir
William Butts. The collections on Sidney's death may have helped
to set the fashion, but it is not until the seventeenth century that
they are truly common."[21] Thus, along with the collections for
Bucer, Charles and Henry Brandon, and much later for Butts, the
Sidney volumes are the earliest in the English tradition of which
Milton's *Lycidas* is probably the best-known single poem.[22]

Baker-Smith contends that the academic volumes "guaranteed

20. Dominic Baker-Smith, "Great Expectation: Sidney's Death and the Poets," in Van
Dorsten et al., eds., *Sir Philip Sidney: 1586 and the Creation of a Legend*, p. 84.

21. G. W. Pigman III, *Grief and English Renaissance Elegy* (Cambridge: Cambridge
University Press, 1985), p. 53. Buxton also mentions an earlier collection of elegies but
does not provide details. See, in addition, Alberta T. Turner, "Milton and the Convention of the Academic Miscellanies," *Yearbook of English Studies* 5 (1975), pp. 86–93.
Turner takes the 1587 volumes to be the starting point. Yet she cautions against too firm
a notion of the conventions at work in the actual manufacture of the miscellanies:
"Although Cambridge had published eight or more volumes of occasional verse between
the death of Sidney, in 1587, and 1625, when Milton matriculated, and although Oxford
had published an even larger number of similar volumes during the same period, the
patterns of authorship, editing, and publication were not fixed" (p. 86). These unfixed
patterns do not, however, affect the extreme conventionality of the individual poems,
especially the ubiquitous recurrence of pastoral elegy.

22. For a recent study of the development of the elegy, see also Dennis Kay, *Melodious
Tears: The English Funeral Elegy from Spenser to Milton* (Oxford: Clarendon Press, 1990).

the Sidney legend a learned audience, and, potentially at least, an international one, but the act of embalming his memory in a learned tongue also works to politicize it" (p. 81). He later speculates on the exact import of that politicizing message: "The Oxford and Cambridge volumes are probably to be seen as part of a wider political campaign to exploit Sidney's death in favour of an interventionist policy in the Netherlands. They give an official stamp to the myth" (p. 90).

This "official stamp" has never been conclusively analyzed, perhaps partly because the elegies themselves have not inspired close readings. As a result, learned opinion varies widely on the meaning and power of the myth. Ringler, for instance, insists that "Sidney has been unintentionally maligned by his admirers. He is a different, and at the same time a far greater man, than his praisers have made him out to be" (p. 9). To the contrary, Hamilton observes of Sidney that, for us at least, "there is no man apart from the legend, no face under the mask" (p. 8). This diametric opposition, while puzzling, is nevertheless a strong testimony to the coherence and legitimacy of the Sidney myth. Yet it is not necessary to agree wholly with either Ringler or Hamilton to recognize the difficulty of trying to avoid the myth. If there is no face under the mask, as Hamilton urges, then it is probably because the further we are removed from Sidney the less apt we are to ignore the mask. Indeed, we can see how Sidney might have been "maligned by his admirers," especially insofar as the mask they fashioned was so adaptable to different kinds of self-serving flattery. But, although Ringler's objections have a good deal of merit, to divine the man under the "official stamp" of the myth, or to separate man and myth, is a biographer's dubious task. Ours is, rather, to interpret the myth-making process and to determine how that process contributes to the formation of English literary genealogy.

MOTIVES OF THE ELEGISTS

Even amid the wide diversity of *encomia Sidneii*, a normative version of Philip Sidney emerges. The norms result partly from the demands of elegiac genres: "Elizabethan and Jacobean memorial literature," as Alan Hager observes, "is unequivocal praise, but the genres themselves are panegyric."[23] Hager explains that the memorial literature "is compromised by two propagandist motives" (p. 3): the interventionist policies of the radical Walsingham-Leicester faction and the causes of the Protestant League; and, considerably subtler, "Elizabeth's own aims of upholding the notion of her court as the late flowering of chivalry" (p. 4). According to Hager, "Sidney is metamorphosed from the complicated, often-neglected courtier into the ideal of chivalric heroism and courtesy, an ideal that would serve to control the impetuosity of some of [Elizabeth's] courtiers" (p. 4). In this scenario, Elizabeth personally controls the Sidney legend, presumably by manipulating its dissemination. As in the efforts of the Walsingham group, the literary encomia would have been useful to the monarch predominantly as political propaganda.

But the elegists often have different interests from the courtiers or from the queen. We might say that they have literary motives as well as political obligations, insofar as the two can be separated in the period. Moreover, it is as tempting to subsume literary motives in sociopolitical conditions as it is to see a sharp dichotomy between literature and politics. But neither approach satisfactorily describes the effect of the elegies for Sidney on English literary genealogy. Before Sidney's death, and especially before the elegies of the 1590s, poets are less self-consciously concerned with literary descent. As Daniel Javitch has observed, "on the rare occasions when early Elizabethan writers discuss their motives for writing verse, they do reveal that by writing poetry, they sought to display abilities that might serve to secure membership at court."[24] In the later part of Elizabeth's reign, however, the ambition to contend in a literary fashion with Continental vernacular tradition has become, thanks in part to Spenser and Sidney, a viable possibility.

Thus, the poetry written for Sidney's death marks a transitional phase in English literary history. Along with the Elizabethan de-

---

23. Hager, "The Exemplary Mirage," p. 3. Hager is intent on showing the limitations of Sidney's hagiography in characterizing his vexed relations to Elizabeth and her court. He is concerned that "Sidney's death . . . may have contained deeper irony than the distortion, *post mortem*, of a complex career into one of simple heroism and virtue" (p. 7). Hager makes a very good case. For our purposes, however, marking how Sidney's literary followers used the "distortion, *post mortem*" is more important than correcting the distorted impression.

24. Javitch, "The Impure Motives of Elizabethan Poetry," p. 228.

sire to entrench a vernacular English literature, we also find a nascent interest in imitating poetic descent over and above the direct imitation of specific poets—and, in this regard, the conceived presences of the genealogical past come to have considerable importance. Similarly, while the notion of literary genealogy certainly owes something in this period to heraldry and genealogical fanaticism, which were surer paths to patronage than literature, it is evident, nevertheless, that the establishment of an English literary tradition owes as much to the genealogical management of past and present literatures as to the influence of contemporary English social conditions. This is not to argue for a purity of "literary" motives, of course, but merely to emphasize their importance in later Elizabethan poetry. The restless social positionings of treatise writers and poets, although outwardly of strategic political import, are finally meaningless without the recognition of a deep structure of literary genealogy. Indeed, Sidney's elegists are excellent examples of this deep structure, even while their ostensible political motives continue to alarm new-historicist readers and to obscure the literary element of their hunt for genealogy.

We might conjecture, for example, that the elegists promulgate the Sidney myth to obscure their hunt for literary genealogy because, demonstrably, that genealogy will be a forgery if it attempts to graft the English vernacular onto a Latinate tradition. The widespread elegizing conveys the sense of an instant artifact, presuming an English tradition to be a fait accompli. The literary aspirations of a generation are hidden beneath the apparently mechanical imitation of classical elegiac verse forms, which appeared repeatedly for the first time in the commemorative volumes. There is virtually no vernacular tradition of funeral elegy, contractual or otherwise, before 1587. The Bucer elegies are in Latin, as are most of the elegies for the Brandons, though some of these were later translated.[25] But they are not pastoral elegies. In fact, there are precious few examples of pastoral elegy at all in England before the Sidney volumes, with the notable exception of Spenser's "Novem-

25. See Pigman, *Grief,* pp. 52–56. In the elegies for Butts (1583 or 1584), Pigman points out, Anthony Cade "has Apollo, Athena, and the Dryads, Fauns, Nymphs, and Muses weep for Butts" (p. 56). But this too is in Latin, and, in any case, we do not find the same aspiring (and successful) Elizabethan poets among Butts's elegists whom we find among Sidney's.

ber" eclogue. Apparently, Sidney's death, probably because of his courtly fame, provides a novel criterion by which poets are able to link their productions simultaneously to a contemporary social circumstance and to the ancient tradition exemplified by Theocritus, Bion, Moschus, and Virgil.[26]

It has long been assumed that Philip Sidney is the ideal subject for commemoration in Elizabethan England. For example, Montrose suggests that "Sidney was in a position to actualize rhetorical and poetic *topoi;* to live out the ubiquitous humanist debate about the relative merits of action and contemplation, the major literary dialectic of heroic and pastoral kinds" ("Celebration," p. 7). This may be true, though it is by no means clear that Sidney himself had any intention of living out the "ubiquitous humanist debate." Nor would I say that he managed to reconcile the merit of contemplation with his courtly and diplomatic ambitions.

The conflation of action and contemplation is, more precisely, the result of and a reason for the legend: it is an invaluable commodity, not to gentleman–amateur poets like Sidney, but to less well-born professionals who must propagate the myth to validate their own unarmigerous social status. Montrose concludes that "Sidney's *Defence of Poetry* is a witty, impassioned, and eloquent defense of literary writing as a fit occupation for gentlemen, as an instigation to virtuous action and as an intellectual form of virtuous action in and of itself" (p. 23). But the attenuation of the Sidney myth by university men and professional writers suggests that the value of his influence lay in demonstrating literary writing as a "fit occupation" particularly for those who were not gentlemen but who needed the example of a perfect gentleman to validate their activities.

Baker-Smith observes that "[t]he dominant theme of the Sidney elegies . . . is his Scipionic resolution of conflicting talents" (p. 97). Citing John Palmer's neo-Latin "Martis et Mercurii Contentio," a mythological debate from the Cambridge *Lacrymae* in which Mars urges arms and Mercury the arts, both claiming the right to

26. The elegiac tradition in the rest of Europe, that is, the systematic imitation of Theocritus, Bion, and Moschus, is only about a century old by the time of Sidney's death. See G. Norlin, "The Conventions of the Pastoral Elegy," *American Journal of Philology* 32 (1911), p. 294: "The publication of the editio princeps of Theocritus in Milan, in 1481, and the Aldine edition, which contained also the elegies of Bion and Moschus, in 1495, started the fashion of singing the loss of kin or friend in musical numbers studiously echoed from the dirges of Theocritus, Bion, Moschus and Virgil."

Sidney, Baker-Smith comments: "This theme of a diversity of talents pervades all the commemorative volumes: in essence it is an expression of the general culture proposed by the humanist curriculum and appropriated by the courtier, but in Sidney's case its authentic application is supported by the strong sense of waste which occurs in so many elegies."[27] The "sense of waste" permits the elegists to bewail Sidney's martyrdom, a very popular theme. In fact, the untimely death of the young hero rather conveniently saves the elegists, as in Palmer's case, from too close a scrutiny of Sidney's credentials as the ideal Elizabethan. If the elegists do not actually invent the Martial versus Mercurial conflicts for the sake of dramatic presentation, then they exaggerate the slenderest evidence to their own ends. And we should recognize the extent to which this particular exaggeration of Sidney's diversity, more than any hyperbole surrounding his deeds, becomes the myth that we continue to honor in one way or another today. Indeed, it is a myth based on a considerable amount of truth, though Sidney did more writing than fighting. But Sidney probably never reconciled the two kinds of activity in his own life, and it is doubtful that he chose his periods of inaction. We should realize, moreover, the overwhelming extent to which the myth reflects a conventional literariness of presentation. Sidney's "Scipionic resolution"—or his supposed ability, in Montrose's phrase, "to actualize rhetorical and poetic *topoi*"—is the elegists' justification for idealizing the young hero.

Yet Fulke Greville, whom above all (as Sidney's close friend and himself a writer-politician) we might expect to subscribe to the conflated myth, seems rather clearly to remember Sidney as a man of action:

Because if his pupose [*sic*] had been to leave his memory in books, I am confident, in the right use of Logick, Philosophy, History, and Poesie, nay even in the most ingenuous of Mechanicall Arts, he would have

27. In fact, John Palmer's elegy raises some unsettling questions about the diversity of talents. After Mars and Mercury debate, Pallas speaks up, asserting her rights and begging Jove to award Sidney to her. Jove agrees, but as a result the envious Mars cuts off Sidney's life. "Clearly," Baker-Smith notes, "Pallas, the armed goddess of wisdom, is a peculiarly apt figure for Sidney's realization of the Scipionic ideal. . . ." But I am not sure how clear this is: even if Palmer means to acknowledge that Sidney contained the dual wisdom—the arms and the arts, the action and contemplation so dear to the elegists—still his assassination suggests the impossibility of reconciling or resolving conflicting talents, at least in this world.

shewed such tracts of a searching, and judicious spirit; as the professors of every faculty would have striven no less for him, than the seaven Cities did to have *Homer* of their Sept! But the truth is: his end was not writing, even while he wrote; nor his knowledge moulded for tables, or Schooles; but both his wit, and understanding bent upon his heart, to make himself, and others, not in words or opinion, but in life, and action, good and great. (Pp. 20–21)

However biased Greville may be, his account of Sidney's intentions could not be construed as helpful to a generation of poets whose "end" *was* writing and for whom extraliterary action represented a very real competition. Perhaps it was lucky for them that Greville's *Life* was not published until 1652. Greville's "truth" would have been anathema to young Elizabethans who needed the conflated Sidney as a precursor to their own literary undertakings. The elegies in large measure support this claim. And we should not forget that, whereas Spenser and many others cast the dead Sidney as a shepherd—implying contemplation as action, noble Virgilian *otium*—Sidney casts himself as a pointedly active forester in *The Lady of May.* [28]

Thus, even the notion of Sidney as an ideal subject for commemoration is best understood as a literary motive. [29] It can be futile to seek a definitive line between the Sidney myth and the facts of his life. Similarly, the process of Greville's and the elegists' representations is more important than the "truth" of their significations. The evident intent of each version of the myth differs: some, like Greville, seek to put Sidney in the best possible light; others to put poetry in the best light. There were probably other suitable candidates besides Sidney for the ideal Renaissance figure, as successful as scholars and more so as military men or courtiers—though, as Buxton reminds us, "it is difficult for us to realize that Sidney was one of only four or five men of any note in his generation to be

28. See Montrose, "Celebration," pp. 10–13 passim. Also Stephen Orgel, "The Lady of May," rpt. Arthur Kinney, ed., *Essential Essays for the Study of Sir Philip Sidney* (Hamden, Conn.: Archon Books, 1986), p. 14. Orgel's point, however, is that the Queen blunders in (not) choosing the "foster." But she doesn''t blunder at all; she rejects Sidney's political trap.

29. Surrey was also an ideal subject for commemoration, as we know from the mid-century poetic miscellanies and other sources, but he never acquired the same force as a genealogical source for Elizabethan writers, perhaps in part because he was not an Elizabethan himself.

killed in action."[30] In any case, Sidney died in the nick of time. And, although the elegists began by attempting to lionize the patron and soldier Sidney, they finished by canonizing the poet Sidney. After all, despite the extreme claims of Sidney's prowess in the field, nobody now thinks of him as a great Elizabethan general or warrior. To the contrary, the mythologized defender of a militantly Protestant foreign policy—whose funeral, incidentally, Elizabeth refused to attend—becomes in the decades following his death, not a Scipio or a Cincinnatus, but almost exclusively the exemplar and defender of English poetry. He is transformed, largely by means of the instant artifact of an elegiac tradition, into a primary genealogical authority of English literature. His "conceived presence" allows poets to aspire to forms of patronage conventionally reserved for courtiers who defend the Crown with arms.

THE EARLIEST ELEGIES, 1587

Although a vernacular elegy might not have had the international audience of its neo-Latin counterpart, there was an undeniable propriety to immortalizing Sidney in the mother tongue. After all, it was English poetry that Sidney championed and wrote, and the *Defence* demonstrates his commitment to the theory as well as the practice of vernacular writing.

The elegists try all the forms, tailoring classical epideictic tradition to the nascent prosody of English verse.[31] For instance, James VI of Scotland contributes a Sidneian sonnet which opens the *Academiae Cantabrigiensis Lacrymae* (ed. Alexander Neville, Cambridge, 1587).[32] John Philip, Angel Day, and George Whetstone

30. Buxton, "The Mourning for Sidney," p. 47. He adds that others were Sir Richard Grenville, Sir John Wingfield, and Robert Devereux.

31. This is not meant to be an exhaustive list of the vernacular elegies but a representative sample of different approaches. Among the longer elegies I do not discuss are Thomas Churchyard's A. W.'s "Eclogue, Made Long Since Upon the Death of Sir Phillip Sidney" (in Francis Davison's *A Poetical Rhapsody*, ed. H. E. Rollins, 2 vols. [Cambridge, Mass.: Harvard University Press, 1931]), and Michael Drayton's fourth *Eclogue, Ideas The Shepheards Garland*.

32. It should be noted that the facsimile edition of the elegies compiled by Colaianne and Godshalk contains a number of different volumes, including the Cambridge *Lacrymae* and the Oxford *Peplus* and *Exequiae*, some volumes with page numbers and

all write, and publish separately, ambitious narrative poems in rhyme royal; Philip's is the longest, over 350 lines, Whetstone's is almost as long, and Day's about half that length. Published with Whetstone's, we find "A commemoration of the generall mone," by B. W. (his brother?), which is approximately seventy lines of rhymed iambic hexameter couplets; the poem laments the burial of the martial Sidney, and the hexameters are probably intended to imitate Virgilian verse. Similarly, Francis Davison's *A Poetical Rhapsody* includes four poems in English quantitative verse, a doomed style, which, it was argued at the time, more closely resembled the classical models; though not published until 1602, these elegiac hexameters, according to Davison, were written some years earlier. The use of "quantity" rather than rhyme had been one of Sidney's passing interests, and the quantitative tributes to him also represent an acknowledgment of his part in the controversy.[33]

In *Brittons Bowre of Delights* (1591), Richard Jones published Nicholas Breton's "Amoris Lachrimae, A most singular and sweete Discourse of the life and death of S. P. S. Knight." The first poem in the miscellany, it is fairly long, over sixty six-line stanzas in iambic pentameter, rhymed *ababcc;* the narrative wanders eccentrically from Sidney's history to pastoral lament to first-person reflection. *Brittons Bowre* contains as well five anonymous poems on Sidney's death, three of which are first-letter acrostics spelling out his name; in addition we find a lengthy epitaph in poulter's measure, alternating iambic hexameter and iambic heptameter lines. This epitaph is followed by an epigrammatic abstract, "The summe of the former in foure lines."

Most of the early elegists do not refer to Sidney as a poet at all. Even George Whetstone, who purportedly knew Sidney well and had even been at Zutphen with him, muddles his literary achievements. As Colaianne and Godshalk point out, "although Whetstone was familiar with Sidney's 'Archadia,' he also gives Sidney

---

some without. Thus we also find duplicate page references. I have conventionalized typography.

33. The first of these poems contains a mysterious bogus genealogy. It is entitled "An Epigram to Sir Phillip Sydney in Elegicall [*sic*] Verse, Translated out of Iodelle, the French Poet." According to Rollins's note, however, "as Bullen points out, Etienne Jodelle, siegneur de Limodin, had died in July, 1573, thirteen years before Sidney's death" (2:173). On quantitative verse, see Attridge, *Well-Weigh'd Syllables.*

credit for writing the 'Shepherds Calendars' " (p. xi). Similarly, James VI, despite his "Sidneian" contribution to the *Lacrymae* and his interest in poetry, makes no specific mention of Sidney's poetry but laments the loss to all the arts:

> Thou mighty Mars the Lord of souldiers brave,
> And thou Minerve, that dois in wit excell,
> And thou Apollo who dois knowledge have,
> Of every art that from Parnassus fell
> With all your Sisters that thaireon do dwell,
> Lament for him . . . (Colaianne and Godshalk, *Lacrymae* Sig.k1r)

Typically, the arts of war and of wisdom are mixed. The reference to the Muses, which is somewhat conventional in imitations of classical monody, anyway covers the spectrum from Calliope to Terpsichore. James can by no means be said to praise Sidney's vernacular productions above, say, his Dutch exploits or his re-knowned patronage of scholars. Nothing could be more eloquent of this, I think, than that James's sonnet is followed in the Cambridge volume by an anonymous Latin translation, "Idem latine per eundem Regem." In 1587 the value of the vernacular, in confrontation with its learned counterpart, is still doubtful.

One of the hexameter poems in *A Poetical Rhapsody* is a medita-tion exclusively on the state of the Muses after Sidney's death. The lament opens with the speaker's surprise at seeing the Muses "in *London* abiding." At first he wonders whether the Castalian streams have dried up, bringing the Muses to town. Then, however, he doubts that they could be Muses at all because the sounds they make are scarcely beautiful:

> No sound of melody, no voyce but drery lamenting.
> Yet well I wot too well, Muses most dolefully weeping.
> See where *Melpomene* sits hidde for a shame in a corner.
> Heare ye the carefull sighes, fetcht from the depth of her entrailes?
> There weepes *Calliope,* there sometimes lusty *Thaleia.*[34]

Melpomene is by tradition the Muse of tragedy, Calliope of epic poetry, and Thalia of comedy. Sidney wrote nothing in any of these genres—in fact, Terpsichore and Erato, either of whom might

---

34. Davison, *A Poetical Rhapsody,* p. 191. Davison credits the poem to "A. W.," as he does all the elegies for Sidney, but the initials may stand for nothing more than Anony-mous Writer.

represent lyric poetry, are conspicuously absent. It seems obvious, therefore, that the Muses mourn here not so much because Sidney will no longer compose in their special fields, but because he can no longer offer patronage to those who do. Indeed, the poem that follows in Davison's manuscript asks the question, "What could three Sisters do more than nine in a combat?" Again the implication is that Sidney was represented by any and all the Muses indiscriminately, though even banded together they could not defeat the Fates.

In the first stanza of his elegy "Upon the life and death of Sir Phillip Sidney Knight," which is addressed to Walsingham, Angel Day pretends to seek out the Muses' lamentation:

> Where are the drops, the sweet distilling dewes,
>   Of *Ida* fresh, whereon the *Nimphes* do gaze:
> Where moans Thalia with her pleasant layes?
>   fine Erato in gladsome Ditties drest,
>   And faire Caliop', statlier than the rest[?]

Although Day at least mentions Erato, it is still apparent by his inclusion of Thalia and Calliope that, once again, the Muses are not linked precisely to Sidney's work. In fact, a few stanzas later we discover that it is not Sidney's work at all that is on the Muses' minds, but their own:

> It was the choice of all the powers devine:
> The influence self, where *Virtues* erst did flowe,
>   The very worke of all the *Muses* nine.

Day first portrays Sidney as a creation in himself, "the very worke" of the Muses, rather than as a creator. In this version the Muses, reflecting one of the meanings of their name, are similar to poets— similar, predictably, to Day himself—who fashion the subjects of their elegies, feigning sorrow.[35] Day asserts that the Muses had twined together one perfect self, "The rarest *Tipe* of courtly gentlenes/Adorned erst with stem of noblenes." Complete with a reference to the Dudley family tree, the "stem of noblenes," Day effectively congratulates the Muses on their production of an ideal figure of the court.

---

35. See E. R. Gregory, *Milton and the Muses* (Tuscaloosa: University of Alabama Press, 1989), pp. 22–34.

In acknowledging Sidney's writing, Day mentions only "A book by him penned, called the Countesses of Pembrooks Archadia." This is the margin note beside the stanza that begins "Archadia now, where is thy soveraigne guide," in which Day mourns the loss of "sondry meeters, wounde from the finest wit" and "the deintiest shepheards sound." Day expresses an extremely high opinion of the poetry, if not accounting Sidney a serious bard, then at least admitting his appeal:

> Sugred Sidney, Sidney sweete it was,
> > That to thy soile, did give the greatest fame:
> Whose honny dewes, that from his quil did passe,
> > with honny sweetes, advaunst thy glorious name. . . .

This praise is still addressed to "Archadia," whose soil gains "the greatest fame" and whose "glorious name" is advanced by Sidney's sweet verses. Day is comparing Sidney favorably to others who have written about Arcadia, from Theocritus to Sannazaro: "Far was it from the skill if any one,/To wade in thee [Archadia], so far as he hath gone."

Yet, as much as Day praises Sidney's *Arcadia,* he does not wish to immortalize Sidney merely as a poet. He invokes the Muses "On Sidneis Tombe your learned tunes to sing," and asks that they might "Be ayding to my skillesse fainting pen,/That hardly dare presume of such a one." Day wishes to present the full picture of Sidney, and he quickly merges the poet with the patron and the knight: "So full of weight, with humours so divine:/ were all his wordes, his workes, and actions fraught." The elegy proceeds to recount Sidney's valor, with a close description of the battle at Zutphen. In fact, the larger number of stanzas is given over to the scene of Sidney's wound, "whereof a musket shot arose," and to his remarkable courage after the bullet pierced his thigh. In the familiar deathbed scene, moreover, Day does not allude to Sidney's poetic achievements. Rather, and most significantly, Day concludes his praise with a suggestive reminiscence of his material contribution to his "Souldiers":

> How oft his bountie did to them abound,
> > To salve such wants as they might not provide.
> From whose relief he never yet could hide,
> > But what distresse or wracke so ever came:
> His purse and aide was prest to help the same.

Day's recognition of the value of Sidney's purse, over and above his value as a model poet, seems clear by the end of the poem. He was a model *for* poetry, Achilles rather than Homer; and that relationship seldom arises in the English context without patronage being in mind. Indeed, in the last stanza Day again alludes to Sidney as a generous patron, "Whose bountie so did binde,/The heartes of all, to whome he was so kinde." For Angel Day, Sidney's fame finally rests on his bounty, not on his pen.

This is the typical view in elegies before the nineties. The earliest stage of the Sidney legend emphasizes his comprehensive patronage of all the arts. In addition, as much as Sidney was accounted "a generall *Maecenas* of Learning," he was also perceived as a larger-than-life hero, an Alexander of the age. These elements are related insofar as payment earns the praise of one's deeds by poets. But the conflation of patronage and heroic deeds, or patronage *as* heroism, is exemplary in the encomia for Sidney, although it becomes more common later in the century, as in the many verse praises of Essex. The earliest elegists use Sidney as a subject for song much as Virgil in the Eclogues used Caesar or Gallus, and thereby they attach themselves to an extant classical and Continental literary tradition. Although there is a far greater advantage to "erecting" Sidney as a uniquely poetic precursor, as Spenser and others come to realize within the decade, the elegists' first impulse after his death is to build monuments to him as a fallen knight and aristocratic patron and to attract the attention of other patrons to their own skillful monument building.

So George Whetstone, whose marginalia tells us "It is flattery to praise the living, and justice to Commend the dead," reveals the advantage of calling on his own muse to sing Sidney's praises: "Live-men have eares; when Tombes are deafe and poore,/Yet thus my name, shall with the best remayne" (Colaianne and Godshalk, "On the Life Death and Vertues . . ." Sig.B1v). This is the pride and optimism of a poet immortalizing a prince. In fact, in the previous stanza Whetstone alludes to Alexander's wish to have had Homer "his victories to spreade." With a frank Elizabethan acknowledgment of what is in it for him, Whetstone undertakes to glorify Sidney as an Alexander of his time.

Whetstone's elegy—according to Whetstone, at any rate—represents a different sort of poem from the work of writers who preceded him. In his address "To the Reader," he justifies his relatively short delay in publishing the elegy with a castigation of less circumspect contemporaries:

Courteous reader, divers of my frendes . . . have charged me to be remisse . . . But I satisfied my frendes, with this reason that I certifie unto the generall reader, *vid.* that the error that I sawe some hasty writers to commit, for lacke of true instruction, and the injurie that they did, unto so worthy a gentleman, in publishing his History, not having knowledge of the one halfe of his vertues, (to shunne the blame of two such capitall wronges,) moved me to be headfull, that I published nothing but truth of so true a Knight.[36]

As Whetstone rescues Sidney from "hasty writers" by whose errors his history has been lost, Sidney rescues Whetstone's virtue by making him "headfull" that he publish nothing but the truth about "so true a knight." The exchange is explicit, and both the live poet and the dead knight benefit. Indeed, the last sentence reminds us that good writing imitates life, or as Whetstone himself puts it earlier, that great lives live on in the "imitation of their posteritie." Nothing could be more helpful than this interchange in aligning the writer with his subject. Whetstone's verse ostensibly partakes of Sidney's virtue by the very act of imitating Sidney in words. The alignment between them is presumed to be so clear that Whetstone even uses it to excuse his dilatory publication, "which," he assures the reader, "cannot come to late, when good Sir Phillip Sidney liveth ever." It is impressive that Whetstone matches his own slow writerly effort to Sidney's eternal fame— fame, of course, that his own elegy claims to guarantee.[37]

36. This avowal appears in Colaianne and Godshalk, but there are no page numbers to the Whetstone text.

37. Delays in publishing a tribute to Sidney, epitomized by Spenser's nine years, seem to have stirred a fair amount of contemporary comment. Thomas Moffett, for example, in *Nobilis,* tries to excuse his six-year delay, pointing out that he "was ashamed, forsooth, to have been seen tearless in the season when not only the fennel and the pine but also the willow and the oak were stained with mutual tears." His reason for delay is that early and excessive lamentation would have been intemperate, and that especially those men who felt Sidney's loss most powerfully have been led to believe that early publication would do more harm than good: "This way of thinking has prompted very many, even those holding the name of Sidney in the highest reverence, up to the present to suppress rather than to publish their expressions of sorrow—fearing, doubtless, lest those that too bitterly bewail one renowned for every virtue . . . haply may wound rather than honor him" (ed. and trans. Virgil B. Hetzel and Hoyt H. Hudson, [San Marino, Calif.:

Whetstone's chief concern in the poem is to establish Sidney's accomplishments in different areas. He describes his noble birth, his "riche" martial and "decent usuall apparrell," his Continental tour, his poetry, his religious translations, his patriotic zeal, his wound ("A smaller wound, leaves many in the fielde"), and his loyalty "To God, to Prince, and to the common weale." The language is deliberately stylized; despite Whetstone's promises, he is more attentive to a memorial tone than to "truth": he echoes Elizabeth at her most stylized, referring to herself as England's "Prince." Although Whetstone's sort of transparent mythologizing now strikes us as pointless, his praise indicates sources of the Sidney legend to which we still subscribe. For instance, Whetstone insists on making it clear that Sidney was as English as could be.

> In Italy his youth, was not begilde.
> By vertue he their vices did forbeare:
> Of this bie-speache he evermore had care,
> An English-man that is Italionate:
> Doth lightly prove a Devell incarnate. (Sig.B2r)

The final couplet is a translation of a so-called proverb that Roger Ascham quotes in *The Scholemaster: "Englese Italianato, e un diabolo incarnato"* (Ascham, *Scholemaster,* p. 229). Ascham quotes the proverb in his jeremiad against Italy and Italian books, and Whetstone is merely echoing a now-venerable prejudice. The aversion to excessive Italian influence, or to its discovery, is important to the early formulation of the Sidney myth, particularly because the first elegists and historians used Sidney as a political (and stridently Protestant) ideal. This aversion becomes less pronounced when the elegists begin to emphasize Sidney's value as a poet over and above his transient value as a political figure. It is impossible, however, not to compare Geoffrey Shepherd's remark, in 1965: "But Sidney

---

Huntington Library, 1940], pp. 69–70). Thus Moffett's defense is that he can now contemplate Sidney in relative tranquility and perhaps even rejoice in Sidney's life. In this respect his apology resembles Whetstone's, though in neither case do we have an actual accusation to which the writers might have been responding. That such accusations existed we know, though the ulterior motives of the accusers and defenders are difficult to discern. Nevertheless it is noteworthy that literary publication of any kind could have had such apparently institutional value. (See Davison's *Poetical Rhapsody,* 2:63, for an accusation of Spenser; and Baskervill's comment in the Spenser *Variorum,* p. 489.)

was no Italianate Englishman" (p.45). That Shepherd can echo Whetstone so closely, and with similar insistence, perhaps testifies to our continued obliviousness to the change in the elegists' characterizations of Sidney after about 1591.

Whetstone acknowledges that Sidney was a poet. But he quickly qualifies the writing of poetry as just one endeavor among many.

> Needes must they say the Muses in him sounge,
> His Archadia, unmacht for sweete devise:
> Where skill doth judge, is held in Souveraigne price.
> What else he wrote, his wish was to suppresse,
> But yet the darke, a Dyamond cannot drowne:
> What be his workes, the finest wittes doe gesse,
> The Shepheardes notes, that have so sweete a sounde.
> With Lawrel bowghes, his healme, long since, have Crownd,
> And not alone, in Poesie he did passe:
> But ev'ry way, a learned Knight he was. (Sig.B2v)

This is flattering criticism of Sidney's writing, yet Whetstone cannot let the praise stand on its own, apparently for fear that Sidney might be taken for a mere poet. So he adds a rider denying the possibility that his hero frittered away his time in "Poesie" alone. He may be a "learned Knight," but Whetstone's couplet strongly implies that the kind of learning under discussion far surpasses poetry. Whetstone confirms the normal Elizabethan opinion that poetry is simply a youthful pastime, a theme that echoes throughout Sidney's biography. Indeed, it will be remembered that Sidney himself somewhat defensively refers to the *Arcadia* as his "toies." And Hubert Languet, commenting on Sidney's rather protracted stays at Wilton after 1577 (where he wrote the *Arcadia*), chides the young man for his withdrawal: "I am especially sorry to hear you say that you are weary of the life to which I have no doubt God has called you, and desire to fly from the light of your court and betake yourself to the privacy of secluded places to escape the tempest of affairs by which statesmen are generally harassed."[38]

Of course, Sidney's privacy was not entirely his own choice. It is

38. *The Correspondence of Sir Philip Sidney and Hubert Languet*, trans. S. A. Pears (London, 1854; rpt. New York, 1971), pp. 155, 187. Quoted in Michael Brennan, *Literary Patronage in the English Renaissance: The Pembroke Family* (London and New York: Routledge, 1988), p. 46.

a commonplace that he was exiled from court and public affairs several times by the Queen's displeasure. He would have preferred to serve the state in an active capacity. As Edward Berry recently observed, "[o]nly when he was denied such service, kept from 'fitte imployments' by the 'unnoble constitution of our tyme,' as he put it to his friend Edward Denny, did he turn seriously to poetry."[39] Sidney was prevented, chiefly by a lack of royal preferment and sometimes by active royal prohibition, from rejoining the courtly "tempest of affairs," though the elegists understandably never connect Sidney's poetry to his courtly failure. For good reasons Elizabeth did not seem to like young Philip, and she was especially reluctant to help him after he published his letter against her marriage to Alençon. Montrose concludes that "Sidney's persistent attempts to gain patronage and to influence government policy were wholly unsuccessful" (p. 11). But if the early elegists were aware of Sidney's frustrations in these areas, they utterly suppress this knowledge in their poetry. It is no part of their enterprise to present what we would consider a realistic portrait. They are more concerned to show, as Whetstone does, Sidney's commendable prudence in balancing his private and public lives. Consequently they characterize Sidney's poetry as neither entirely frivolous nor quite serious. It is, according to much of the elegiac hyperbole, as good as poetry can be, but it is never represented as a worthy career in itself. Rather, the fact of the poetry exemplifies Sidney's commendable prudence in balancing his private and public lives.

Sidney had not gone entirely unnoticed as a man of letters, even though he himself preferred to be seen as a man of action. As Michael Brennan explains,

Edmund Spenser and Gabriel Harvey appear to have been the individuals most responsible for the formulation, in its earliest stages, of Sidney's public reputation in England as a man of letters. In *Gratulationes Valdinenses* (1578), a collection of poetic panegyrics, Harvey addressed him as one "In quibus ipsae habitent Musae, dominentur Apollo"; Spenser

---

39. Edward Berry, "The Poet as Warrior in Sidney's *Defence of Poetry*," *SEL* 29 (1989), p. 21. Berry goes on, echoing Johan Huizinga, though perhaps overstating the case: "For men of Sidney's position, poetry was at best a courtly game—to be pursued with great energy and passion, perhaps, like other games, but not to be confused with the serious business of life" (p. 22). For contrast with "men of Sidney's position," see Miller, *The Professional Writer in Elizabethan England;* and Helgerson, *Self-Crowned Laureates.*

dedicated *The Shepherd's Calendar* in 1579 to "the noble and virtuous gentleman most worthy of all titles both of learning and chivalry M. Philip Sidney"; and the following year, the *Familiar Letters* of Spenser and Harvey again referred to Sidney's literary pursuits.

Strangely, these determined efforts to publicise Sidney's commitment to literature did not stimulate any widespread appreciation during the 1580s of his poetic skill. (P. 50)

Perhaps it is not so strange as Brennan suggests that not even Spenser and Harvey could "stimulate widespread appreciation" of Sidney's poetic achievements. Sidney's poetic contemporaries would have been reluctant to encourage a comparison of Sidney's poetry and their own—assuming, of course, that they even knew of Sidney's work. Their praises are confined to Sidney's deeds, to his rank and person. It is for the elegists of the next generation to recognize the value to their own status of honoring a near contemporary as a poetic precursor.[40] If, as John Buxton declares, "Sidney set the English Renaissance on its course" (p. 255), then he did so only after his death. It is largely as a result of the gradual change in Sidney's reputation, from courtier-hero to poet-hero in the early 1590s, that we now construe him as a *primum mobile*. Even Buxton's notion that, with the help of Dyer and Greville, "Sidney planned his campaign to make English poetry comparable to the poetry of Renaissance Italy" (p. 102) reflects that later myth.

Indeed, most of the early elegists emphasize that Sidney's true career was his loyalty to the Crown. The multiplicity of his interests supposedly underscores the loss to England of so variously capable a courtier. Moreover, the detailing of Sidney's abundant accomplishments allows writers to demonstrate their rhetorical skills—and, most important, to link their own rhetorical copiousness to patriotic loyalty. For instance, in the preface to "The Life, Death, and Funerals, of Sir Philip Sidney knight" (1587), John Philip lists in one long sentence a superb review of Sidney's worthy behavior as well as a defense of his loyalty. This tour de force, in a letter addressed to Robert Devereux, Earl of Essex, follows the characterization of Sidney as both a "Phenix" and "the flower of curtesie":

40. As Helgerson notes in *Self-Crowned Laureates,* a literary "generation" may sometimes be displaced by another within a few years, for we are speaking about attitudes and not literal familial descent.

This even this most worthy Knight passing his pilgrimage in this ter-
restriall vale of too manifold miseries, so behaved himself that for the
exercise of perfect pietie, he was honoured and highly esteemed of all
men, to the poore he was mercifull, to the learned liberall, to Sutors a
great comfort, to the fatherless favourable, to the widowes, helpfull, and
to saye the truth, his hande, his heart, and pursse, was alwayes ready to
support the distressed, with goodmen he was delighted, and with them
alwaies ever conversant, and as he himself had scaled *Pernassus* and sat
with *Citheria* amongst the *Muses,* so gloried he in wisdome and the lovers
of the same with the perverse, the frowarde and mallicious suche as were
contemners of truth, enemies of her majesties most royal person, and
conspiring *Catalins* against their native countrie, who can saye that
sweet *Sidney* was ever touched with one spot of disloyaltie: nay, who can
not say, but that he carried in his secreat bosom a hart undefiled, a cleare
conscience, & a mind garnished with innocence. (Colaianne and Godshalk, Philip's preface, Sig. 2Ar)

Even in this jumble the order of praiseworthy deeds is notable:
according to Philip, Sidney was primarily a patron, a supporter
first and foremost of the poor, the learned, the fatherless, and also
the widowed. The "generall Maecenas" has somewhat branched
out in Philip's version, but the chief lesson is that his "pursse" was
always open, "ready to support the distressed."[41] Such a lesson, we
presume, is aimed at Robert Devereux, with John Philip's support
in mind. To that end, perhaps, Philip alludes to Sidney's poetic
achievements, paying the obligatory compliment that Sidney "had
scaled *Pernassus* and sat with *Citheria* amongst the *Muses.*" It is not
clear to which work Philip is referring, and he might simply be
echoing the official line on the martyred courtier. Speculation is
irrelevant, in any case, because Philip's objective, as we see in his
next phrases, is to link Sidney's familiarity with the Muses to his
political loyalty.

Actually it is difficult to miss the association, even in Philip's
tortured syntax, between "the perverse, the frowarde and mallicious suche as were contemners of truth, enemies of her majesties

---

41. The extent of Sidney's patronage of scholars and poets is still not clear. His free
spending, however, whether to support general learning or for his own use, anticipated
inheritances he never received and put him into massive debt. As is well known, after
Sidney's death his father-in-law, Francis Walsingham, went bankrupt paying off the
creditors.

most royal person" and those who would disdain poetry and wisdom. Indeed, an amalgam of loyalty and poetry not only characterizes Sidney but effectually unites him with all those who profess their loyalty through poetry. This is an eloquent point, a call for a limited meritocracy, placing writers and scholars who vie for substantive patronage alongside those to the manor born. Philip's preface only intimates this point. The second stanza of the elegy, however, which is ostensibly spoken from the grave by Sidney himself, explicitly articulates the argument for merit, drawing particular attention to the equal clay of all births.

> I neede not I, record my bloud, ne birth,
>> For whych to you my parentage is knowne:
> My mould was clay, my substaunce was but earth,
>> And now the earth enjoyes agayn her owne,
> My race is runne, my daies are overthrowne.
>> Yet Lordings list, your patience here I crave,
>> Heare Sydneis plea, discussed from his grave. (Sig. 2A1r)[42]

Throughout the elegy Philip repeatedly emphasizes Sidney's importance to the common man. It seems to be Philip's objective to establish that Sidney's death and funeral somehow unite men of gentle and common blood, or that they are brought together in Sidney's person. For instance, the mourners who march past the bier, whom Sidney thanks for their grief, consist of the poor, the yeomen, and the "gentles." The sight of Sidney's standard trailing on the ground "in greivous dolefull wise,/Made rich and poore, with plaints to pearce the skies." Philip implies that Sidney's death has a leveling effect on class differences, that it "Gave all estates occasion meete to mourne."

Much of the elegy involves an anti-Catholic diatribe in which Rome, "that cage of birdes uncleane," has invaded England to seduce souls away from Elizabeth. Philip accuses Rome, and presumably the Catholic Spanish against whom Sidney was fighting, of sowing division among English Protestant subjects. Sidney is

---

42. Fulke Greville also has Sidney speak from the grave. According to Lanham, Greville puts "his apologia for a might-have-been foreign policy into the mouth of one who had died heroically trying to carry it out. . . . Sidney seems to come from the grave to defend again that implacable hatred toward Catholic Spain which united and inspired Walsingham's war party" ("Sidney: The Ornament of his Age," p. 324).

cast as the Queen's avenging knight, prepared to defend Protestantism and to warn off those in England who would follow Rome with what Milton was to call "privy paw":

> You that do with your curssed wils to have,
>   And daily strive your country to betray,
> Heare Sidney speake to you from out his grave,
>   That pearst aloft, by treason to leave sway,
> Though that your pranckes in secreat you do play,
>   Yet God your grudge will bring to each man's sight,
>   And in his wrath with vengeance you requight. (Sig. 2A2v)

With Sidney's help Elizabeth then triumphs: "Of poperie she the puddels hath made cleane." Moreover, in Philip's extended praise of the Queen ("Twentie nine yeares you have her grace possest"), Sidney personally urges a general humility:

> To God and Prince remember then your bow,
> Live subject like and then take this from mee,
> Redoubled thrice her happie daies shalbe. (Sig. 2B1v)

To have Sidney urge humility to "God and Prince" seems somewhat ironic in light of his open defiance of the Earl of Oxford on the tennis court. It will be remembered that Elizabeth censured Sidney precisely because he overstepped his rank. Of course it is true that Sidney always obeyed the Queen herself, as when she ordered him back from Drake's excursion. Still, his tantrum demonstrates at least some resistance to a life of subjectlike behavior.[43]

Although Philip seems to share Sidney's militantly Protestant vision, nevertheless he sounds an unusual antiwar theme in the elegy. He represents the martyred Sidney as the awful harvest of armed hostilities. Curiously, Philip shows patent contempt for the "band of marshall wights" who attend Sidney's burial. They are naifs, he contends, "Their muskets borne so out of order clean,/As though they knew not what the war did meane." Earlier in the poem, as in his preface, Philip refers to Catiline:

43. See F. J. Levy, "Philip Sidney Reconsidered," *ELR* 2:1 (1972), pp. 5–18; rpt. Kinney, ed., *Essential Essays,* esp. p. 5. Levy suggests that the quarrel with Oxford, "that Court popinjay," symbolizes Sidney's decision to be recognized as a statesman rather than a courtier. It strikes me, to the contrary, that such ill-considered behavior holds dubious promise for future statesmanship. In any case, Sidney's attitude toward the earl could scarcely be misconstrued as humility.

And you that carpe with Catiline for spoyle,
And would convert your quiet peace to war,
Have some remorse unto your native soyle,
Let not the Pope procure you thus to jarre. (Sig. 2B1v)

A description of Zutphen follows as Sidney recounts that last day on the battlefield. Then Philip, always in Sidney's persona, allots a stanza each to Leicester, Warwick, Pembroke, Essex, and Sidney's brother. Presumably these men know the import of converting "quiet peace to war," and, while recognizing the necessity of fighting, deeply regret the pointless loss of men like Sidney who have been sacrificed to the Pope.

Even in this section of the elegy the rich and poor are juxtaposed in bereavement: "Care clad my friends, their harts a sunder cleft,/ my servants minds were overwhelmed with griefe." Indeed, as the mournful procession passes the corpse, after the lords, the "Lord Maior," and "Senators most grave," Philip emphasizes that Sidney's "friends" included those of much lower social status:

Wert these my friends in order passed on,
  The gentle crew of Grocers comly clad.
These, these my friendes, their loving friend did mone,
  they for their friend to mourne occasion had. (Sig. 3A2r)

The word "friend" appears four times in this short passage, in puzzling conjunction with the grocers. They are rich guild members, who, like the ironmongers and goldsmiths, are likely to end up as gentlemen (or their sons will). Moreover, the grocers are clearly superior to the misguided "marshall wights" who are behind them in the funeral procession; like the nobles, the grocers are friends. And even if we accept "friend" in its Elizabethan sense, less as an affectionate than as a practical relation, nevertheless we must acknowledge something exceptional in Sidney's hypothetical friendship with "the worshipful company of Grocers," as Philip glosses them in the margin. This seems to be part of the persistent effort throughout the elegy to establish the measure of Sidney's worth in his appeal to all classes. It is doubtful that any really poor people were in the procession, though it may have been the official piety that the poor cheered or wept from the sidelines. Thus, when Sidney bids adieu in the last stanza, Philip reminds us that "Your Sidneis wordes remember rich and poore."

"AMORIS LACHRIMAE"

Four years after the first collections of elegies were published by Oxford and Cambridge in 1587, the year after Sidney's death, Nicholas Breton published "Amoris Lachrimae" (1591). Here we begin to discern a change in attitude toward Sidney. Although we do not know exactly when Breton wrote the lament, the prominence of the speaker over Sidney in the poem indicates a date later than 1587. My argument does not depend on this date, however, and I would be reluctant to point to any single year as a watershed. Rather, as I mentioned earlier, the change in Sidney's reputation should be seen as gradual, taking place over nearly a decade. Breton's long poem is helpful in this regard because in it we observe, perhaps for the first time in any extended sense, the use of Sidney as an abstract quantity.

Breton does not overtly acknowledge that Sidney was a poet. He begins in an obligatory fashion, showering praise on Sidney's "Valure and Vertue, Learning, Bountie, Love."[44] He asserts that "His hands was [sic] free to helpe the needie hart," doubtless an oblique reference to his patronage; and, poetry notwithstanding, Breton maintains that Sidney's "onely joy was honour of the fielde" (p. 8). The furthest Breton goes in associating Sidney with literature is to establish in prosopopoeia how much he is missed: "Nature and Art are got about his grave,/And there sit wailing of each others losse." Beauty also mourns "with her blubbered eyes," as do Love, Care, Patience (uncharacteristically "pricking of her fingers ends"), and Pity. Breton is careful to include the Muses, who "sit and rend their shriveled heares" (p. 9), but they are distressed, evidently, by the sounds of Love and Beauty lamenting rather than by the loss of a poet. It would be difficult to suggest that Breton, any more than Whetstone or Philip or Angel Day, sees Sidney as the first poet of the English tradition.

Yet Breton's elegy is different from the others in its grandiose evocation of the speaker's predicament. Admitting that "through [sic] my penne can never halfe expresse,/The hideous torments of my heavie heart," he proceeds to "set down some touch of my distresse,/That some poore soule may helpe to beare a part" (p. 8).

---

44. *Brittons Bowre of Delights* (1591), ed. Hyder Edward Rollins (New York: Russell & Russell, 1968), p. 6.

His pretext for writing is to share his pain, and, significantly, to view Sidney's absence as both a unifying condition and as a kind of inspiration. This is not precisely the same as regarding Sidney as a genealogical original, but, nonetheless, it represents a departure from the monument-building of the first elegists. For instance, Breton consciously invokes his muse as a kind of salve to Sidney's death, and thereby himself becomes the protagonist of the rest of the poem:

> I live, oh live, alas, I live indeede,
> But such a life was never such a death,
> While fainting heart is but constrainde to feede,
> Upon the care of a consuming breath:
>   O my sweete Muse, that knowest how I am vexed,
>   Paint but one passion how I am perplexed. (P. 9)

Indeed, though Breton is not a particularly profound versifier, he has a knack for paradox and the inverted phrase:

> To live in death is but a dying life,
> To die in life, is but a living death,
> Betwixt these two is such a deadly strife,
> As make me draw this melancholike breath. (P. 8)

Again and again, the inversion of Sidney's fate becomes Breton's inner passion. Consequently, his introspection replaces the usual mundane recapitulation of Sidney's life achievements. Sidney (or the loss of Sidney) appears in the poem as that abstract quantity that renders Breton's life as barren as any death. In fact, in a clever turnabout, Breton mourns for his own life because, without Sidney, it is as endless as Sidney's death: "Thinke what a death of deathes I have endured," he moans.

Breton alludes to the "losse of such a daintie friend," incidentally acknowledging that he knows Sidney better in death than he could in life. Cursing "cruell Death," he despairs in life now that his "love" is gone:

> For I have lost the honour of my love,
> My love hath lost the honour of my life,
> My life and love doth such a passion prove. (P. 10)

Again the inverted phrases produce a version of the speaker's passion, this time uniting all of Sidney's supposed attributes in Breton—love, honor, passion. As the elegy continues, Breton personifies Sidney as "Love," alternating between the upper-case personification and the lower-case emotion: "My heavenly Love, heavens lov'd as well as I"; or, "Oh heavenly Love, heavens will I looke for never,/Till in the heavens I may beholde thee ever"; or, yet again, "Such lacke of love, such mourning for a friend" (p. 10). In the end this alternation serves to confound Breton's inmost feeling with Sidney's being; the "lacke of love," for example, is both a lack of Philip Sidney and a lack of passion in the speaker now that his "friend" is gone. Mourning the loss of Sidney becomes, in part, an exercise in mourning the loss of Breton's will to live.

Such personal lamentation is distinctive in Elizabethan vernacular elegies. Peter Sacks has suggested that "One of the major tasks of the work of mourning and of the elegy is to repair the mourner's damaged narcissism."[45] Yet, so far as I can tell, Breton is more intent on documenting his "damaged narcissism" than on working through his loss toward some reparation. The connection between the act of mourning and the writing of poetry is of paramount importance. Writing does not provide a remedy for the pain, but rather an advertisement of it:

> And on thy tombe I wil with teares engrave,
> The death of life that for thy lacke I have. (P. 13)

All the elements of the poem converge in these lines. Breton's inversions of life and death, of love and lacke, will coalesce in the graphic representation on the tomb. Tomb inscription is a well-established tradition in the period, connected with Roman lapidary writing. But Breton plans to immortalize Sidney with his tears on the stone, an image perhaps intended to recall ink on paper. The elegy's final couplet repeats the sentiment more literally.

> Upon thy Tombe I will these wordes set downe,
> That all the world may read of thy renowne. (P. 16)

45. Peter Sacks, *The English Elegy: Studies in the Genre from Spenser to Yeats* (Baltimore: Johns Hopkins University Press, 1985), p. 10. Sacks is referring in this passage to Freud's theories on the "work of mourning." He explores, as he puts it, "a significant similarity between the process of mourning and the oedipal resolution" (p. 8). See also Joshua Scodel, *The English Poetic Epitaph: Commemoration and Conflict from Jonson to Wordsworth* (Ithaca and London: Cornell University Press, 1991). Scodel suggests that "[d]eath rituals generally seek to bring about or affirm the new status of the deceased. The person who has been violently torn from the living must be incorporated into the world of the dead, however conceived, so that he or she can be related in a new way to the community of the living" (p. 89).

Breton is overgoing the traditional "laureate hearse" on which elegiac documents would be pinned. Instead, his elegy will be graven on the tomb itself and his words, more than anything else, will have the renown attached to Sidney. This is the final replacement of his "lacke" with his "love" or "Love."

It is noteworthy, moreover, that "Amoris Lachrimae," which Breton calls "the onely true Anotamie of love" (p. 16), should be written in English rather than in Latin. The words on Sidney's tomb will be English poetry, and, therefore, the vernacular tradition that Sidney championed will confirm his (and, incidentally, Breton's) fame. Breton seems consciously to distinguish the vernacular from the scholarly languages:

> The Scholers come with Lachrimis Amoris,
> As though their hearts were hopelesse of reliefe,
> The Soldiers come with Tonitru Clamoris,
> To make the heavens acquainted with their griefe:
>   The noble Peeres in Civitatis portis,
>   In hearts engraven come with Dolor mortis.
>
> The straungers come with Oh che male sorte,
> The servants come with Morte dila vita,
> The secret friends with Morte pui [*sic*] che morte,
> And all with these Felicita finita:
>   Nowe for my selfe, Oh dolor infernale,
>   Da videre morte, & non da vivere tale. (P. 15)

The descent from the Latin is clear. Scholars, soldiers, and peers of the realm mourn the dead knight in the learned tongue. Strangers, servants, and secret friends, whoever they are, mourn Sidney in Italian. Among these latter we find Breton himself. While he may humbly take his place with the citizens below noble rank, the vernacular he chooses is Dante's, Petrarch's, and Ariosto's—the language of the most renowned poetry of the period.

In fact, however, the words on Sidney's grave were a translation from French. Sidney was buried in St. Paul's (despite his fame no monument was ever erected), and on the pillar above his grave, according to W. H. Bond, "were fixed his crest, coat of arms, and colors, and beneath them a simple tablet of wood bearing an anonymous epitaph."[46] Bond reflects that "the most ironic paradox

---

46. William H. Bond, "The Epitaph of Sir Philip Sidney," *MLN* 58 (1943), p. 253.

of all was the fact that Sidney's epitaph was not original, and that it
was not even English to begin with. It was merely a clever adaptation of the epitaph written by Joachim du Bellay for Guillaume
Gouffier, Seigneur de Bonnivet" (p. 256). Perhaps the adaptation
of the French poem is more appropriate than Bond recognizes. In
any case, the original, as Anne Lake Prescott notes, spawned at
least five English imitations: "This minor but clever piece must
have pleased English readers because it so handily magnifies the
great soldier into a universe of admiration while simultaneously
compressing him into one brief huitain":

> Le France & le Piemont, & les Cieux & les Arts,
> Les Soldats & le Monde ont faict comme six parts
> De ce grand Bonivet: car une si grand' chose
> Dedans un seul tombeau ne pouvoit estre enclose.
> La France en a la Corps, qu'elle avoit eslevé:
> Le Piemont a le Coeur, qu'il avoit esprouvé:
> Les Cieux en ont l'Esprit, & les Arts la Memoire:
> Les Soldats le Regret, & le Monde la Gloire.[47]

The epitaph above Sidney's grave follows the original with reasonable fidelity:

> England, Netherlands, the Heauens, and the Arts
> The Souldiers, and the World, haue made six parts,
> Of the noble Sydney: for none will suppose,
> That a small heape of stones can Sydney enclose.
> His body hath England, for she it bred,
> Netherland his blood, in her defence shed:
> The Heauens haue his soule, the Arts haue his fame,
> All Souldiers the greefe, the World his good name. (Bond, p. 254)

The epitaph is lost now, but it remained a shrine in London, a kind
of tourist attraction, until well into the seventeenth century. We
have testimony of its existence in several sources, including John
Eliot's *Ortho-Epia Gallica* (1593), Dekker's *The Guls Horne-booke*
(1609), and Anthony Stafford's *Niobe: or His Age of Teares* (1611),
which quotes the epitaph in full.

Of the other English versions of Du Bellay's poem, Ralegh's is
best known; as Prescott says, he pushes the conceit even further
and divides Sidney into eleven or twelve parts.

---

47. Prescott, *French Poets and the English Renaissance*, p. 60. In contrast to Bond,
Prescott gives Bonnivet's first name as François.

England doth hold thy lims that bred the same,
Flaunders thy valure where it last was tried,
The Campe thy sorrow where thy bodie died,
Thy friends, thy want; the world, thy vertues fame.

Nations thy wit, our mindes lay vp thy loue,
Letters thy learning, thy losse, yeeres long to come,
In worthy harts sorrow hath made thy tombe,
Thy soule and spright enrich the heauens aboue.[48]

Ralegh's elegy for Sidney appeared in both *The Phoenix Nest* (1593) and later in Spenser's *Astrophel* collection. It is difficult to determine if he imitated Du Bellay's huitain directly or responded to the anonymous English epitaph. But his tribute, with considerably more grace than Breton's, merges the Continental and English vernaculars in the same way that he (and myriad others) merged Mars and Minerva in Sidney's persona. More than the anonymous epitaph writer, who did little besides change the place-names, Ralegh subsumes his models in a new original. There is nothing particularly surprising about Ralegh's relation to Du Bellay in terms of *imitatio*. But an additional, uncanny layer appears when we recognize the similarity between Ralegh's linguistic or poetic imitation—his simultaneous dependence on and transformation of his models—and the genealogical relation of the dead Sidney to his elegists.

THE ASTROPHEL COLLECTION

By far the best-known vernacular elegies are in the *Astrophel* collection, appended to Spenser's *Colin Clouts Come Home Again,* which did not come out until 1595. Baker-Smith explains that along with Spenser's poetry "pieces by Matthew Roydon, Raleigh and (probably) Dyer which had originally appeared in *The Phoenix Nest* in 1593, are reprinted with other laments by the Countess of Pembroke (or, more probably, Spenser) and Lodowick Bryskett to make up a sequence which is framed by Spenser's own lines" (p. 88).

48. *An Epitaph upon the right Honourable sir Philip Sidney knight: Lord governor of Flushing,* in *Spenser: Poetical Works,* ed. J. C. Smith and E. de Sélincourt (Oxford University Press, 1912), p. 559, lines 44–51. The "Epitaph" appears anonymously in this edition. I will use Smith and de Selincourt for Bryskett's and Roydon's elegies and, of course, for all of Spenser's works. I have here again normalized typography.

Although one might not characterize the poems of *Astrophel* precisely as a sequence, nevertheless Spenser's lines initiate and frame a fairly consistent view of Sidney as a poetic figure. Ralegh's "Epitaph," and especially its famous epithet of Sidney as the "*Scipio, Cicero,* and *Petrarch* of our time" (Smith and de Selincourt, p. 559), seems to be a throwback to the earlier elegies. Throughout *Astrophel,* as we see best in Spenser's title poem, the war general and the public man are subsumed in the poet. The "Maecenas of learning" is gone from Spenser's "Astrophel," and the other elegies in the collection seem to follow suit. It has been argued that the collection would have been put together by the printer rather than by Spenser. But Spenser must have been aware of the arrangement of the poems to some extent. For instance, "Astrophel" ends with a stanza introducing "The Doleful Lay of Clorinda"; and "The Doleful Lay of Clorinda" (which Baker-Smith suspects that Spenser wrote) ends with a reference to Bryskett's poem, the next in the collection ("Hight *Thestylis,* began his mournfull tourne"). The brief anticipatory verses between these poems may not indicate that Spenser had control of the collection precisely, but perhaps his awareness of the order of selections helped to influence the general character of the book.

Spenser's "Astrophel" is a striking departure from earlier praise of Sidney. While Sidney remains a martial hero in some of the later elegies, the dead knight is judged by Spenser to have been misguided in his foreign exploits, more like a hubristic Adonis than an exemplary Alexander. The shepherd Astrophel is a consummately brilliant courtier who does not recognize the value of his own verse. Moreover, Spenser unambiguously indicates the destructive potential, both to the poet and to the man, of Astrophel's monomaniacal devotion to Stella, for whom the young swain abandons poetry. But the abandonment of poetry leads Astrophel to his death on foreign soil. There can be no mistaking Spenser's critique of Astrophel's poor judgment in turning to the active life merely to entertain Stella. Both Stella and Astrophel himself are indicted as disastrously bad judges of poetry's value, and both of them pay with their lives in Spenser's denouement.[49]

In contrast, Lodowick Bryskett's "The Mourning Muse of The-

---

49. See chapter 2 for an extended discussion of Spenser's "Astrophel."

stylis" ends with stunning praise of Sidney's wartime achievements. But the poem is curiously bifurcated. At first Bryskett accuses Mars of abandoning Sidney in battle: "Ah dreadfull *Mars* why didst thou not thy knight defend?" (13). He wonders if it was because of a "wrathfull mood" or a "fault of ours" (14), meaning the Britons', that Mars permitted Sidney to be killed. He admits that Mars "hast in Britons valour tane delight of old" (17), and that there is fame and renown in "glorious martiall deeds" (19). But, for Bryskett at least, Sidney's death clearly does not redound to Britain's glory; it represents Mars's betrayal of "woful England" (24) rather than a heroic and honorable sacrifice. Perhaps in suggesting that Mars was not on England's side, Bryskett hopes to criticize the foreign policy that led to the Zutphen adventure; or perhaps he merely wishes to echo the conventional outcome of the Mercury-Mars contention.

Like Spenser, Bryskett compares Sidney to Adonis (though, unlike Spenser, he also likens Stella to Venus). And if we assign the familiar traits of Adonis to Sidney, then we are inclined to regard the dead knight more as a lover and somewhat incompetent hunter than as a martial hero. But Bryskett seems to have something else in mind. Inexplicably he reverses himself at the end of "The Mourning Muse of Thestylis" and describes Mars honoring Sidney:

> And *Mars* in reuerant wise doth to thy vertue bow,
> And decks his fiery sphere, to do thee honour most.
> In highest part whereof, thy valour for to grace,
> A chaire of gold he setts to thee, and there doth tell
> Thy noble acts arew [*sic*], whereby euen they that boast
> Themselues of auncient fame, as *Pirrhus, Hanniball*
> *Scipio* and *Caesar,* with the rest that did excell
> In martiall prowesse, high thy glorie do admire.
> (Smith and de Sélincourt, p. 550, ll. 182–89)

Gone without explanation is Mars's anger at the Britons. Sidney now sits on a golden throne admired for his "martiall prowesse" by the great generals of antiquity. In fact, Mars himself becomes the epic poet and tells of Sidney's "noble acts," an unusual role for the god of war.

The promulgation of the Sidney legacy has much to do with the availability of a figurehead for canonization. It is much more useful to aspiring poets, and much less threatening, to avoid the poetry and to invent a martyred poet. Following a convention of pastoral elegy stemming from Moschus, elegists repeatedly emphasize Sidney's wasted youth and talent, just as they wonder at the incomprehensibility of the divine plan. Thus, also in "The Mourning Muse of Thestylis," Bryskett decries Sidney's unfulfilled promise:

> Mourne, mourn, great *Philips* fall, mourn we his woeful end
> Whom spitefull death hath pluct untimely from the tree,
> While yet his yeares in flowre, did promise worthie frute
>
> (Ll. 10–12)

Bryskett characterizes the untimely plucking from the tree as the loss of a poetic persona who is also a shepherd knight. He summons to mind Sidney's most famous literary posture by describing Stella's grief—the same Stella who, for all practical purposes, exists only in Sidney's poetic fiction:

> Ah that thou hadst but heard his lovely *Stella* plaine
> Her greevous loss . . .
>   She wroong her hands with paine
> And piteously gan say . . .
> What cruel envious hand hath taken thee away,
> And with thee my content, my comfort and my stay?
> . . . .
> O greedie envious heav'n what neede thee to have
> Enricht with such a Iewell this unhappie age,
> To take it back againe so soone?
>
> (Ll. 93–112, passim)

According to G. Norlin, "There is expressed in almost every dirge, ancient or modern, a feeling of bitter resentment against the cruel fate which blasts life in the bud or cuts it off in the fullness of its flower" (p. 306). Bryskett is participating in a conventional lament as old as the form, though new to English poetry since Spenser's "November," but nevertheless his choice of aggrieved mourner is significant. From a biographical perspective, it is odd that Stella should be in such pain. After all, as everybody who knew Sidney would have known, and as the sonnets themselves suggest, Penelope Rich, the putative model for Stella, had married someone else. Bryskett's aim, however, is not to write a history or to revise the outcome of Sidney's sonnet sequence. Rather, he wants to underscore the loss to England and English letters of a consummately writerly figure.[50]

In Bryskett's second poem in the *Astrophel* collection, "A pastorall Aeglogue upon the death of Sir Phillip Sidney Knight," he abandons praise for Sidney's martial prowess and makes no mention of Sidney's role as a patron (except in calling him "liberall"), to which his reputation as an Alexander is often linked. Rather, Bryskett mourns the loss to the pastoral world of a shepherd-poet, a worthy shepherd-peer, as he puts it earlier, "pluct vntimely from the tree."[51] In the debate between Lycon and Colin (who is probably meant to be Spenser), the latter characterizes the dead man as, above all, a poet:

> *Phillisides* is dead. O lucklesse age;
> O widow world; O brookes and fountaines cleere;
> O hills, O dales, O woods that oft haue rong
> With his sweet caroling, which could asswage
> The fiercest wrath of Tygre or of Beare.
> Ye Siluans, Fawnes, and Satyres, that emong
> These thickets oft haue daunst after his pipe,
> Ye Nymphs and *Nayades* with golden heare,

---

50. "The Mourning Muse of Thestylis" was entered on the Stationer's Register in 1587. If Bryskett did not revise the poem between 1587 and its publication in *Astrophel*, then his focus on the writerly Sidney is precocious. We should note, however, that Bryskett knew Sidney very well, had been his traveling companion during the Continental tour, and would have been aware of the efforts of Harvey and Spenser to establish Sidney's credentials as a man of letters. His precocity would help to distinguish the elegists who knew Sidney from the contractual elegists or, in Breton's phrase, "secret friends."

51. "The Mourning Muse of Thestylis," p. 550, line 11. It is conventional to acknowledge that Sidney was "untimely plucked," though usually the elegists are referring to the flower called Astrophel rather than to a tree, as in Bryskett's line. For instance, in "The Doleful Lay of Clorinda," the Countess of Pembroke (or Spenser, if he is the author) makes much of the "fairest flowre" and asks "What cruell hand. . . ,/Hath cropt the stalke which bore so faire a flowre?/Vntimely cropt, before it well were grown" (p. 549, ll. 31–33). On the other hand, Spenser inverts the convention and transforms Astrophel and Stella into a flower after their deaths. He advises a representative transformation of the "herbe" which until then had been called Starlight or Penthia: "From this day forth do call it *Astrophel*" (196). Moreover, in a further inversion, Spenser suggests that whenever passing the Astrophel flower, one should "pluck it softly for that shepheards sake" (198). Unlike the typical plucking of youth by untimely death, which constitutes a sudden truncation, the plucking that Spenser recommends is meant to prolong Astrophel's existence in memory.

That oft haue left your purest cristall springs
To harken to his layes, that coulden wipe
Away all griefe and sorrow from your harts.
Alas who now is left that like him sings?
When shall you heare againe like harmonie?
So sweet a sownd, who to you now imparts?

(Ll. 111–23)

The unanswerable questions seem to be conventional in funeral elegies of the period. The Countess of Pembroke (or Spenser), in "The Doleful Lay of Clorinda," asks "Who euer made such layes of loue as hee?" But her question, like Bryskett's three, serves a descriptive more than an interrogative function. Sidney is established as an irreplaceable poet in the same moment that the loss of his poetry is mourned. This characterization of him, unaccompanied by the mandatory mention of his patronage, is an innovation peculiar to the later vernacular elegies.

Matthew Roydon's reprinted elegy is another case in point. Roydon seems to suggest that Sidney's extraordinary potential as a soldier, by making Mars jealous, caused his death:

Then *Pallas* afterward attyrde,
Our *Astrophill* with her deuice,
Whom in his armor heauen admyrde,
As of the nation of the skies,
    He sparkled in his armes afarrs.
    As he were dight with fierie starrs,

The blaze whereof when *Mars* beheld,
(An enuious eie doth see afar)
Such maiestie (quoth he) is seeld,
Such maiestie my mart may mar,
    Perhaps this may a suter be,
    To set *Mars* by his deitie.

(P. 557, ll. 163–74)

But Astrophil never actually performs any martial feats in Roydon's elegy. His martial appearance alone irritates Mars; dressed up in sparkling armor, Astrophil presents a threat not so much for what he does as for the looks he might attract. There is an irony in this that Roydon may or may not intend: Sidney was wounded precisely because he was *not* wearing the proper armor to cover his thighs. Astrophil's "maiestie," or magnanimity, may characterize him as a larger-than-life hero, but Roydon's chief aim is to mourn the passing of a poet. Whereas Pallas "afterward" attires Astrophil with her device—a heraldic symbol, which incidentally gets him killed within three stanzas—the many stanzas before the arming elaborately describe a shepherd-poet.

Roydon's Astrophil is not a rounded courtier who commands both words and deeds, but rather a versatile verbal performer: "The Muses met him every day,/That taught him sing, to write, and say." And Roydon is not sparing in his praise of the poet: "Did never Muse inspire beneath,/A Poets braine with finer store." As Astrophil, Sidney becomes the fabled poet of a nascent English tradition. Roydon consoles Stella with her lover's preeminence as a poet:

> Then *Astrophill* hath honored thee,
> For when thy bodie is extinct,
> Thy graces shall eternal be,
> And live by vertue of his inke. (Ll. 145–48)

The characterization of an English poet as "eternal" is also a novelty of the later elegies for Sidney. Whereas Sidney's first elegists promised an ability to praise prospective patrons by praising Sidney, the later elegists attach their own poetry to a grand and permanent tradition by pretending to follow Sidney's example as a poet. Roydon, for instance, connects himself to that "eternal" Sidney in the last line of the elegy: "And here my pen is forst to shrinke,/My teares discollors so mine inke." We recall that Stella's graces will be made eternal by "the vertue of [Sidney's] inke." The repetition of the word "inke" may well represent Roydon's attempt to unite his own verse with Sidney's already enshrined poetry.

The aggrandizement of Sidney as a poet is the first step in the invention of an English literary genealogy. We have noted the shift in the characterizations of Sidney in the nineties and observed that that shift resulted from the need to establish a poetic family tree from which writers could descend. Pastoral elegy supplied the link with classical authors and placed English literature squarely in the line of descent from Continental authors like Sannazaro, Castiglione, Marot, and Tasso. It should be remembered that, as Ellen Lambert has pointed out, "[t]he ten years following Sidney's death in 1586 mark the height of the pastoral elegy's popularity in England, with Sidney himself, the flower of the Elizabethan world, untimely plucked, its chief subject" (p. 143). That the elegiac genre served the purpose so well is significant, and, moreover, leads us to surmise that it is an instant artifact in English literary history.

The *Astrophel* collection contains the roots of Sidney's canonization as a poet. His reputation as a patron and soldier begins to lose importance beside his reputation as a poet. In the earlier elegies Angel Day, George Whetstone, and even Nicholas Breton appeal to Sidney's renowned stature as a patron and soldier to advance their cause. They do not recognize a need to withhold their praise of Sidney's public persona for the sake of enhancing the strength of their own poetic origins. On the other hand, the later elegists, led by Spenser, abandon in particular praise of Sidney's patronage and erect a chiefly poetic precursor from whom to descend. This shift in the characterization of Sidney, though by no means absolute or completely precipitous, indicates the beginning of a change in the Elizabethan attitude toward poetic genealogy. We might locate the first self-conscious roots of the English poetic family tree in the elegiac transformation of Sidney from a patron and soldier into a poet.

TWO

Rhymes to Please the Dead

Spenser's "Astrophel"

Whereby we stand opposed by such means
As you yourself have forg'd against yourself . . .
—*Henry IV, Part One*, V. i

Spenser's contribution to Elizabethan literary genealogy has the deceptive appearance of self-sacrifice. As is well known, he published *The Shepheardes Calender* some time before Philip Sidney's death and nearly two decades before Sidney's canonization as the first poet of the modern English tradition, a canonization Spenser forcefully encouraged in several different poems. Yet, despite his legitimate literary priority, Spenser falls in step with Sidney's other elegists and, being sure to take his place at the head of the queue, often feigns coming behind his dead contemporary. We cannot help but notice Spenser's intent in both "Astrophel" and "The Ruines of Time" simultaneously to establish and to join an English literary succession. Yet, while "Astrophel" canonizes the dead shepherd-knight as an originary and, to a certain extent, an inspirational force, in the final analysis we recognize that Spenser dissociates himself from Sidney's courtly frivolities and puts into "Astrophel" as much criticism as praise. Nevertheless, we must acknowledge how enduringly Spenser represents Sidney as a poet, which in itself was unusual at the time, and how persuasively he casts Sidney, by a kind of genealogical back-formation, as a vernacular predecessor.

It should be remembered that the canonization of Sidney as a poet did not occur immediately after his death. The first volumes of elegies published by Oxford and Cambridge in 1587, as well as the numerous commemorative verses of the early 1590s, tended to characterize Sidney chiefly as a patron and a soldier and only incidentally as a poet. As I suggested in chapter 1, not until the publication of Spenser's *Astrophel* collection do we find a clear shift from soldier to poet in the characterization of Sidney. The appearance of the *Arcadia* and *Astrophil and Stella* mainly provided public acknowledgment of privately held convictions regarding Sidney's literary value and, moreover, might well have had a reverse effect, paradoxically confirming the anachronistic construct of Spenser's literary descent. Contemporary readers might have noticed, for example, that Sidney occasionally borrows from *The Shepheardes Calender,* and they would perhaps have recognized the difference between literary fact and Spenser's literary figuration.[1]

It might be argued that Spenser never expressly claims Sidney as a poetic father, as he does Chaucer. But it is difficult to deny that again and again Spenser portrays Sidney/Astrophel as a prototype; he clearly resists the idea that his own earlier poetry be acknowledged as the chronologically leigimate source of Sidney's verse. In "The Ruines of Time," for instance, the eclogue Sidney sings in the Elysian fields explicitly antedates—as well as postpones—Spenser's elegy; and in "Astrophel" the "dolefull plaint" the poet evokes is indisputably belated, while Astrophel's piping and versifying occur in an earlier, originary time. Yet, although Spenser never claims priority in poetic history, neither will he entirely admit his debt to the ambiguous Sidney/Astrophel compound. At times, Spenser rejects Astrophel and even seems to relish the conflicting logic of eulogistic revisionism. At other times, however, his posture toward Sidney is well-nigh reverential.

Such bold contradictions abound in Spenser's attitude toward Sidney, and understanding their inevitability helps us to appreciate not only a local literary relationship, but also the contradictory

---

1. There are of course earlier English poets in Spenser's pantheon, particularly Chaucer and Skelton, but our conception of them as part of a coherent tradition of genealogical antecedents owes much to Spenser's formulation of Elizabethan literary descent. As Alastair Fowler has said, "Spenser occupied a uniquely strategic position between literary worlds. . . . He not only wrote well but wrote first; so many aftercomers have modeled themselves on him, directly and indirectly, that one may say he invented much of poetic form as we know it" ("Spenser's Names," in *Unfolded Tales: Essays on Renaissance Romance,* ed. George M. Logan and Gordon Teskey [Ithaca: Cornell University Press, 1989], p. 32.) I would add that Spenser's "uniquely strategic position" also permitted him to invent much of English literary genealogy as we know it.

impulses inherent in the forging of a new literary system, a new poetry, and a new literary genealogy. Perhaps, as Richard Helgerson has suggested, Spenser's attitude reflects the conflict between his own ambitions as a laureate poet in contrast to—and even in a struggle against—the ambitions of an amateur poet. Helgerson maintains that, until Spenser, the literary system was dominated by amateurs like Sidney, while "[t]he task of the laureates was to take this system and make of it a vehicle for a very different sort of identity."[2] Spenser manages to use the system for his own ends by changing his ends from those traditionally associated with poetry. Helgerson points out that whereas among amateur poets "[t]he lesson of poetry was . . . to stay away from poetry and from everything associated with it" (*Self-Crowned Laureates*, p. 64), Spenser maintained a view that poetry, because of its didactic function and moral value, was not to be dismissed as a youthful toy.[3] As we shall see, this view has particular importance in "Astrophel," and Spenser's condemnation of the shepherd-knight's capricious use of poetry serves virtually to enact the two sides of the debate. Thus the notion of a "laureate" poet is helpful in distinguishing Spenser from the highborn amateurs who abounded in the period, as well as in separating him from his professional contemporaries. But we should be careful not to polarize the distinctions too much. Emphasis on the social oppositions between these groups of writers, though based on real differences in their practical aims for poetry, often fails to account for shared notions of literary descent and shared participation in the forging of literary genealogy.

Much recent scholarship has focused on Spenser's ambitions in the Elizabethan courtly milieu.[4] His career as a poet in a society

2. Helgerson, *Self-Crowned Laureates*, p. 35. As my discussion shows, despite a few differences in emphasis, I am indebted to Helgerson's study of Spenser as a laureate poet. In addition, I have found his earlier study of first-generation Elizabethan writers quite useful; see *The Elizabethan Prodigals*, especially p. 5, where Helgerson describes an anxiety of absence among poets who work without established literary models. We should probably bear such an anxiety in mind in our reading of Spenser's "Astrophel," particularly insofar as Spenser seems divided between canonizing and castigating his elegiac subjects.

3. We would probably do well to remember, however, that this typical Renaissance posture regarding poetry as frivolous is itself an imitation of Horace, who, in his epistle to Maecenas, declares: "Nunc itaque et versus et cetera ludicra pono" (And so now I put aside my verses and other toys), *Epistles*, I.i.10.

4. See, especially, Louis Adrian Montrose, " 'The perfecte patterne of a Poete': The Poetics of Courtship in *The Shepheardes Calender*," *TSLL* 21 (1979), pp. 34–67; also

unsympathetic to poetry as a vocation has received deserved attention in recent years. But, while attempts to formulate a sociology
of poetry have unearthed new and provocative information about
the period, the concentration on the Elizabethan political context
has tended to obscure the relation of texts to the *literary* con-
struction of a literary past. This tendency is particularly unfortunate where Spenser is concerned because, more than any other
English author, Spenser manipulates his own English literary genealogy at the same time that he attempts to transcend the bonds
of national literature with generic and formal universality. Indeed,
we encounter awkward limitations when we try to read Spenser as a
response to or as a representation of local power relations, even
though the mode of allegory, his most persistent figurative device,
at times calls out to be translated into something like Elizabethan
journalism.[5] Although it is inevitable that we should compare
Astrophel to Sidney, I have tried whenever possible to underscore
Spenser's habit of blurring the line between literary figuration and
putative social reality.

SIDNEY'S OBSCURE OBLIVION

The establishment of a shared literary descent partly explains
Spenser's long delay in publishing a commemoration of Sidney,

---

Montrose's "The Elizabethan Subject and the Spenserian Text," in *Literary Theory/Renais-
sance Texts,* ed. Patricia Parker and David Quint (Baltimore: Johns Hopkins University
Press, 1986), pp. 303–40; Stephen Greenblatt, *Renaissance Self-Fashioning: More to Shakespeare* (Chicago: University of Chicago Press, 1980); Richard Helgerson, *Self-Crowned
Laureates;* David Norbrook, *Poetry and Politics in the English Renaissance* (London: Routledge, Kegan Paul, 1984).

5. In the course of the chapter I have indicated my skepticism about reading poetry for
its social dimension, though I have not attempted to offer a systematic critique of New
Historicism or cultural materialism. At present there seems to be a burgeoning negative
reaction to these two related approaches. See, for instance, James Holstun's recent
"Ranting at the New Historicism," *ELR* 19 (1989), pp. 189–225. Holstun raises some
valuable objections to any totalizing view of culture, condemning what he sees as the
replacement of Tillyard's older totalization with "a high-tech version of the Elizabethan
world picture" (p. 199): "Even though we have replaced an 'order model' of the Elizabethan world picture with a 'power model,' each canonical cultural artifact remains a
cultural synecdoche" (p. 203). But whereas Holstun urges a more minute examination of
the material aspects of culture, I am inclined to investigate the opposite end of the
spectrum: the methods of literary transcendence, that is, bogus genealogy, regardless of
whether (or *because*) such transcendence is itself a myth of canonical perspective.

although there were apparently financial reasons as well for the delay. The preoccupation of Sidney's earlier elegists with their subject's martial exploits would have made it difficult for Spenser, without losing his credibility, to disparage Astrophel's military side and to favor his poetic side. A delay of nearly ten years after Sidney's death and five years after the first publication of his works permitted Spenser to recast Sidney as a poetic predecessor. The delay allowed him, moreover, to position himself in self-righteous contrast to Sidney's literary ambitions while, at the same time, claiming a genealogical connection to his newly created antecedent.

Despite the inestimable good it did Sidney's reputation, Spenser's delay apparently caused some malevolent gossip in the Sidney circle. In the dedicatory epistle to "The Ruines of Time" (1591), Spenser condemns the "frends" who upbraided him for not writing an elegy.[6] "Suffer their names to sleep in silence and forgetfulnesse," he writes to the Countess of Pembroke, suggesting that her "noble house" and family should cease to support Spenser's accusers. The ground of their accusations, according to Spenser, is that he has neglected the "bandes of duetie" with which he was "tied" to Sidney. To Spenser's consternation, these accusers "haue now sought" to appropriate those ties for themselves by publicly disparaging him. Spenser explains that, apparently because of this upbraiding, "I haue not shewed anie thankfull remembrance towards him or any of them." This seems a petty (or pouty) response to a bit of Elizabethan gossip and a flimsy excuse for not writing an elegy to satisfy his erstwhile patrons. But in this relatively insignificant situation we have a clear demonstration of Spenser's laureate egoism: he has failed to join the public lamentation for Sidney because he has been replaced by other elegists in the "bandes of duetie" that he had previously established with the family.

The dedicatory epistle reminds us how unblushingly practical Spenser could be about poetry, and it foreshadows the deliberate reluctance to write an elegy that Spenser dramatizes in the poem. Despite its ostensibly apologetic aim, the letter insinuates that a decline in support from Sidney's surviving family members has helped to cause Spenser's silence. The poem itself echoes this

6. Smith and de Sélincourt, *Poetical Works*, p. 471. All further references are to this text.

sentiment. While "The Ruines of Time" contains Spenser's longest and most explicit praise of Sidney prior to the publication of "Astrophel," the poem also offers the not-so-veiled warning that, apart from Sidney's own extant work, the poetry needed to memorialize Sidney has yet to be written. In catalog format, "The Ruines of Time" laments the passing of such Elizabethan lords as Leicester, Burghley, and the Earl of Bedford, in verse units from two lines to a few stanzas. In contrast, when Spenser arrives at Sidney, he spends ten stanzas heaping praise on him. Referring to Sidney's mother, Lady Mary, he calls Sidney her "sacred brood of learning and all honour" (l. 279); he describes Sidney presenting his body to God "as a spotless sacrifise" (l. 298), and he urges Sidney to "inspire" him from heaven with his "sacred breath" (l. 315). But, significantly, the moment of inspiration never occurs in "The Ruines of Time." Twice Spenser promises to "sing" for Sidney, and twice he demurs before he can begin—first to the Countess of Pembroke, "thine owne sister, peerles Ladie bright" (l. 317), and then to Sidney's own song, "thine own selfes valiance" (l. 324). For all their flattery, these lines dramatize a curious and, I think, deliberate reluctance on Spenser's part to write a full-fledged elegy for Sidney. Spenser's poetic readiness, his inspiration as it were, is obstructed by the Sidneys' poetry.

Spenser graciously acknowledges that the Countess of Pembroke is better equipped than he would be to mourn the dead Sidney, contending "That her to heare I feele my feeble spright/Robbed of sense, and rauished with joy" (ll. 320–21). But, poetic paradoxes aside, there is a bitter undertone to Spenser's demurral. Being "robbed of sense" describes a theft as much as it does a transcendental experience. And while "rauished" can mean "enraptured" or "entranced," its primary sense denotes violation and being seized or carried off against one's will. At the risk of straining the point, we might add that it is chiefly women, rather than men, who are ravished—for instance, the *OED* cites Shakespeare's *Troilus and Cressida:* "The rauish'd Helen, Menelaus Queene"—and, while "ravished" is fairly common in Spenser, perhaps his use of the word in this context signals his displeasure with the exchange of roles that allows the countess, by singing in his place, to rob him of livelihood and fame. Further, Spenser's pretense of not entering the contest because he will surely lose is a reminder that he has not yet written mourning verses. In dramatizing his displacement by the countess, he underscores the considerable discrepancy between the countess's poetic gifts and those of the New Poet.

Spenser goes on to describe a heavenly poetic convocation in which Sidney sings for himself, perhaps hinting that, until Spenser joins in, such hallowed events have yet to take place on earth. He imagines Sidney and the mythological poets of the past conversing in rhymes:

> Whiles thou in *Elisian* fields so free,
> With *Orpheus,* and with *Linus,* and the choice
> Of all that euer did in rymes reioyce,
> Conuersest, and doost heare their heauenlie layes,
> And they heare thine, and thine doo better praise.
>
> (Ll. 332–36)

Not only does Sidney receive the "better praise" of the lyric poets Orpheus and Linus, as if victorious in a Pythian contest. The scene in the Elysian fields also contains the particular irony that Sidney lives on and continues singing in heaven while, on earth, his fame depends on the songs sung about him:

> So there thou liuest, singing euermore,
> And here thou liuest, being euer song
> Of us, which liuing loued thee afore,
> And now thee worship, mongst that blessed throng.
>
> (Ll. 337–40)

The stanzas on Sidney end with this irony, with the question of immortality unresolved.

Yet, in the transitional stanza that follows, arguably meant as a contrast to Sidney, Spenser rather ruthlessly explains the dangers of not being Sidney, of being neither a poet nor an honored member of society:

> But such as neither of themselves can sing,
> Nor yet are sung of others for reward,
> Die in obscure obliuion. (Ll. 344–46)

It is difficult not to hear a threat in these lines, directed perhaps toward Sidney's family. To some extent, by not writing a spontaneous elegy, Spenser has cast himself as a paid mourner, silent until rewarded. He strongly hints that his song could prevent Sidney's disappearance into "obscure obliuion."

VERSES ARE NOT VAINE

Once Spenser finally publishes "Astrophel," however, he plays down his own importance as a poet. The character of Astrophel, the type of the shepherd-knight, appears in the poem first as a youthful courtier, then as a careless masker and ardent lover, and finally as a dubiously competent soldier on a foreign battlefield. While Spenser certainly praises Astrophel at times, the elegy also displays an ambivalence about its subject. Indeed, my argument is that Spenser divides the courtier from the courtier's poetry deliberately to engineer his own descent from an original literary product at the same time that he repudiates its producer. Both Astrophel and Stella die in the poem; both are actually Sidney's creations borrowed to represent their creator and his lover, a kind of autobiography by proxy. Their deaths demonstrate how Spenser's own imagination buries and replaces Sidney's poetic inventions.[7]

"Astrophel" is the first poem in the collection of the same name that is appended to *Colin Clouts Come Home Againe* (1595). It has not, for the most part, impressed its readers. The Variorum records Palgrave's reflection that nothing of Spenser's "so completely and so unexpectedly disappoints."[8] Some critics suspect that Spenser wrote the poem hastily, as a sort of obligation, betraying a curious stiffness in his attitude toward Sidney. For instance, early in this century Robert Shafer maintained that "[a]n elegy had to be written, for some reason the quality of inspiration could not be summoned at the moment, and perhaps it was from a lack of material with which to round out an adequate poem that Spenser had recourse to borrowings more strikingly inappropriate then than now."[9] In a similar vein, C. S. Lewis constructs a complete scenario around the publication of the poem, casually disparaging it as

---

7. Helgerson points out that "laureate self-fashioning demanded rigorous exorcism and denial" of certain sites and characters—the Bower of Bliss, Jonson's vice figures, Milton's Satan—because the laureates are very much present in the poems and are therefore threatened by "metamorphic loss of identity" (*Self-Crowned Laureates,* p. 10). Spenser's execution of Stella, as well as his often severe censure of Astrophel's behavior, reflect his strong will to fashion his own poetic identity.

8. Variorum, 7: pt. 1, p. 487.

9. Robert Shafer, "Spenser's *Astrophel,*" *MLN* 28 (1913), p. 226. Despite the unappreciative critique of the poem, Shafer's brief article is significant because it calls attention to Spenser's debt to Bion's "Lament for Adonis."

unworthy of Spenser's other writing and barely worth the trouble to read. He begins with a speculative history of the "elegies by various hands on the death of Sidney":

Spenser's own contribution to this collection is *Astrophel*, a poem difficult to date. *A priori* we should expect it to have been written soon after Sidney's death in 1586; especially since Ludovic Bryskett's contribution, *The Mourning Muse of Thestylis,* appears in the Stationers' Register in 1587. But then in the Dedicatory Epistle to the *Ruines of Time* (1590) Spenser confessed that at that date he had still failed to elegize Sidney. It is not impossible that he had already written *Astrophel* and rightly judged it unworthy of the occasion. Nine years later, anxious once more to fill up a volume for the press, he might have glanced at the old manuscript and suffered one of those recrudescences of partiality which are among the dangers of a literary life. In such a mood, with an eager publisher at his elbow, he might come to think that it would just do after all. If so, he was mistaken, but not dreadfully mistaken. *Astrophel* has none of the elaborate ugliness of *Daphnaida.* It is merely insipid. The eighth stanza has some merit. [10]

Lewis's unflattering speculation about the poem's publication history reflects the longtime reluctance among critics to read "Astrophel" as much more than an obligatory exercise on Spenser's part. Until fairly recently, in fact, the poem's very provocative genealogical relations have gone largely unnoticed and, with them, Spenser's most transparent account of the lineage of Elizabethan poetry.

In the last two decades, however, as study of Sidney has flourished, interest in "Astrophel," though hardly overwhelming, has begun to grow. For instance, both Peter Sacks and Ellen Lambert have analyzed the generic complexities of the poem, considering "Astrophel" a valuable Elizabethan example of pastoral elegy and an undeniable precursor to Milton's *Lycidas.* [11] And, with the increase in attention, "Astrophel" has received more appreciative criticism. Harold Bloom, in his prefatory note to a collection of essays on Spenser, calls the poem "Spenser's beautifully modulated

10. C. S. Lewis, *English Literature in the Sixteenth Century, Excluding Drama* (Oxford: Clarendon Press, 1954), pp. 371–72.

11. Sacks, *The English Elegy,* esp. pp. 51–63; Lambert, *Placing Sorrow,* esp. pp. 220–21, n. 11.

lament for Sir Philip Sidney."[12] Even such careful praise would have seemed utterly hyperbolic in Lewis's day.

But the disparity among learned readings does not obviously result from aesthetic division, or from changed ideas of what a good poem should be or do. Those, like Palgrave, who fault the poem for its chilly appreciation of Sidney's attributes incorrectly consider the subject of "Astrophel" to have been the life of Philip Sidney. They are predictably disappointed, therefore, to discover the "real" Sidney's minimal role in the poem. Where they presumably expect to find a Shelleyan revival of the hero, they encounter instead Spenser's deliberate interment of Sidney, his grief itself walled up in poetic conventions. According to Shelley in *Adonais*, " 'tis Death is dead" when the poet (Keats) dies and his voice becomes one with nature. He is not to be mourned, for he is not really gone but "is a presence to be felt and known."[13] The immortality of the poetic voice supposedly triumphs over Death in the exact moment when Death exercises its irresistible will. But, so far as I can tell, Shelley's notion of the killing of Death is a later feature of the English elegy, owing more to Milton's revival of Edward King than to Spenser's "Astrophel." Critics who regard Spenser's elegy from even a proto-Romantic vantage point tend to be disappointed in the poet's lack of effort to revive his dead friend.

In contrast, critics who suspect that the subject of "Astrophel" is Spenser's poetic lineage are more inclined to approve the elegy. They understand that, though Spenser mourns the loss of the shepherd knight, he cannot explicitly return Sidney to the fold (as the fold's leader, to boot) without contradicting his own position in the literary genealogy. As Peter Sacks has argued, Spenser's belated elegy for Sidney "is clearly an assured bid for inclusion in the company of poets" (p. 52). According to Sacks, Spenser turns the very belatedness of "Astrophel" to his literary advantage: "Spenser is now speaking directly to his fellow poets, commanding their audience. Some of these poets are the other elegists whose poems are published here with Spenser's. In fact, Spenser has maneuvered these poets, all of whose elegies preceded his in time,

12. *Edmund Spenser*, ed. Harold Bloom (New York: Chelsea House Publishers, 1986), p. x.
13. See *Adonais*, stanzas 41 and 42.

into a position of posteriority and dependency. It is he now who leads the mourning, introducing their poems after his."[14] Nearly all the poems in *Astrophel* acknowledge Sidney as a poet rather than as a patron of the arts. In this respect, as a collection, they represent an institutionalization of the new Sidney of the 1590s, less patron and soldier than first poet of the modern English tradition. Consequently, Spenser's "Astrophel" not only "leads the mourning," as Sacks suggests, but also heads the family of poets who descend from Sidney.

This literary descent naturally depends on the acceptance of Sidney as a man of letters rather than as a mere courtier. As W. L. Renwick long ago pointed out, "in *Astrophel* Spenser happily ignored the patron for the poet" (Variorum, 7: pt. 1, p. 489). Spenser and Gabriel Harvey, alone among Elizabethans, had asserted Sidney's literary skill as early as the 1570s. In a way, therefore, Spenser's anachronistic placement of "Astrophel" before other poems in the collection represents a reassertion of these earlier claims and of his own perspicacity.

But, above all, Spenser needs Sidney as an absence, not as what Shelley calls "a presence to be felt and known." In fact, Shelley's famous characterization of Sidney in *Adonais* is at odds with Spenser's; it is a demonstrably post-Miltonic misreading or revision of "Astrophel":

> Sidney, as he fought
> And as he fell and as he lived and loved
> Sublimely mild, a Spirit without spot,
> Arose. (Ll. 401–4)

Because the notion of a "Spirit without spot" has so often captured the attention of upholders and debunkers of the Sidney myth, we seldom speculate on the last word of this description. Yet it would be more problematic, especially for Spenser's agenda, to imagine Sidney arising from death than to see him as a spotless figure. For Spenser, Sidney himself is a silent object of mixed appreciation rather than an active presence in the form of a revived poet. Even the effusive John Philip, though he portrays Sidney speaking from

---

14. *The English Elegy,* p. 52. As Lewis noted, Bryskett's elegy was entered on the Stationers' Register in 1587; Ralegh, Roydon, and Dyer published theirs in *The Phoenix Nest* (1593).

the grave in his elegy, nevertheless does not exactly resurrect the dead knight.[15] Sidney's utility to Elizabethan poets is the empty slot he leaves behind. True, it takes almost a decade for poets to realize that they can use Sidney's absence by claiming him as a precursor of Elizabethan poetry. But once they recognize this possibility, they are far too conscious of their invention to allow their recently created dead patriarch to arise: the creation by fiat of a poetic savior would have been too obvious and its discovery might have cast suspicion on their serious effort to establish a poetic lineage.

Consequently, we might take "Astrophel" to be Spenser's pointedly serious contribution to the notion of English poetry as the product of specific genealogical descent. Although the poem is included in the same volume with *Colin Clouts Come Home Againe,* Spenser's treatment of Sidney in the two works is markedly different. In *CCCHA* Sidney, in the persona of Astrophel, appears among the English courtiers whom Colin praises, as opposed to those whom he disparages for their vanity and excess. Spenser moreover makes a point of praising Astrophel's poetic skill, comparing him favorably to Daniel and others who have survived him. "All these," he asserts, referring to the best of the piping swains of Cynthia's court,

> All these, and many others mo remaine,
> Now after *Astrofell* is dead and gone:
> But while as *Astrofell* did liue and raine,
> Amongst all these was none his Paragone.
> (*CCCHA*, ll. 448–51)

This is unqualified praise of Sidney's poetry, echoing Spenser's high esteem for Sidney's gifts in "The Ruines of Time." As in the earlier poem, however, we get the clear sense that Spenser is speaking as an outsider, as a poet patently not a member of the group of whom "was none [Astrofell's] Paragone." There seems little suggestion in *CCCHA* that Spenser was seeking to integrate himself in a genealogy. Indeed, Colin Clout already has an explicit genealogy of his own, descending from Skelton and probably the French.

Yet, while Spenser does not seek to join the group of English

15. See John Philip, "The Life, Death, and Funerals of Sir Philip Sidney Knight," in *Elegies for Sir Philip Sidney,* ed. Colaianne and Godshalk, (no pagination).

poet-courtiers—in fact, Colin sings his song in Ireland, to his own provincial group of swains and shepherdesses—he nevertheless manages to establish Sidney's literary priority. In listing Cynthia's noteworthy waiting-women, Colin eventually comes to Stella:

> No lesse praisworthie *Stella* do I read,
> Though nought my praises of her needed arre,
> Whom verse of noblest shepherd lately dead
> Hath prais'd and rais'd aboue each other starre. (Ll. 532–35)

In competition with Astrophel's, Colin's verse is belated and irrelevant. Further praise of Stella would be superfluous, Colin implies, so Spenser impishly omits any specific praise at all. (This omission anticipates his somewhat unflattering portrait of Stella in "Astrophel.") But the genealogical point is established: Sidney's poetry precedes Spenser's, and, at least to some degree, provides a model.

It is difficult to gauge the importance of Spenser's praise for Sidney and the Sidney family in *CCCHA* in contrast to his much more qualified approbation in the microscopic appraisal of "Astrophel." Certainly both poems, like "The Ruines of Time," confirm Spenser's ongoing engagement with the Sidney legacy; in *CCCHA* he praises the Countess of Pembroke (whom he calls Urania) above all the other nymphs of Cynthia's court, emphasizing that she is "sister vnto *Astrofell*" and thereby representing the Sidneys as the first family of the poem. Whether this representation is history or hyperbole remains unresolved, as Spenser probably intended. But the gap between the monumental encomia of *CCCHA* and the revisionism of "Astrophel" provides Spenser with valuable maneuverability, allowing us to glimpse his literary aspirations in the chinks of the temple wall. In the final analysis, Spenser's various roles as recipient of patronage, as commemorator of Sidney's achievements, and as poetic descendant are vexed by ambivalence regarding the Sidney legend and by his own salient ambition, both political and literary.

Spenser's strongest opinions and his last words on the subject of Sidney, coded as they may be, find lasting expression in "Astrophel." The poem is explicitly a "Pastorall Elegie" and contains six-line stanzas rhymed *ababcc;* its measured nostalgia recalls Virgil's elegiac mode in the Eclogues and probably owes something to Clement Marot's elegy, in his *Complainctes,* "De Madame Loyse de Savoye."[16] In addition, as Prescott suggests, Spenser's elegy "loosely follows Ronsard's 'Adonis' (1563), itself in part an adaptation of Bion's great lament for the lover of Aphrodite."[17] Bion's "Lament for Adonis" is an ancient dirge, differing from pastoral elegy, according to Ellen Lambert, because "there is not—and cannot be—a distinction between the dying hero and the natural world that mourns him: for Adonis is no less than (and no more than) the incarnation of nature's own annual death and rebirth."[18] But, differences aside, the notion of Adonis as a vegetation deity seems to have contributed to Spenser's formulation of his Astrophel character. Freely adapting, Spenser's narrative tells the story of a "Gentle Shepheard born in *Arcady*"; the stages in the tale schematize a familiar idealized version of Sidney's life: golden youth, poetry and love for Stella, adventure and death on "forreine soyle," Stella's desperate grief, which causes her own death, and finally their joint transformation into "one flowre that is both red and blew." (Stella's death is unique to Spenser's poem among the elegies, and, of course, has no parallel in history, whether we take Stella to be Penelope Rich or, as de Sélincourt maintains in his introduction to the *Poetical Works,* the Lady Francis [*sic*] Walsingham.)

Spenser is eager, moreover, to demonstrate the centrality of poetry in the psychological and social development of his Astrophel character. On a general level, Spenser thematizes poetry as prudent judgment in "Astrophel," and any rejection of the work of the poet, either by the poet's addressee or by the poet himself, he punishes with death. Thus both Astrophel and Stella die, one because he drops poetry to woo his love with action and the other because she rejects the poetic wooing in the first place. Not only is

16. On Spenser's debt to Marot see Annabel Patterson, *Pastoral and Ideology: Virgil to Valéry* (Berkeley: University of California Press, 1987). As Alastair Fowler has pointed out (*Unfolded Tales,* p. 33), E. K. mentions Marot's elegy as a place, in addition to Skelton's poem, where Colin Clout's first name appears.

17. Prescott, *French Poets and the English Renaissance,* p. 109; see also p. 110: "The original significance of the story adds resonance to Spenser's poem—Sidney was a "pattern" whose loss was deeply felt in England—but naturally Spenser recognizes not only the flower into which Astrophil [*sic*] changes but the happiness of his soul in Heaven, a reward more readily available to English captains than to a demigod."

18. Lambert, *Placing Sorrow,* p. 24. On "Astrophel" and Bion's "Lament for Adonis," see Henry G. Lotspeich, *Classical Mythology in the Poetry of Edmund Spenser* (Princeton: Princeton University Press, 1932), p. 32; and also, Shafer, "Spenser's *Astrophel*."

the poet-lover misunderstood and consequently driven to prove himself in hazardous adventures, but he also misunderstands himself. Sacks calls attention to "Spenser's hostility or at least ambivalence toward Astrophel," concluding rightly that "Spenser's critique assumes added interest when one recalls that Astrophel's choice is equated by Spenser with a rejection of language. For Astrophel was not content with a merely verbal wooing or praising of Stella, and chose instead the unmediated and here almost suicidal pursuit of violent action" (pp. 53, 54).

Astrophel's miserable end is a warning both to poets and to their audiences. The misunderstood "self," to the extent that it existed in the period, is reflected for Spenser in the misunderstanding of readers. As interiority and desire give way, in language, to outward signs of love or grief, it becomes necessary to make what for Spenser may be the critical choice of civilized life. Either one regards poetic representation as sufficient to bear truth or one rejects poetic representation as mere feigning and requires physical proof as testimony of the truth of intent. Of course, this conflict adumbrates the debate over the *vita activa* and the *vita contemplativa,* in addition to sounding a familiar note about the value of poetry to society and the importance, therefore, of patronizing poets.[19] But, more significantly, the plot of "Astrophel" warns audiences not to spurn poetic texts and warns poets to trust, in Angus Fletcher's terms, their "prophetic moments." So the warning applies to Spenser himself as he sets out prophetically to mourn his poetic antecedent, just as it applies to Elizabeth in reading *The Faerie Queene* and to Spenser's peers in reading "Astrophel." The message is manifestly the acknowledgment of Sidney as a poetic precursor and the replacement of Sidney's (failed) poetry with Spenser's elegy.

The failure of Astrophel's verses results essentially from a mistaken notion of poetry's function. Astrophel uses poetry as a courtier would use flowers or jewels: to persuade his beloved to act. When the verses fail to accomplish this end, he abandons poetry for other means:

> Ne her with ydle words alone he wowed,
> And verses vaine (yet verses are not vaine)

19. See Fraser, *The War against Poetry,* esp. pp. 29–76.

> But with braue deeds to her sole seruice vowed,
> And bold atchieuements her did entertaine.
> For both in deeds and words he nourtred was,
> Both wise and hardie (too hardie alas). (Ll. 67–72)

The phrase "verses vaine" echoes *The Faerie Queene,* Book 3, the canto in which Paridell woos and rapes Hellenore.

> And otherwhiles with amorous delights,
>> And pleasing toyes he would her entertaine,
> Now singing sweetly, to surprise her sprights,
>> Now making layes of loue and louers paine,
> Bransles, Ballads, virelayes, and verses vaine. (3.10.8)

In both stanzas the conventional courtly use of poetry as "pleasing toys" prefigures destruction, leading Hellenore to rape and abandonment and Astrophel (and Stella) to death.[20] Although by no means identical, Paridell and Astrophel are in a sense linked by the vanity and presumed ephemerality of their verses. To the contrary, Spenser divorces his own verses from theirs by the very fact of self-citation. His own courtly behavior aside, Spenser's verses are not vain because they endure to be quoted.

The echoes between the poems indicate Spenser's contempt for Astrophel's false courtliness, though, in contrast to the formidable Paridell, Astrophel appears to be both an erotic and an eristic bumbler. This is not to ignore Spenser's praise of Astrophel, whom he calls "wise and hardie." But Astrophel's wisdom, like his hardiness, is undercut by Spenser's descriptions of his impulsive behavior. Not only is Astrophel "too hardie"—presumably too physical to lead a contemplative life—but he also misunderstands the objective of good poetry. Whether because he is too enamored of Stella to think straight or because he is a flawed reader of his own work, Astrophel recklessly abandons his writing to pursue the "bold atchieuements" that will kill him. (Not only "hardie," he is

---

20. In a well-known argument on the opposition of artifice and nature in *The Faerie Queene,* C. S. Lewis cites Paridell's "verses vaine" as an example of the false art that Spenser identifies with courtliness and therefore condemns. Lewis claims that Spenser "is not at home in the artificialities of the court, and if, as a man, he was sometimes seduced, as a poet he never was." See *The Allegory of Love: A Study in Medieval Tradition* (New York: Oxford University Press, 1958), p. 328. In a passage on the House of Busirane, Lewis adds: "Any moralist can disapprove luxury and artifice; but Spenser alone can turn the platitude into imagery of such sinister suggestion" (p. 329). Similarly, given Astrophel's eventual end, the imagery of his wooing of Stella has a certain "sinister suggestion" about it.

foolhardy in Spenser's view.) But it is not bad or inferior composition that sends him off to other ventures. To the contrary, Astrophel has "enchanting skill" on the oaten pipe, and his songs hold an
irresistible charm for "many a Nymph." Rather, Astrophel's self-
banishment results from his callow, amateurish notion that poetry
is, as Helgerson puts it, "a mere ribbon in the cap of youth" (*Self-
Crowned Laureates*, p. 55), an adolescent game to be abandoned for
the more serious matters of Elizabethan adulthood. For Spenser
such an attitude is corrupt. It degrades the value of poetry and
leads the poet into the vanity and the dangers of the *vita activa*.
Spenser emphasizes Astrophel's error (and Stella's ignorance) by
allowing "bold atchieuements" to replace the "hymnes of immor-
tall praise" that Astrophel composed for his love; the contrast
between a bold achievement and a hymn makes it easy enough, at
least in the world of the poem, to identify the morally appropriate
act. Again we think of Paridell and the comparison is unfavorable,
both because of Paridell's inescapably deplorable character and,
further, because Astrophel is only a poor man's Paridell, in much
the same way that Paridell is only a poor man's Paris. If Paridell is
scarcely the echo of an epic hero, then Astrophel is the echo of an
echo.

As a consequence of a kind of misreading of his own verse,
Astrophel's militarism becomes courtly entertainment in place of
his poetry, constituting an abuse of both militarism and poetry. To
an extent, the condemnation of war in "Astrophel" is generic, an
inherent trait of pastoral poetry. Yet, the poem's sharp scrutiny of
Astrophel's choice seems to exceed the generic criteria. Further,
Spenser's elegy is not only a "dolefull plaint" on the subject of
Sidney's death, but it is also a bitter complaint about the abuse of
poetry (and poets) by courtly amateurs and their frivolous readers.
In addition to what Sacks terms "inclusion in the company of
poets" (52), we find Spenser stipulating here that his audience be
only other shepherd-poets:

> Hearken ye gentle shepheards to my song,
> And place my dolefull plaint your plaints emong.
>
> To you alone I sing this mournfull verse. (Ll. 5–7)

The poet is not a suitor, and his song, "Astrophel," is to be compared only to other poems of the same kind by judges who are his
vocational peers. This is very different from placing poetry along-

side feats of prowess in a kind of competition for a lover's rewards. Spenser elaborates on this theme, prevailing on any accidental reader who is not a shepherd to remember, above all, whom the poem is written for:

> To you I sing and to none other wight,
> For well I wot my rymes bene rudely dight.

> Yet as they been, if any nycer wit
> Shall hap to heare, or couet them to read:
> Thinke he, that such are for such ones most fit,
> Made not to please the living but the dead. (Ll. 11–16)

There is a curious bifurcation in these lines. The poet sings to his fellow shepherds "and to none other wight." Yet the "rymes" have been made "not to please the living but the dead." Although the audience for the lament consists of other (living) writers of similar poetry, the final judgment of the poem depends on its favorable reception by "the dead." If we take "the dead" in a collective sense, then we can imagine in the verb "to please" the poet's anxious effort to attach his poem to a tradition. More specifically, however, "the dead" refers to Sidney alone. The dead knight is at once the subject of the elegy and the final judge of Spenser's poetic performance. And, since Sidney's imagined judgment of Spenser is so important, the poem presents itself unmistakably as the product of a genealogical literary relationship comparable to that presumed to exist between classical poets and their contemporary imitators. Of course, in Spenser's version, it is necessary for Sidney to be a failed predecessor, so that Spenser can simultaneously claim the existence of a lineage and supersede the immediate past.[21] This double gambit raises our skepticism about Spenser's genealogy as literary history, and it reminds us that we are engaged in tracing tropes of literary descent rather than strictly historical details. Nevertheless, part of Spenser's objective is to reform previous concepts of the placement of poems in English literary history—to form, in other words, the concept of a hereditary poetic tradition in the minds of a readership accustomed to thinking about contemporary poetry as frivolous, casual, and uniformly parvenu.

---

21. One senses in Spenser early stirrings of the agonistic relationship with the past identified by Harold Bloom, or the burden noted by W. J. Bate. At the same time, however, Spenser has the conventional humanistic impulse to reconstruct lost lineages.

ASTROPHEL'S ONELY FAYLING

At the beginning of the poem, Spenser taps the Elizabethan obsession with genealogy. Just as Elizabethans recognized exiguous claims of legitimate descent among competing families, Spenser demonstrates an awareness in the poem of the dubious nature of his own literary descent. He does this by identifying Sidney as an antecedent, a historical deception he had already introduced in "The Ruines of Time," and by suggesting that Sidney (or the poet Astrophel) doubles as his own precursor. Just as Sidney's death is effectively the reason for the poem's existence, Sidney's poetry (specifically *Astrophil and Stella,* published in 1591) is the original from which the Sidney character, Astrophel, descends. In a sense, therefore, the character Astrophel is self-begotten. This makes it possible to see Astrophel as simultaneously both literary father and first literary son.[22]

Spenser calls attention to this seminal ambiguity in the opening stanzas of the poem. Astrophel is "borne in *Arcady,*/Of gentlest race that euer shepheard bore" (ll. 1–2). But we find no mention of his father in the brief description of his childhood. Rather, we find "the Nymph his mother" (l. 14) to have been influential in his early years; Astrophel is "In comely shape, like her that did him breed" (l. 16), an inherited resemblance that has no paternal counterpart. (In "The Ruines of Time," too, Spenser's genealogy of Sidney excludes the paternal branches.) One might argue that the omission of Sidney's father in conjunction with the emphasis on his mother is Spenser's way of praising the noble blood of the Dudleys, Sidney's mother's family. As Spenser could have known, Sidney was very proud of his maternal descent. In the *Defence of the Earl of Leicester* (ca. 1585), which is a reply to genealogical slurs on his uncle, Sidney expostulates on his lineage: "I am a Dudley in blood,

---

22. We might compare this genealogy to Spenser's extended meditation on distorted generation in the Garden of Adonis episode of *The Fairie Queene*. There is, first of all, the implication that Venus, in searching for Cupid, has incestuous designs. (This implication is manifest in a comparison of Spenser's model, Ovid's *Metamorphoses* 10, in which Venus searches the same sites not for Cupid but in a feverish passion for Adonis.) In addition, we find that both Adonis and Amoret have strange parental relations: Adonis's father, for example, is actually also his grandfather, as a result of his mother Myrrha's seduction of *her* father Cinyras. The genealogical confusions are manifold, and their suggestiveness, while expressly complicating Spenser's characterization of Adonis as the "Father of all formes," cannot but resonate if we think of Astrophel as self-begotten.

that Duke's daughter's son, and do acknowledge, though in truth I may justly affirm that I am by my father's side of ancient and always well esteemed and well matched gentry, yet I do acknowledge, I say, that my chiefest honour is to be a Dudley."[23] Possibly Spenser wishes to acknowledge Sidney's "chiefest honour," if not to capitalize on it with the surviving family members. Nevertheless, the paternal amputation serves Spenser's literary purposes insofar as it provides a way to represent Sidney's putatively fatherless status in English poetic tradition.

It should be added that Spenser's genealogical reference, though very slight to our eye, would not have escaped the Elizabethan reader. As John Guillory points out, in a discussion of *The Faerie Queene*, "[i]t is difficult to overestimate the importance of genealogy, accurate, fudged, or totally fabricated, to anyone with 'pretensions' in Renaissance England—including, of course, the dubious House of Tudor."[24] We are justified, therefore, in imputing a fair amount of importance to the absence of Astrophel's father in the poem. Like Sidney, whose father had no title and no fortune to pass on to his son, Astrophel is at a disadvantage in the courtly milieu, a disadvantage reflected in Stella's rejection of him. Indeed, Astrophel's subtle social inferiority helps to explain Spenser's otherwise puzzling observation that the shepherd-knight was "In one thing onely fayling of the best,/That he was not so happie as the rest" (ll. 11–12). Astrophel's unhappiness presumably is due to his yearning for Stella, or at least we suspect as much with our prior knowledge of Sidney's sonnets. But in Spenser's poem Stella herself does not even appear until the tenth stanza, and Astrophel's "onely fayling," the unhappiness of stanza two, is never explicitly linked to his disappointment in love. Thus, we might speculate that Astrophel's "onely fayling" is, partly at least, his lack of a highborn sire. Moreover, although Astrophel is superior in physical and mental attributes to "all the pastors of his daies" (l. 9), he is nevertheless unable to secure the love from Stella that would keep him at court. The criticism of Stella, while certainly supported by the biographical details of the sonnets, also serves as a criticism of the genealogical pretensions of the Elizabethan court.

23. Duncan-Jones and Van Dorsten, *Miscellaneous Prose of Sir Philip Sidney*, p. 134. The duke to whom Sidney refers is Northumberland.

24. Guillory, *Poetic Authority*, p. 50. See also Lawrence Stone, *Crisis of the Aristocracy*, p. 25.

But I do not think that "Astrophel" can be reduced to a schematic representation of the levels of prestige and power at court. As a belated elegist Spenser perhaps had more freedom to criticize the court openly: the period he writes about is long past, and he masks his condemnations as praise for the dead. The lateness of his elegy (and the fame of his subject) may help Spenser to evade rigidly hierarchical rankings of shepherds and nymphs, but, nevertheless, we should remain skeptical about the so-called conventional uses of the pastoral genre in which he is working.

Louis Adrian Montrose has suggested, for instance, that although Renaissance pastorals "direct criticism or hostility against courtly decadence or the inequities of courtly reward, such anticourtliness tends to measure either the court's distance from its own high ideals or the courtier's distance from the satisfaction of his ambitions."[25] Provocative as this definition may be, however, it does not explain Spenser's ambiguous anticourtliness in "Astrophel." In contrast to Montrose's notion of "the inequities of courtly reward," Spenser castigates Astrophel for not being satisfied with the court's response to his verses. The poem condemns Astrophel for harboring or developing the wrong ambitions, especially insofar as those newer ambitions involve laying aside the literary aspirations that the courtly audience (with the exception of Stella) has already approved.[26]

The social appurtenances of Astrophel's world, embodying the

25. Louis Adrian Montrose, "Of Gentlemen and Shepherds: The Politics of Elizabethan Pastoral Form," *ELH* 50 (1983), p. 426. Although I have often found Montrose's speculations interesting, by and large it seems as though he does not read pastorals as individual poems in a nascent vernacular tradition but as captions beneath a familiar (and relatively stable) Elizabethan social tableau. Perhaps this reluctance to distinguish among poems explains why he quotes virtually no pastoral in his essay on pastoral form. He appears to regard genre as an end rather than as a model and, therefore, interprets all poems in the pastoral "genre" to represent exactly the same cultural paradigm. This would be scandalous interpretation if applied, say, to epic or tragedy, and should seem equally so in regard to pastoral. As I have suggested, we cannot read "Astrophel" in the reductively oppositional terms we encounter in Montrose's definition of anticourtliness and ambition.

26. This is not to suggest that Spenser is oblivious to the relation between social exigencies and the familiar complaints of other Elizabethan poets. But the social model, like any trope, is subsumed in the poem's relation to other poems, to different and earlier uses of the same trope. It cannot work the other way around: the social model cannot be somehow "real" while everything else in the pastoral is a trope. The subtlety of Spenser's social observations in "Astrophel," exemplified by the curious double significance of Astrophel's (or Sidney's) fatherlessness, adumbrates the poem's insistently literary concerns.

typical landscape of Elizabethan pastoral, can best be understood according to poetic norms. Not even "nature," the supposedly zero-grade background of all pastoral poetry, can have a transpoetic value. As Harry Berger, Jr., observes in his discussion of the pastoral of *The Shepheardes Calender*, "[i]t isn't merely that 'nature' is a cultural category and an abstraction selectively defined according to the norms of any particular culture, . . . but that the primary referents of nature terms in pastoral are literary conventions and contexts."[27] Berger explains that even the typical pastoral metaphors of "hard" and "soft" nature, idyllic versus worldly experience, are best understood as tropes of literary responses to literary tradition.[28] Berger concludes, therefore, in *The Shepheardes Calender* "[w]hat results is not a 'fall' into hostile 'nature' or Mantuan's 'predatory world' . . . or any other external environment, but a fall into an inadequate response to the environment" (p. 42). An "inadequate response" would be the source of the poet's obsession (and perhaps anxiety) because it represents, at the same time, a claim to genealogical position in relation to other similar (and possibly more "adequate") responses.

When Spenser begins "Astrophel" by placing his poem among the other "plaints," he is expressing a literary preference for the mode or subgenre of plaintive over recreative pastoral. He immediately points out that his "rymes" are really meant to please the dead because, in addition to wanting to honor the dead Sidney, he wants to be judged according to the conventions historically appropriate to his subgeneric choice. More than Sidney's death or Spenser's social obligation to write a memorial poem, it is literary

27. Harry Berger, Jr., "Orpheus, Pan, and the Poetics of Misogyny: Spenser's Critique of Pastoral Love and Art," *ELH* 50 (1985), p. 42.

28. See Erwin Panofsky, "*Et in Arcadia Ego:* Poussin and the Elegiac Tradition," in his *Meaning in the Visual Arts* (Garden City, N.Y.: Doubleday, 1955), p. 297: "There had been, from the beginning of classical speculation, two contrasting opinions about the natural state of man, each of them, of course, a 'Gegen-Konstruktion' to the conditions under which it was formed. One view, termed 'soft' primitivism in an illuminating book by Lovejoy and Boas [*Primitivism and Related Ideas in Antiquity* (Baltimore, 1935)], conceives of primitive life as a golden age of plenty, innocence and happiness—in other words, as civilized life purged of its vices. The other, 'hard' form of primitivism conceives of primitive life as an almost subhuman existence full of terrible hardships and devoid of all comforts—in other words, as civilized life stripped of its virtues." See also Panofsky's essay "The Early History of Man in Two Cycles of Paintings by Piero di Cosimo," in his *Studies in Iconology* (1939; reprint, New York: Harper, Row, 1962), especially p. 40.

tradition that Spenser reviews and responds to in "Astrophel," what Berger calls the "nature of books" as against the "book of nature" (p. 42). Spenser's particular gift is that, while appearing to vacillate between literary tradition and social realities, he manages to convey the sense that the pull of literary tradition is too strong to be resisted.

Whereas in "The Ruines of Time" Spenser alludes to the Sidney family's sudden parsimony toward him, in "Astrophel" the social facts of Sidney's life themselves become speculative, part and parcel of Spenser's ongoing speculations on the relation of eros to ethos and of poetry to the genealogical continuity of imagination. In effect, sociohistorical realities, such as Sidney's birth or his escapades in the Netherlands, function as tropes of actual behavior in the same way that Stella's death in the poem functions as a trope of her presumed emotional desolation (or of Spenser's hostility toward her for rejecting Sidney's poetry). Not surprisingly, therefore, we come upon the collision between social and what might be termed "poetic reality" in the description of the smitten Astrophel's attempts to impress Stella. On returning briefly to the crucial passage quoted earlier, Spenser's agenda, his intention of demonstrating the futility of seeing poetry as a social grace, begins to become clear:

> Ne her with ydle words alone he wowed,
> And verses vaine (yet verses are not vaine)
> But with braue deeds . . . (Ll. 67–69)

It is impossible to ignore that Spenser's parenthetical observation is a revision of the first half of his own line. Allegorically, this self-revision could refer to any number of relations: for example, the relation of the first half of Spenser's life to the latter half, or the first verses for Sidney (in "The Ruines of Time") to these elegiac verses in "Astrophel," or even the first half of *The Faerie Queene* to the second. But the reflexiveness of the revisionary juxtaposition is finally less significant than the notion that revision itself is a trope of Spenser's genealogical relation to Sidney.

Within the poem the parenthetical remark is a narrative correction of Astrophel's abuse of poetry. If it is true that "verses are not vaine," then one is inclined to ask who believes that verses *are* vain. Does Stella? Does Astrophel himself? Or is such a belief the result of a general consensus, the common Elizabethan notion that poetry is a youthful frivolity? Spenser's parenthesis ostensibly puts these questions out of court, though they never entirely disappear; even in the last part of the poem, we remain skeptical about the sincerity of mourners who might earlier have dismissed a youthful poet's verses. But eventually it proves irrelevant whether Stella or the Elizabethan gentry regards verses as vain. Spenser's characterization of Astrophel depends, rather, on our recognizing that the "sclender swaine" himself considers his verses vain and therefore engineers his own destruction.[29]

Since Spenser so pointedly condemns Astrophel's view of poetry as just another gaudy trinket in the courtier's bag, we are inclined to question his motive in casting Astrophel as an originary figure of any kind.[30] But, in fact, feigning a literary descent from someone whose attitude toward poetry he does not fully endorse serves Spenser in two ways. Not only does the troubling figure of the self-martyred shepherd-poet in "Astrophel" contrast Elizabethan literary reality with Spenser's more exalted view of poetry, but that troubling figure also supplies the exact literary subject matter that Spenser can use to separate himself from the courtly "past." Astrophel's verses contain the ideal elements from which the New Poet can fashion his literary descent. These verses, first taken as forms of idleness (even by the author himself), can be reinterpreted by a later generation of "shepheard peares" as forms of labor, "never vaine" but fruitful. Thus Spenser, by rereading and reinterpreting "earlier" poems, can repudiate his precursor at the same time that he invents him.

In several recent discussions of *The Faerie Queene,* critics have

29. It is difficult to determine whether Spenser judged the *Arcadia* to be less serious writing, though, in any case, his condemnation is aimed at a particular courtly attitude rather than at specific texts.

30. See Helgerson, *Self-Crowned Laureates,* p. 63, where the author asserts that, for the sake of his "laureate ambitions," Spenser was the first of his generation "to abandon all social identity except that conferred by his elected vocation" of poet. I think Helgerson overstates his case insofar as he reads Spenser's poetry almost exclusively as an annotation on his "career," but the point is well taken that Spenser's attitude toward poetry stands in marked opposition to that of most of his contemporaries. In fact, Helgerson's later conclusions regarding Spenser's return to pastoral in Book 6 of *The Faerie Queene* should resonate in our reading of "Astrophel": "Unlike the other poets of his generation, Spenser responds to . . . pressure not by renouncing, but rather by affirming, the value of poetry. The sometimes hostile active world belongs, he lets us see, to the realm of mutability. Poetry alone has access to the unchanging forms of moral and aesthetic perfection" (p. 97).

noted the significance of Spenser's use of Virgilian georgic and his emphasis on labor as a critique of prevalent Elizabethan courtly attitudes.[31] We find evidence of a similar emphasis at a pivotal juncture of "Astrophel." Before Spenser introduces Stella, sportive nymphs forsake "christall wells and shadie groues" to attend the young shepherd. (This occurs in the eighth stanza, to which Lewis laconically ascribed "some merit.") But it turns out that these nymphs are not completely otiose, as one expects nymphs to be, because they bring to Astrophel "mellow fruit if it were haruest time." They are apparently working nymphs who participate in the harvest at least to gather fruit.

The nymphs' gifts, despite Astrophel's disdainful attitude toward them, represent commendable productiveness. Though Astrophel might not have cared a "whit" for any of the nymphs "Ne for their gifts vnworthie of his wit," Spenser notes with apparent irrelevance that these gifts were "not vnworthie of the countries store." But, of course, this is not an irrelevant observation: it provides a contrast with the nonproductive, demonstrably unworthy Stella, and it underscores the proper response to poetry. In addition, the parallel use of "vnworthie" in subsequent lines (50–51) represents Spenser's revisionism again, the litotes of the second line intended to correct Astrophel's negative perception of the gifts. This mirroring of language, in which the reflected usage represents the recasting of its original, characterizes both Spenser's genealogical relation to Sidney and the relation of true poetry to courtly toys. For the "not vnworthie" gifts are also mirror images of poetic verses, the products of labor and love. In responding to Astrophel's pipe with the worthy products of the countryside, the nymphs attempt to effect an equal exchange, the sort of transaction that would make Spenser's linguistic revisionism unnecessary. Presumably, if Astrophel's perceptions of love, duty, and poetry were not distorted, neither "verses vaine" nor "gifts vnworthie" would require immediate correction by the belatedly detached elegist. We infer that, essentially as fruits of labor, the nymphs' gifts are

31. See Low, *The Georgic Revolution,* esp. pp. 35–70; William Sessions, "Spenser's Georgic," *ELR* 10 (1980), pp. 202–38; Andrew V. Ettin, "The Georgics in *The Faerie Queene,*" *Spenser Studies* 3 (1982), pp. 57–71; and Jane Tylus, "Spenser, Virgil, and the Politics of Poetic Labor," *ELH* 55 (1988), pp. 53–77. Tylus points out that "the language of patronage regularly coincided with the language of agrarian labor and organic process" (p. 54).

appropriate responses to Astrophel's song—the kind of response Stella never makes. Thus, Astrophel's rejection of the nymphs as lovers not only foreshadows his own rejection by Stella but also supplies the didactic key to his misguided and lethal adventurism.

The linking of "whit" and "wit," moreover, is Spenser's wry comment on how little Astrophel's wit is worth for turning down the fruits of labor. The rhyme does not so much "please" the dead Astrophel as pun at his expense. Spenser implies that these harvested fruits would have wooed Astrophel if he had had a whit's worth of wit. Instead, Astrophel ignores the "mellow fruit" and turns to the "ydle words" with which he hopes to woo Stella. The movement from labor to idleness is ominous in the poem, especially in view of the strict Elizabethan censure of it in law, church doctrine, and daily practice. As Stephen Greenblatt reminds us, "[i]t is difficult to recover the immense force which this charge of idleness carried; some sense may be gauged perhaps from the extraordinary harshness with which vagabonds were treated."[32] Indeed, we might also gauge the force of the charge of idleness by the harshness with which Spenser treats Stella.

The turning point of the poem, therefore, is the moment at which Astrophel chooses to abandon his "verses vaine" and to try "hardie" deeds. Spenser portrays him as his own least imaginative critic, a pathetically ideal match for the obtuse Stella. They continually reflect each other's distortion, as, for instance, when Stella sees her wounded Astrophel and "She likewise did deforme like him to bee" (l. 156). Spenser is damning Stella by faint praise, and the irony of the line is that neither Astrophel nor Stella would be in such a fix if Astrophel had not already "deformed" himself to please her.

Much hinges on Astrophel's poetic persona. Unable to read his own verses as the nymphs (and Spenser) read them, and therefore unable to recognize his most important value to the courtly society, Astrophel turns to action in its most conventional mode: the pursuit of martial glory. Ordinarily, in Spenser as well as in much of the poetry of the period, such martial bravura would be the subject of effusive, highly stylized praise. Sidney's earlier elegists, for example, again and again compare the dead hero to Alexander

---

32. Greenblatt, *Renaissance Self-Fashioning*, p. 183.

while they describe his governorship of the Netherlands in the terms of a holy Protestant mission.[33] In "Astrophel," however, Spenser unambiguously shows the young shepherd's military exploits to be the empty gestures of a courtier. Astrophel has no legitimate quest. He performs his "hardie" deeds for his own motives, propelled neither by Gloriana's desire, as Prince Arthur is in *The Faerie Queene,* nor by the selfless patriotism of Cincinnatus, who, as Anthony Low notes, "easily exchanged his plow for weapons and the tactics of war when he was called upon to save the state" (p. 10). Astrophel has no plow to exchange, as his attitude toward the fruits of harvest amply demonstrates; in addition, his exchange of his shepherd's life (and syrinx) for the weapons and tactics of war occurs too easily in Spenser's judgment. Just as there is a personal desperation in Astrophel's repudiation of his "verses vaine," there is also a suspect facility in his adaptation to "hardie" escapades. Whereas the glory of Cincinnatus was his ability to labor with equal strength and productivity in peace or war, the dereliction of Astrophel is his facile disregard for genuine labor in poetry, love, and war. Half an Arthur and half a Cincinnatus, Astrophel hollowly imitates both versions of martial excursion for his own lovelorn purposes.

Early in the poem Spenser characterizes Astrophel as a playful courtier virtually indispensable to the pleasures of the court:

> And he himselfe seemd made for meriment,
> Merily masking both in bowre and hall.
> There was no pleasure nor delightfull play,
> When *Astrophel* so euer was away. (Ll. 27–30)

Presumably calculated to flatter, this praise instead reverberates as a description of frivolity and shallowness when Astrophel impetuously decides to "entertaine" Stella with "bold atchieuements." It is impossible to forget that Astrophel "seemd made for meriment" and, consequently, we suspect that his apparent resolve to do "braue deeds" is merely a continuation of the "masking both in bowre and hall." Even the war in the Netherlands Spenser calls a "perilous game," which suggests the continuity between that ear-

---

33. See in particular the elegies of Angel Day and John Phillip, in Colaianne and Godshalk, eds., *Elegies for Sir Philip Sidney.* Compare, too, Ralegh's famous characterization of Sidney as a Scipio of his time.

lier "meriment" and the later ill-starred gambit. Spenser's criticism of Astrophel is that he is always at play, always masking. And this critique is pointedly aimed at Astrophel's irresponsible behavior as a poet in contrast to Spenser's behavior.[34] As we remember from the first lines of *The Faerie Queene,* the serious poet abandons masking, however unwillingly, to sing martial exploits:

> Lo I the man, whose Muse whilome did maske,
>> As time her taught, in lowly Shepheards weeds,
>> Am now enforst a far vnfitter taske,
>> For trumpets sterne to chaunge mine Oaten reeds. (1.Pr.1)

Invoking the Virgilian *rota* as the model for a poetic career, Spenser accepts his poetic duty "to chaunge" his shepherd's pipe for "trumpets sterne."[35] In contrast, Astrophel attempts to exchange his pipe, not for a different poetic instrument, but for arms. Spenser condemns this exchange as a courtly obtuseness to the value of poetry and the contemplative life beyond adolescence. Although one might exchange a plow for a sword as Cincinnatus did, one should only exchange one kind of poetry for another, superior kind.

Low suggests that "[n]ot only did Sir Walter Ralegh and Sir Philip Sidney write gracefully crafted poems; they also produced deliberate and lasting works of art by shaping their own lives" (p.

---

34. There is a provocative irony in Spenser's implied accusation that Astrophel has abandoned a higher calling for a lower. As Helgerson notes, "[t]he second world of poetry was allowed for its beauty, with the Neoplatonic hope that such beauty might lead to virtuous action. But the allowance was grudging and the hope slim. . . . Colin Clout could not be blamed, as Philisides could, for abandoning a higher calling to become a shepherd. But Spenser could. He, like Sidney, had been given an education that destined him for public service, an education that defined poetry not only as different from action but as opposed to it" (*Self-Crowned Laureates,* p. 61). Perhaps, therefore, Spenser's irascible condemnation of Astrophel is a guilty reflection of his own secret impulse to abandon public life and to pursue poetry to the exclusion of all mundane distractions—an impulse diametrically opposed to Astrophel's, a perfect mirror image.

35. Donald Cheney points out that the lines also echo "the introduction to the *Aeneid* as the Renaissance knew it." See *Spenser's Image of Nature: Wild Man and Shepherd in 'The Faerie Queene'* (New Haven and London: Yale University Press, 1966), p. 18. Cheney is referring to the spurious "Ille ego" opening, which was probably incorporated from an advertisement attached to the poem and was thought for centuries to have been from Virgil's hand. See Low, *Georgic Revolution,* p. 3; and also Ettin, "The Georgics in *The Faerie Queene,*" who, in a discussion of Spenser's imitation of Virgil's career, notes "that Spenser, his *Georgics* unwritten, is navigating around the middle passage in his progression through the genres" (p. 60). It is precisely Astrophel's lack of appropriate "navigation" that Spenser finds unacceptable.

4). In fact, the shaping of their lives was probably more important to them than their poetry. Sidney preferred to think of himself as a man of action and often expressed some disdain for his literary toys. It is significant, therefore, that Spenser accuses him of being a less-than-serious poet, exactly what Sidney himself claimed to be. Further, Spenser makes this accusation virtually at the same time that he and the other elegists of the 1590s begin to revise Sidney's reputation from that of renowned patron to that of precursor poet. But even if Spenser's allegations regarding Sidney's seriousness as a poet are unfounded or unjust, nevertheless Sidney must be seen as a *poet* to be considered frivolous with his gifts. Paradoxically, Spenser's denial of Sidney's poetic will supplies the foundation for a literary genealogy with Sidney as the most plausible English progenitor.

Despite his mournful praise of Astrophel, Spenser obviously disapproves of his elegiac subject's behavior. References to the idleness and vanity of the young knight who chooses to fashion himself in the image of a soldier strongly indicate as much. And the nymphs' failure to effect an exchange of harvest fruit for Astrophel's piping balefully anticipates Astrophel's failure to exchange his "verses vaine" for the true labor of war. He never matures as a poet, nor can he transform himself into an instant Alexander. In fact, one condition precipitates the other: more than any other factor in the poem, Astrophel's failing as a poet causes his failures elsewhere. He is "deformed" on the battlefield, where he sacrifices his poetic gifts for a delusion of active heroism.

Elizabethan readers of Spenser's one-quarter-finished epic inevitably would have contrasted Astrophel's failure with Spenser's disciplined fulfillment of the Virgilian formula, his repudiation of "Shepheards weeds" (which, ironically, he dons again in the elegy) to perform the "vnfitter taske" of completing *The Faerie Queene*.[36] The back-formation of a modern English literary genealogy has a clear advantage for the putatively belated author of "Astrophel." By creating a flawed poetic original, Spenser illumines his own superior poetic achievement.

36. He dons "Shepheards weeds" again in Book 6, but only to emphasize the end of that particular stage of development. Considering Colin Clout's relation to Spenser—not to mention Spenser's relation to Skelton—we might read the pastoral of Book 6, just as we might read "Astrophel," as an anatomy of literary descent and literary ambition.

THREE

"A Fire Now, That Lent a Shade"
Ben Jonson's Conversion of the Sidney Legacy
and His Crowning of Shakespeare

> To me the difference forges dread.
> —*The Winter's Tale*, IV. iv

It is a critical commonplace to acknowledge Ben Jonson's conservative and even intractable resistance to change, whether that change is manifest in architecture or poetry, hospitality or stagecraft. Yet throughout Jonson's poetry we find evidence of the favorable representation of willed change, or conversion, and Jonson clearly distinguishes between glib, courtly transformations and the human effort to convert one substance or one self into another substance or self.

We should probably not be surprised to find Jonson favorably disposed to certain kinds of self-generated change. That he exerted a profound effort toward his own social and intellectual conversion is well-known and was part of his legend even during his lifetime. We find references to Jonson's dubious background everywhere, in both disparaging and complimentary contexts. While the success of his work is often emphasized by allusion to his great achievement in leaving behind his lowly origins, his failures are sometimes ascribed half-humorously to his inability to outgrow those same vulgar roots. Perhaps Mildmay Fane (Earl of Westmoreland), in his brief obituary for Jonson, most unabashedly gives expression to the centrality of Jonson's unpedigreed status in the appreciation of his poetry. We detect an uneasy mixture of awe and condescension in regard to Jonson's self-conversion:

> He who began from Brick and Lime
> The Muses Hill to climbe;
> And whilom busied in laying Ston,
> Thirsted to drink of *Helicon;*
> Changing his Trowell for a Pen,
> Wrote straight the Temper not of Dirt but Men.
>
> Now sithence that He is turn'd to Clay, and gon,
> Let those remain of th'occupation
> He honor'd once, square Him a Tomb, and say
> His craft exceeded farr a Dawbers way.
> Then write upon't, He could no longer tarry,
> But was return'd again unto the Quarry. [1]

Fane's poem is, to an extent, about conversion and reconversion. Jonson "began from Brick and Lime" both occupationally and in the sense that he had humble, earthbound origins. After his death, he "is turn'd to Clay" once more and "return'd again unto the Quarry." But along the way Jonson exchanges his trowel for a pen and, by his remarkable success with the new implement, comes to deserve a tomb crafted by his erstwhile fellow masons. Not only does Fane call to the service of his metaphor the universal Biblical-biochemical conversion of human clay, but he also calls attention to Jonson's exceptional ambition and massive effort to convert himself from a bricklayer to a poet, to ascend from the society of tomb builders to the ranks of those for whom tombs are built. Of course, the completeness of Jonson's self-conversion remains somewhat ambiguous, since, in the end, Fane returns the ex-Dawber to the quarry from which he emerged.

We find in John Taylor the Water-Poet a similar meditation on Jonson's self-conversion. In his funeral elegy for Jonson, Taylor supplies a brief (and somewhat inaccurate) biography, emphasizing Jonson's climb from obscurity. Most interesting, however, is Taylor's assertion that it is a lie to call Jonson a bricklayer's son:

> A lying rumour up and downe doth run,
> Reporting that he was a *Bricklayers* Sonne,
> Which if 'twere true was no disgrace or scorne,
> For famous *Virgil* in a ditch was borne,

---

1. *Ben Jonson,* 11 volumes, ed. C. H. Herford and Percy and Evelyn Simpson (Oxford: Clarendon Press, 1947), 11:493. All further references are to this edition.

And many men of meane obscure degree,
Have risen to the height of Soveraignty. (11:424, ll. 115–20)

Virgil's obscure birth provides a genealogical rebuttal to the rumor of Jonson's humble origins. And, in addition, Taylor connects Jonson to the sovereign powers in the same way that Jonson aggrandizes himself as a poet. According to Taylor, "A reverend Preacher was *Ben Jonson's* Sire," and as a preacher's son he had an "innated inclination" to learning. But when the preacher died, Jonson's mother then married the bricklayer, who forbade Jonson his studies.

Then was he forc'd to leave the *Academ,*
And lay by Learning (that unvalued Iem)
Beholde a *Metamorphosis* most strange,
His Books were turn'd to *Bricks,* a suddaine change,
The like was never seene since the creation,
Papers transform'd to *Stones* (a hard translation)
He from decent *Scholars* suit *Nonsuited,*
His habit all with lime and sand polluted,
His writing pen a *Trowel,* and his reading
Was joyning *Brickbatts* close, and morter spreading.
(Ll. 153–62)

Taylor describes the metamorphosis from scholar to bricklayer so that he can emphasize Jonson's self-willed reconversion to scholar. While laboring as a bricklayer, he had "more lofty study in his mind," and brooded continually on the Muses:

These were the sacred *Nine* he built upon;
And they embrac'd his love, infus'd his braines,
With heavenly raptures, and transcendent strayns,
That by their influences, learned *Ben,*
Layd by the *Trowel, Brick's* turn'd Books agen. (Ll. 176–80)

Although the Muses "by their influences" help to change Jonson's bricks back to books, Taylor clearly accords a great deal of the responsibility for the reconversion to Jonson himself. Whereas Fane's poem ends with some ambiguity, Taylor has no doubt that Jonson was never meant to hold a trowel and that once he laid it by he never returned to the quarry.

Fane's and Taylor's fascination with Jonsonian self-conversion is apt. Conversion is very much a part of Jonson's life and often turns up as a metaphor in his poetry. For instance, Jonson alludes to his self-conversion from soldier to poet in "To True Soldiers":

> I sweare by your true friend, my *Muse,* I love
>   Your great profession; which I once, did prove:
> And did not shame it with my actions, then,
>   No more, then I dare now doe, with my pen. (8:69)

But there are different kinds of conversion in Jonson's scheme—or, perhaps more accurately, there is conversion, which has positive connotations, and there is a kind of negative transformation. This latter tends to appear in poems on courtiers, as in the epigram "On Court-Worme," where Jonson suggests a dubious change from innocence to worldliness or vanity:

> All men are wormes: But this is no man. In silke
>   'Twas brought to court first wrapt, and white as milke;
> Where, afterwards, it grew a butter-flye:
>   Which was a cater-piller. So't will dye. (8:31)

Cryptic as these verses are, Jonson seems unquestionably condemnatory of the transformation from the silken whiteness of the caterpiller to the doomed butterfly.

In "Inviting a Friend to Supper" Jonson demonstrates the distinction between conversion and mere change. Neither the meal nor the wine, a beverage notorious for its powers to change personalities for the worse, will adversely affect the host and the guest. Jonson insists that "at our parting, we will be, as when/We innocently met" (ll. 38–39). We detect a familiar resistance to the facile transformations that Jonson abhors elsewhere. The conversion in the poem is digestive and economic, redirecting an array of commodities to the specific pleasure of the diners, just as Jonson converts or transfers the ownership of the "rich *Canary*-wine,/ Which is the *Mermaids,* now, but shall be mine" (ll. 29–30). Similarly, we witness the promise to convert living animals to meat, a graduation from random existence to utility, from nature to human entertainment. Indeed, the entire poem exercises a force of conversion. The host carefully transforms everything he mentions—from hens to lemons to Livy—into a presentable economy of hospitality.

Metaphorically, the term conversion has economic, religious, digestive, alchemical, and even literary significance, inasmuch as

imitatio is itself a form of conversion. Jonson refers to all these
different kinds of conversion, in both encomiastic and satirical
contexts. More than any other poet of his generation, he is obsessed
with varieties of change, and his condemnations often single out
hasty or impatient transformations as a prime vice. In "An Epistle
to Sir Edward Sacville," he explains that quick changes cannot
produce glorious results, that only by degrees does genuine change
occur:

> Men have been great, but never good by chance,
> Or on the sudden. It were strange that he
> Who was this Morning such a one, should be
> *Sydney* e're night! or that did goe to bed
> *Coriat,* should rise the most sufficient head
> Of Christendome! And neither of these know
> Were the Rack offer'd them, how they came so;
> 'Tis by degrees that men arrive at glad
> Profit in ought; each day some little adde,
> In time 'twill be a heape; This is not true
> Alone in money, but in manners too. (8:156, ll. 124–34)

The passage borrows its sentiment nearly intact from Plutarch's
moral epistle, *Quomodo quis suos in virtute sentiat profectus,* a lesson of
which is that no one who becomes truly virtuous could be ignorant
of his conversion. As readers of Jonson we should bear such a lesson
in mind. Even in praising the virtues of others, Jonson never loses
sight of his own self-conversion from obscurity to greatness. His
standards are set by his own gradual achievement.

Jonson's use of Sidney as an example of perfection achieved by
degrees is not a little ironic, given the facts of Sidney's life. Sidney
after all achieved his greatness more or less overnight, as a young
martyr. This is not to suggest that Jonson intends to belittle
Sidney's achievement. His praise is probably aimed at Sidney's
manners and at his virtues as the flower of Elizabethan chivalry,
rather than at his poetry. But, nevertheless, in comparing the two
men as poets, we cannot but notice that, more so than Sidney,
Jonson comes to greatness by slow degrees. He remarks further to
Sacville:

> Yet we must more then move still, or goe on,
> We must accomplish: 'Tis the last Key-stone
> That makes the Arch. (Ll. 135–37)

Even if Sidney represents a preeminent model of virtue, he could never be said to have laid the keystone in the arch of his life, since his life was snatched away from him so suddenly. Rather, it is the figure of Jonson that lurks heroically behind this passage. The image of the unfinished arch calls our attention to his occupational self-conversion, for no one would be better qualified to lay the last keystone than a onetime bricklayer.

KING AND POET IN "TO PENSHURST"

With the same heroically high standards in mind, Jonson converts the Sidney legacy to his own use as a poet. Once we begin to read Jonson with an eye to his literary genealogy, we recognize that, in addition to striving for a classical poetic lineage, he seeks as well to establish a unique place for himself in the English literary family tree. Indeed, if Sidney is invented by his elegists as the first precursor of English poetry, then Jonson invents himself as the first belated poet in the tradition. He probably borrows his irascible consciousness of generational conflict from the widespread social mobility of the period. But the application—or conversion—of that consciousness explicitly to poetic descent is his own.

In Epigram 9, Jonson announces that "I a *Poet* here, no *Herald* am." The distinction between poet and herald is important, as it will be for Milton, because just as it distinguishes Jonson from what he would take to be a lower social rank, it also separates his discourse from the merely nunciatory. Jonson is inclined to be instructional, to delight and to bring profit in verse, rather than merely to honor his subjects. This is a stance worth remembering in connection with Jonson's praise of Sidney in "To Penshurst," as well as in the poems to Sidney's daughter, the Countess of Rutland. A patina of didacticism, familiar in so much of the poetry and drama, covers Jonson's attitude toward his most prominent antecedent—and, indeed, his attitude toward genealogical descent itself.

For example, Jonson begins Epigram 79, "To Elizabeth, Countess of Rutland," with exceptional praise of Sidney:

> That *Poets* are far rarer births then kings,
>   Your noblest father prov'd: like whom, before,
> Or then, or since, about our *Muses* springs,
>   Came not that soule exhausted so their store. (8:53, ll. 1-4)

The first line echoes a favorite comparison, Jonson in this case judging poets superior to kings rather than their equals.[2] He moreover characterizes Sidney's poetic production as the most significant in England to date ("our" muses being the English ones, presumably). Spenser notwithstanding, Sidney is erected in the poem as the unequivocal first poet of the nation. Thus his fatherhood is revealed to be twofold: he is at once the Countess of Rutland's biological father and also a father figure to the poets who follow him, not least among them the aspiring Jonson himself.[3] The several genealogical strains come together in the curious comparison of Sidney's poetry to his daughter.

> Hence was it, that the *destinies* decreed
> (Save that most masculine issue of his braine)
> No male unto him: who could so exceed
> *Nature,* they thought, in all, that he would faine.
> At which, shee happily displeas'd, made you:
> On whom, if he were living now, to looke,
> He should those rare, and absolute numbers view,
> As he would burne, or better farre his booke. (Ll. 5–12)

Both his own poetry and the countess are Sidney's progeny. But his writing, "that most masculine issue of his braine" (l. 6), though the zenith of English literary achievement, pales in value before the glorious attributes of his child. Jonson establishes a conflict between *techne* and *phusis,* between Sidney's art and Nature's creation of the Countess of Rutland. This conflict recalls the well-known passage of the *Defence:* "Nature never set forth the earth in so rich tapestry as divers poets have done; . . . Her world is brazen, the poets only deliver a golden" (Shepherd, *Apology for Poetry,* p. 100). But in Epigram 79 Nature is victorious, and—according to Jonson's somewhat heavy-handed logic—Sidney would himself admit the inadequacy of the so-called "golden world" of his poetry. Indeed, in confrontation with Nature's accomplishment in his daughter, Sidney would burn his book.

Genealogy is the subtext of Jonson's praise in the epigram, and

2. See below, p. 138, and note 12.

3. There may indeed be a conflation of biological and poetical fatherhood in the countess. Although he does not mention her poetry in Epigram 79, Jonson claims in the *Conversations with Drummond* that the Countess of Rutland was "nothing inferior to her father" in poetry.

he deliberately obfuscates the line between literary and biological descent. Like few others in the Elizabethan period, the Sidney family lends itself to such a conflation of poetry and blood. Yet Jonson's view of the family's genealogical relations is not untroubled. It is difficult to deny, for instance, that Sidney's theory and his poetry are both somewhat compromised by the end of the poem. It is all in a good cause, of course—the admiration of the Countess of Rutland. But the meeting of the model poetry and the model progeny results in the survival of only one of them. And, while this may not be a lesson exactly, Jonson certainly seems to sound a grim note on the viscissitudes of descent relations.

In contrast, Jonson's invocation of Sidney in the "Epistle to Elizabeth, Countess of Rutland," which is the twelfth poem of *The Forrest,* carries no negative implications. The paternal presence appears twice, the first time as both the ideal poet and an ongoing model for his daughter's patronage of Jonson:

> With you, I know, my offring will find grace.
> For what a sinne 'gainst your great fathers spirit,
> Were it to thinke, that you should not inherit
> His love unto the *Muses,* when his skill
> Almost you have, or may have, when you will? (8.114, ll. 30–34)

There may be a slender threat in these lines, that to refuse Jonson would be a "sinne 'gainst your great fathers spirit." But on balance filiation is more rewarding than limiting in the poem, particularly insofar as the countess has inherited Sidney's poetic skill. If she wanted to write, Jonson asserts, she would be as good as her father—or almost as good.

In his second reference to Sidney, Jonson aligns that same poetic skill with his own, after first performing what Richard Peterson calls "his playful impersonation of Orpheus, one of Apollo's reputed sons."[4] As a son of Orpheus, Jonson will immortalize the countess, moving stones to build her "golden *pyramede.*" He disdains the mere erection of a tomb, explicitly contrasting stone monuments and the pyramids of poetry:

> But, *Madame,* thinke what store
> The world hath seene, which all these had in trust,

---

4. Richard S. Peterson, *Imitation and Praise in the Poems of Ben Jonson* (New Haven: Yale University Press, 1981), p. 115.

And now lye lost in their forgotten dust.
It is the *Muse,* alone, can raise to heaven,
    And, at her strong armes end, hold up, and even,
The soules, shee loves. Those other glorious notes,
    Inscrib'd in touch or marble, or the cotes
Painted, or carv'd upon our great-mens tombs,
    Or in their windowes; doe but prove the wombs,
That bred them, graves: when they were borne, they di'd,
    That had no *Muse* to make their fame abide. (Ll. 38–48)

The theme is borrowed from Horace (*Odes,* IV.viii); it had become
all but conventional for poets to commend poetry—usually their
own—as the only lasting monument. But in Jonson's case the
disdain of tombs carries a uniquely personal message, reminding
us that his praise of poetry includes a repudiation of his own
"dawber's" past. Moreover, he associates tomb carving or tomb
painting with traditional genealogy, the "cotes" being the coats-of-
arms of noble families, while he proceeds to reveal his own "rarer"
genealogy, his descent from Orpheus on one side and, by association of "moodes," from Sidney on the other. The conversion for
which his elegists admire him seems a salient feature of the epistle.
Though he is still willing to build a monument to the Countess of
Rutland, he will no longer perform this service with his old tools.
Rather, he promises to "rear" her head with verse:

There like a rich, and golden *pyramede,*
    Borne up by statues, shall I reare your head,
Above your under-carved ornaments,
    And show, how, to the life, my soule presents
Your forme imprest there: not with tickling rimes,
    Or common places, filch'd, that take these times,
But high, and noble matter, such as flies
    From braines entranc'd, and fill'd with extasies;
Moodes, which the god-like SYDNEY oft did prove . . . (Ll. 83–91)

Such "noble matter" flying from brains recalls "that most masculine issue" of Sidney's brain in Epigram 79. In fact, Jonson
makes the connection explicit, holding up "god-like SYDNEY" as
the model poet of "high and noble matter." The ex-dawber has
completed his occupational conversion from builder to true maker.
And Sidney's presence seems to serve a paternal function as much

for Jonson as for the countess, so that aristocratic lineage and literary descent merge.

In scorning the lesser lights of the literary scene, the "Epistle" provides a stark contrast to genuine poetic descent from Sidney. The versifiers of the court—including, implicitly, the rival poet of line 69 who has recently won the Countess of Bedford's patronage (probably Samuel Daniel)—trade in "tickling rimes,/Or common places, filch'd" (ll. 87–88). They are poetasters, superficial plagiarists incapable of sculpting Orphic verse that would endure. Reminiscent of Marlowe's contempt for "jigging veins of rhyming mother-wits," Jonson's snobbish scorn for the rhymes and commonplaces "that take these times" underscores his antipathy to the vagaries of fashion, especially where poetry is concerned.

Jonson's association in the "Epistle" of fashionable versifying with the pointless (though also fashionable) decoration of tombs recalls a theme that he first introduces in "To Penshurst," the second poem in *The Forrest*. The futile luxuriousness of the "touch or marble" from which great men's tombs are constructed in the "Epistle" glances backward in the collection to the contrast of Penshurst Place with the fashionable mansions of Kent. In fact, Jonson specifically says that Penshurst is *not* built of touch or marble. Rather, it retains its original, genuine architecture, and the lesson of the contrast is a genealogical one. Just as in the "Epistle," the genuine poet Jonson descends from Orpheus and Sidney, while the tickling rhymers and filchers seem to descend from ephemeral tomb painters, so Penshurst Place has a bona fide and aristocratic lineage in direct contrast to the filched and transitory status of the fashionable mansions. Indeed, throughout "To Penshurst" Jonson instructs his readers to avoid the seductive allure of fraudulent descent, which is exemplified in the countryside by the houses "built for enuious show." He urges resistance to the symbols of impetuous change, such as the inflated Palladian appointments recently imported from Italianate architecture. One of his chief objections is to the illegitimate architectural genealogy reflected in the showy expansions and decorative agglomerations that proliferated in the English countryside under James. For example, the notorious lantern of the poem's opening lines, "wherof tales are told," clearly represents a corruption of Penshurstian values, a kind of fraudulence invading the balanced continuity of economics and hospitality in the countryside. The lantern epitomizes what Thomas Greene has called "the febrile thirst for transformation," which Jonson repudiates in favor of an "equilibrated energy of the centered self."[5] This is precisely the kind of facile change that Jonson scorns, preferring always prudent conversion by degrees. The "polish'd pillars," "roofe[s] of gold," the "stayre[s]" and "courts" of other country estates are like the multiple disguises of Jonson's most shiftless, conniving "courtling" characters.

Greene maintains that "[t]he subject of *Volpone* is Protean man, man without core and principle and substance" ("Centered Self," p. 337). We might make a similar claim about "To Penshurst," that its subject is the contrast between the Protean ambitions of the lords who merely "have built" and Lord Lisle who "dwells." Excessive, self-serving architectural transformations, usually effected by aristocrats of the period to attract the king for a visit, indicate to Jonson a threatening discontinuity with past social values. His praise of Penshurst emphasizes the bona fide descent of genuine aristocratic values and implies that a bogus and arriviste lineage informs the recently built estates. (This may seem disingenuous of Jonson, given that he is a social bounder himself, but, presumably, his exalted birth as a poet entitles him to a conservative view.) Thus, using the lantern as a pivotal negation of houses, to use Greene's phrase, "without core and principle and substance," Jonson supplies a not-so-veiled warning about the facile alchemy of fashionable transmutations. As William McClung notes, the word "lantherne" in the poem signals a very specific contrast:

The lantern of a medieval house was simply a small louvered opening over the screens passage. . . . But the word in Jonson's time applied to a much larger architectural feature, located in the lantern's position on top of the central block of the hall. By far the most famous was the immense "lantern" of Wollaton Hall, Nottinghamshire (1588), a house of spectactular vulgarity.[6]

5. Thomas M. Greene, "Ben Jonson and the Centered Self," *SEL* 10 (1970), p. 342; p. 333.

6. William McClung, "Jonson's 'To Penshurst,' 1–5, 99–102," *Explicator* 33 (May 1975), Item 78. See also McClung, *The Country House in English Renaissance Poetry* (Berkeley: University of California Press, 1977), esp. chapter 3.

Doubtless, Jonson knew of Wollaton Hall, which was "an Elizabethan sensation," according to McClung. Similarly, as J. C. A. Rathmell suggests, the Earl of Dorset's "vastly expensive remodelling of Knole (eight miles from Penshurst)" would have provided a sharp contrast, again with the lantern as a possible focal point:

Knole was transformed into a magnificent Renaissance palace in which the hall was reduced to the status of a mere antechamber. While Penshurst remained a rambling and essentially uncoordinated "ancient pile," Knole consisted of a series of finely articulated courts with pillared loggias, enormous staterooms decorated with magnificent ceilings, a spacious and brilliantly lighted stair, the whole complex dominated by a commanding lantern-tower. Penshurst had of course a lantern, stair, and courts: Jonson's point is that they are of Anglo-Saxon simplicity. They lack the Italianate luxuriousness "whereof tales are told." By the same token Penshurst is essentially the focus of the local community whereas Knole, during these years of reconstruction, was uninhabited.[7]

Jonson's reference, whether to Wollaton, Knole, or other parvenu atrocities of the period, underscores a restraint at Penshurst in direct contrast to any kind of urgent transformation.[8]

Jonson's antipathy toward the dubious lineage of Italianate fashion in the English countryside becomes, as the poem progresses, an ambivalence toward English poetic genealogy in this, its incipient phase. Philip Sidney is the absent spirit of the poem. His numinous presence in the woods of his brother's estate anticipates and inspires the arrival of later poets, among them Jonson himself. But the sylvan poets who follow Sidney, "taken with his flames," resemble nothing so much as the inflamed and unrequited lovers of Latin and Italian pastoral or love poetry. Their lineage, unlike that of Penshurst itself, is Continental, complicated by contemporary

7. J. C. A. Rathmell, "Jonson, Lord Lisle, and Penshurst," *ELR* 1 (1971), p. 256.
8. Lanterns seem to indicate mockery and falseness to Jonson. In "An Execration on Vulcan," complaining about the fire that destroyed his library, he describes Vulcan wearing "a Lanthorne for a Crowne" (l. 10). The lantern crown represents a mocking memento of Mars's adulterous union with Venus. (Old lanterns were made of horn and, thus, Jonson alludes to Vulcan's cuckold's horns.) Comparably, in *Bartholomew Fair* Leatherhead instructs Littlewit to call him Lantern (or Lanthorne) to mask his true identity from Cokes, whom he had robbed in an earlier scene. A sense of manipulativeness attaches to the false name since, at that moment in the play, Leatherhead is acting as a puppet master. The puppeteers are performing a vulgarized version of the Hero and Leander story, and perhaps we should note the proximity of the name Lantern to the expedient, self-serving corruption of classical literature.

fashion and the fanatical Elizabethan imitation of the Italians. To the contrary, Jonson associates himself with what Rathmell calls the "Anglo-Saxon simplicity" of the estate, raising his own status by the classical origins of his poem in Martial as he confirms the genuine genealogical origins of the Sidney family's hospitality. In praising Penshurst Place for remaining true to a vaguely honorable medieval past, for resisting change, and particularly for representing proof of the virtue of bona fide and uncontaminated descent, Jonson praises his own ability to identify genuine genealogy. But for Jonson to attach himself *as a poet* to the ancient and bona fide line he must separate himself from Sidney's impassioned followers. As Don E. Wayne suggests, in "Why I Write Not of Love" Jonson has already repudiated the older Petrarchan mode in *The Forrest,* and he "has managed to establish a complex structure of relations, coded in aesthetic terms, through which he simultaneously identifies with the name of Sidney and contends with it."[9]

At times, "To Penshurst" seems to be uneasy about Sidney's usefulness as a poetic precursor. The subject of the poem is, to a certain extent, the contrast between the Protean ambitions of the lords who merely "have built" and Lord Lisle who "dwells." For the poet in the poem, this contrast is realized in the comparison of the inflamed sylvans to Jonson himself, to his presence on the estate and to his ability to praise the Sidneys with "equilibrated energy." That Jonson, despite his own very urgent social self-transformation, manages to cast himself as a model chronicler of restraint and genealogical propriety is a marvel of the poem. Nevertheless, the poem's measured praise of proper architectural display, human hierarchy, and reward for production functions as much as a tribute to the Sidneys as to Jonson's discretion and urbane skill. Indeed, in praising Penshurst Place Jonson emphasizes the civilized achievement of genuine aristocratic descent, both social and literary, and he seems to warn us of the retrograde, unrefined nature of arriviste lineages by associating the sylvans'

9. Don E. Wayne, "Jonson's Sidney: Legacy and Legitimation in *The Forrest,*" in *Sir Philip Sidney's Achievements,* ed. M. J. B. Allen, Dominic Baker-Smith, Arthur F. Kinney, with Margaret M. Sullivan (New York: AMS Press, 1990), pp. 233–34. Discussing Jonson's claim regarding his place in English letters, Wayne notes that "Jonson could not have made such a claim without recourse to the legitimating figure of Sir Philip Sidney" (p. 227).

enamored fury with the self-serving Palladian infatuation that informs the recently built estates. And the love-distracted sylvans seem the readiest example of idolaters who, in a fever of fashionable imitation, are trapped as creatures of the forest while, on the other hand, Jonson thrives so visibly as a guest of the great house.

Jonson's own presence in "To Penshurst," however, or the presence of his poetic persona, makes the poem considerably more (and, perhaps, less) than a tribute to the apparent recipients of his praise. In part, as critics have often noted, the poem is also a tribute to the praiser, which effectively undermines its own ostensible literary justification for having been written. Such self-tribute—what Richard Helgerson aptly calls self-crowning—also scrambles the pecking order at Penshurst Place, casting doubt on the inviolability of the Great Chain of Being.[10] The confusion of ranks serves not only as a compliment to the Sidneys' leveling generosity but also as a means by which Jonson distinguishes himself from the other commoners. Wayne notes that "Jonson appears as a 'guest' beginning at line 61. Neither he nor the king is represented as bearing tangible gifts; instead, they receive gifts" (p. 76). One might object that Jonson's gift to the Sidneys is the poem at hand, that his fulsome praise and classical allusions constitute his proper poetic labor, and, as such, unite him with the gift-bearing tenants on quarter-day.[11] Yet, poetic labor notwithstanding, it is difficult to avoid the conclusion that, as Wayne puts it, "Jonson implies an important difference among those who are untitled" (p. 76). Jonson is clearly not a servant, not a tenant, and not a mere appurtenance below the salt at the table—as he had been, to his bristling irritation, during the infamous dinner with

10. See Don E. Wayne, *Penshurst: The Semiotics of Place and the Poetics of History* (Madison: University of Wisconsin Press, 1984), p. 66: "in developing the chain of being on the estate, Jonson places himself in a position next to the king. . . . This is hardly consistent with the order of being prescribed by tradition."

11. See Thomas M. Greene, *The Light in Troy*, p. 283: "Is it excessively ingenious to point out that most of the epigrams, as well as many other poems, are written and entitled 'To' somebody and so constitute a kind of sweet or poisoned gift?" See also G. R. Hibbard, "The Country House Poem of the Seventeenth Century," *JWCI* 19 (1956), p. 159: "The poet is not a menial or hanger-on, but an honored friend and guest, welcomed for himself and for what he has to contribute to the great house;" and Sara J. Van den Berg, *The Action of Ben Jonson's Poetry* (Newark: University of Delaware Press, 1987), p. 118: "If Penshurst at first served the imagination, by the end of the poem Jonson has found a way to make his literary imagination, and literary language, serve the state."

Salisbury. At Penshurst he drinks the "selfe-same wine" as his Lordship and, being an honored guest, all but reigns in tandem with James himself.

But the parity of Jonson and the king is deceptive. It does not represent merely the resolution of a particular kind of class conflict. Rather, the parity of poet and prince constitutes Jonson's representation of complementary (and competing) forms of genealogy, social and literary. As Jonson puts it in *Timber:* "Solus Rex, aut Poeta, non quotannis nascitur" (8.637: "Only the king or the poet is not of everyday birth").[12] Renaissance defenders of poetry from Boccaccio to Sidney had insisted on the divine origins of poetic genealogy, usually citing Orpheus, Amphion, and Musaeus as the creators and the original citizens of society as it had come to be known. In assuming the parity of poet and prince, Jonson simply acknowledges the already commonplace notion that literary and social genealogy can claim equally distinguished and equally ancient origins and that both forms of genealogy are divinely mandated. At his most extreme, as in "To Penshurst," Jonson conceives poets to be ranked in an alternative family tree exempt from the system of social lineage and not to be absorbed into it. Stanley Fish, discussing the poems of invitation in particular, draws a similar inference: "Jonson manages (at least in his poetry) the considerable feat of asserting and demonstrating his independence of the 'poor ties' that supposedly constrain and define him. In short, Jonson establishes in these poems an *alternate* world of patronage and declares it (by an act of poetic fiat) more real than the world in which he is apparently embedded."[13] Fish concludes that Jonson effaces social distinctions in his "alternate world" by draw-

12. A nearly identical sentence recurs in the last line of the "Panegyre" for James, as noted by Robert C. Evans, *Ben Jonson and the Poetics of Patronage* (Lewisburg, Penn.: Bucknell University Press, 1989), p. 94. Other playwrights were aware of Jonson's notion about kings and poets; as Evans points out, during the notorious "poetomachia" of the first years of the century, "Dekker [in *Satiromastix*] seizes one of Jonson's favorite ideas—that true kings and true poets possess similar gifts and comparable responsibilities—and exploits it to great effect" (p. 146). In contrast, see the opening of Epigram 79, "To Elizabeth Countesse of Rutland," which seems, somewhat hyperbolically, to belie the notion of parity and completely to upend the conventional hierarchy: "That *Poets* are far rarer births then kings,/Your noblest father prov'd." Significantly, Philip Sidney, the countess's "noblest father," is the proof of Jonson's assertion.

13. Stanley Fish, "Authors-Readers: Jonson's Community of the Same," *Representations* 7 (1984), p. 38.

138

ing everyone into a community. But Jonson's objective in "To Penshurst" seems to be a less leveling one. If anything, he hopes to realign the conventional social distinctions and, while all castes besides his own may be leveled, to raise himself to a position of symmetrical opposition to the king. He implies that true poetic gifts are incommensurate with courtly genealogy. Poets may be made as well as born, as Jonson writes in his elegy for Shakespeare, but the fact of their existence *as poets* provides them with a separate (but equal) lineage. Thus Jonson's literary relation to Philip Sidney, and especially to Sidney's tree at Penshurst, is as significant in the poem as his social relation to Robert Sidney, Lord Lisle. [14]

Fish has suggested that at the beginning of a Jonson poem "one often finds a meditation on the difficulty of beginning, a meditation that will typically take the form of a succession of false starts after which the poem stumbles on its subject" (p. 28). This is an especially provocative notion when applied to "To Penshurst." Although the poem may not have a "succession" of false starts, the famed opening lines telling us what Penshurst is *not* gently force us to wonder what the house *is*. Even in rereading the poem we have the sensation that, once the negative description is finished, Jonson will begin again with the actual details. But this turns out to be a false sense of anticipation. Rather than clarify the physical description of the house (which would involve revising his own verses), Jonson altogether abandons the "ancient pile." The poem turns from the house to the grounds or park, and, to use Fish's felicitous phrase, literally "stumbles on its subject."

To be accurate, the poem stumbles upward from the house to the high ground, from the medieval stone building to a rustic landscape inhabited by much more ancient creatures of literature and myth:

> Thou joy'st in better markes, of soyle, of ayre,
> Of wood, of water: therein thou art faire.
> Thou hast thy walkes for health, as well as sport:
> Thy *Mount*, to which the *Dryads* doe resort,

14. See Graham Parry, *The Golden Age Restor'd: The Culture of the Stuart Court, 1603–42* (Manchester, England: Manchester University Press, 1981). Discussing the opening lines of the epistle to Robert Wroth, Parry notes that "we hear Jonson claiming equality with his noble friend on the basis of his special status as a poet, who by his learning and his moral eminence deserves to hold a privileged place in a cultivated society" (p. 169).

> Where PAN, and BACCHUS their high feasts have made,
>   Beneath the broad beech, and the chest-nut shade;
> That taller tree, which of a nut was set,
>   At his great birth, where all the *Muses* met.
> There, in the writhed barke, are cut the names
>   Of many a SYLVANE, taken with his flames.
> And thence, the ruddy *Satyres* oft provoke
>   The lighter *Faunes*, to reach thy *Ladies oke.*
> Thy copp's, too, nam'd of GAMAGE, thou hast there,
>   That never fails to serve thee season'd deere,
> When thou would'st feast, or exercise thy friends.
>
>   (8:93, ll. 7–21)

This is truly a sylvan passage in the Jonsonian sense, describing, among other things, a group of what "the multitude call Timber-trees, promiscuously growing."[15] Beech, chestnut, and oak are all organized around Sidney's "taller tree." The trees signify a genea-logical record on the land, and moreover represent a living or present connection between recent events and the mythological past. As Peterson has observed, "In poem after poem Jonson shows his subjects variously thrusting up to stand like outcroppings of the Golden Age; looming like survivals or restorations of antique structures and images; encompassing, and sometimes assuming to the eye, upright shapes that represent inner form; or, finally, metamorphosed into straight trees rooted firmly in English soil" (p. 44). They are family trees which the English soil nurtures, and their link to the Golden Age constitutes, as we shall see, the genealogical justification of both nobility and poetry.

Yet at the same time Jonson regards survival from one genera-tion to the next with some ambivalence, even though he himself became something of a father figure to those "sealed" of the tribe of Ben.[16] In *Timber,* using an ominous botanical image, he warns against oppressive filiation: "Greatnesse of name, in the Father, oft-times helps not forth, but o'rewhelmes the Sonne: they stand too neere one another. The shadow kils the growth" (8:576). The metaphor of shadow and growth resonates in Sidney's "taller tree"

15. This phrase comes from the definition of "Sylva" in the address "To the Reader" of *Underwood,* 8:126.

16. Jonson's attitude toward actual, as opposed to figurative, fatherhood is also complex, as "On My First Sonne" demonstrates with particular poignancy. See Scodel, *The English Poetic Epitaph,* esp. 92–109.

as well as in the contrast between the cumbrous old "standing" oak and the youthful "flowre of light" in the "Cary-Morison Ode."[17] But the worry about tall trees stifling the growth of younger ones was not unique to Jonson. For instance, the metaphor appears with similar import in *The Changeling:*

ALBIUS. Yet may not this concord and sympathise?
Old trees and young plants often grow together,
Well enough agreeing.
LOLLIO. I, sir, but the old trees raise themselves higher and broader than the young plants. (I.ii,21–25)[18]

Extending the analogy, we might note that in the shadows of taller trees mushrooms would grow, just as the notorious "mushroom gentlemen" sprang up in the shadows of ancient families during the period.

It is more significant, however, that Jonson's deleterious shadow echoes a passage from Sidney's *The Lady of May,* lines spoken by Rixus the forester: "O sweet contentation, to see the long life of the hurtless trees; to see how in straight growing up, though never so high, they hinder not their fellows; they only enviously trouble, which are crookedly bent."[19] Jonson would have come across the passage in the 1598 *Arcadia.* We might infer that he considered "*Greatnesse* of name" sufficient to distort Rixus's otherwise "hurtless trees" into the kind that are "crookedly bent" and whose shadows hinder growth.[20] Rixus's speech, moreover, occurs in the climactic debate of the play, after which Queen Elizabeth herself was to choose between the forester and the shepherd. Louis Montrose has suggested that "[o]ppositions of young forester to old shepherd

17. The image of harmful shadows occurs in Virgil's tenth Eclogue: apparently warning "singers" to avoid the shade of juniper trees, Virgil declares "*nocent et frugibus umbrae*" (line 76: "and shadows are harmful to fruit").

18. Spenser's "Februarie" Eclogue, while confirming that old trees shadow the growth of younger ones, also warns that chopping down the venerable oak can be imprudent: "There lyeth the Oake, pitied of none,/Now stands the Brere like a Lord alone,/Pulled up with pryde and vaine pleasaunce" (ll. 221–23).

19. Duncan-Jones and Van Dorsten, eds., *Miscellaneous Prose of Sir Philip Sidney,* p. 29. The passage is cited by Montrose, "Celebration and Insinuation," p. 17.

20. It is possible that Sidney has in mind the difference between field trees, which spread out as they grow, and forest trees, which grow straight up. In current usage, a forester, taking a utilitarian view of trees, refers to the field tree in a forest as a "wolf" tree, for taking more than its share of room. I am grateful to Anthony Low for suggesting this idea.

and of young trees that grow straight to those that are crookedly bent insinuate the intergenerational conflict of temperaments and policies that continues to keep Sidney, as well as Greville and other like-minded friends, from places of real power and sources of substantial income under the regime of Burghley and his queen" ("Celebration and Insinuation," p. 17). For the younger Jonson, who was not a gentleman, the conflict would of course have been somewhat different. Less concerned with "real power" than with "substantial income," his struggle in part is against the towering literary fame of his antecedents. Sidney's legacy threatens to "shadow" Jonson's growth as a poet, mainly because Sidney's inviolate status makes it inadvisable not to claim him as a poetic father. It becomes Jonson's mammoth task, either for the sake of his preferment or of his literary concerns, to separate himself from Sidney without losing the use of Sidney as a precursor among the scanty roots of the English literary family tree (or, in this context, family forest).

Thus, both as a professional poet and as a courtier, Jonson would have been obliged to promulgate the Sidney myth. But as Richard McCoy is correct to point out, "Jonson was one of the first to take a somewhat skeptical attitude toward the legendary figure."[21] Sidney provided a dubious poetic legacy to the man who would set poets and kings side by side. As Don Wayne has noted, "the particular decorum which (Sidney) was so careful to observe in transforming social and political ambition into romantic desire is an indication of the extent to which his muse continued to obey an aristocratic and quasi-feudal ethos."[22] Perhaps Jonson recognizes the balance and propriety of such an ethos in his praise of the smooth functioning of Lord Lisle's country house. But he resists being included in the scheme as a feudal subject. He resists, in effect, the temptation to trade on his descent from Sidney insofar as that descent continues to reduce his own poetic status, not to mention his literary achievement, to a subordinate social position.

It may be possible, therefore, to uncover in "To Penshurst"

21. McCoy, *Sir Philip Sidney,* p. 32.

22. Wayne, *Penshurst,* p. 143. On Jonson's relation to Sidney based on the epistle addressed to Elizabeth, Countess of Rutland, see esp. p. 145: "Here, as elsewhere, Jonson pays homage to Sidney, homage that is perhaps sincere but also obligatory given the status of Sir Philip and the nature of Jonson's relation to the family."

Jonson's precocious revision of English poetic genealogy and perhaps to discern a palimpsest of his famous anger in his accents of
praise.[23] The upward movement in the second stage of the poem
leads to the "Mount" behind the house. Figuratively we make the
climb with Jonson, the honored guest who legitimately enjoys the
"walkes for health, as well as sport" (l. 9). But Jonson is seeking
more than physical exercise. Gaining the high ground, where
Sidney's tree is flourishing, implies as well a kind of rhetorical
health. Although the poet and the king may be of equal birth,
nevertheless the poet's continued effort is necessary to maintain an
ascendency: "To this perfection of Nature in our *Poet*," Jonson
remarks in *Timber*, "wee require Exercise of those parts, and frequent" (8:637). As he climbs toward the "Mount" Jonson suggests
a habit of verbal exercise, which, if he continues upward, would
result in his almost physical parity with the rooted Sidney, the poet
of the Arcadian past.

The metaphorical association of topography and language is a
recurrent theme in Jonson's writing. For instance, railing against
the Schoolmen, he links a writer's relation to ancient authors, his
rhetorical success, and the figurative attainment of a hill:

Nothing is more ridiculous, then to make an Author a *Dictator,* as the
schooles have done *Aristotle.* The dammage is infinite, knowledge receives by it. For to many things a man should owe but a temporary
beliefe, not an absolute resignation of himself, or a perpetuall captivity. . . . calmely study the separation of opinions, find the errours
have intervened, awake Antiquity, call former times into question; but
make no parties with the present, nor follow any fierce undertakers, . . .
but gently stirre the mould about the root of the Question. . . . Then
make exact animadversion where style hath degenerated, where flour-
ish'd, and thriv'd in choisenesse of Phrase, round and cleane composition
of sentence, sweet falling of the clause, varying an illustration by tropes
and figures, weight of Matter, worth of Subject, soundnesse of Argument, life of Invention, and depth of Judgement. This is *Monte potiri,* to
get the hill. For no perfect Discovery can bee made upon a flat or levell.
(8:627–28)

23. See Ian Donaldson, "Jonson and Anger," in *English Satire and the Satiric Tradition,*
ed. Claude Rawson (Oxford: Basil Blackwell, 1984); and David Riggs, *Ben Jonson: A Life*
(Cambridge: Harvard University Press, 1989), esp. the chapter entitled "Angry Young
Man."

The passage vigorously condemns ancestor-worship and concludes, significantly for "To Penshurst," that present-day writers must climb the hill to discover truth in their own language. The landscaping metaphor, "but gently stirre the moulde about the root of the Question," perhaps doubles as good advice for Jonson himself in confrontation with the Bear Oak. Although it may be a very different exercise to "awake Antiquity" than to agitate the roots of immediate precursors, Jonson might well adopt his revisionary stance in regard to recent as well as distant "errours."

Consequently, we might consider *Monte potiri* as an exhortation to revise. "To get the hill" at least in part means to climb higher than past authors, judiciously rejecting or adapting their rhetorical constructions in order to advance one's own discovery of truth. For the poet, who according to Jonson "writes things like the Truth" (8:635), getting the hill would moreover involve "*Imitation,* to be able to convert the substance, or Riches of an other *Poet,* to his owne use" (8:638). This poetic conversion might be flattering or derogatory, respectful or satirical, preserving or revisionary. The imitation of ancient authors was a well-established practice among poets, the subject of voluminous theorizing in sixteenth-century treatises. From the perspective of literary genealogy, imitating a particular author not only affirmed that author's place in the established lineage but also constituted a contemporary author's bid to add his own name to the family tree. Similarly, although no methodology had been explicitly articulated for the imitation or "conversion" of one's contemporaries or immediate precursors, we might presume that the genealogical effects of such a practice would be comparable to the imitation of ancient authors. In a sense, the conversion of immediate precursors would itself have been an imitation of genuine imitation, a kind of genealogical tactic to assert the resemblance between contemporary poetic descent and ancient canonized lineage.

SIDNEY'S SHADOW AND THE "*SECUNDUS HOMO*"

For Jonson the conversion of immediate precursors—especially Sidney—was extremely useful. It confirmed by practice what was by no means a fait accompli: that English poetry, because it supported imitation, must therefore have definable origins and crystallized lines of descent from which Jonson could deliberately swerve. Francis Meres may enthusiastically link the poets of Greece and Rome with English poets, but his assertions are scarcely persuasive.[24] More convincing is Jonson's imitation of Sidney's poetry, through which he probably sought to classicize that earlier generation. Even the opening lines of "To Penshurst," where we find the powerful negative view of artifice so often attributed to Jonson's taste for classical proportion, allude directly to Sidney's *Arcadia*. As G. R. Hibbard points out, "It is generally accepted that when Sir Philip Sidney described Kalander's house in the *Arcadia* it was in fact his own home that he was thinking of. His description is worth quoting because he also recognizes that the house expresses a certain attitude to life, and because it may well have been in Jonson's mind when he wrote *To Penshurst*" ("Country House," p. 163). Hibbard goes on to quote a long passage in which we find several striking similarities to Jonson's descriptions: for instance, in Sidney's phrases "with fitte consideration both of the ayre, the prospect and the nature of the ground" and "[t]he lightes, the doores and staires, rather directed to the use of the guest, then to the eyes of the Artificer" we recognize the inspiration for Jonson's categories "Of soyle, of ayre,/Of wood, of water" as well as "no lantherne, . . ./Or stayre, or courts." By "lightes" Sidney means windows, but nevertheless Jonson's description is close enough to awaken our curiosity about his *textual* relation to the earlier poet.

As is well known, Jonson contradicts himself (off the record) on Sidney's achievement: in *Timber* he recommends "the best Authors to youth first, so let them be openest, and clearest. As *Livy* before *Salust, Sydney* before *Donne*" (8:618); whereas in the *Conversations with Drummond* he complains that Sidney broke the rules of decorum by allowing all characters to speak alike. Similarly, we find conflicting attitudes on the record. At times, as in his benign allusion to Kalander's house, Jonson imitates Sidney with a filial respect. But at other times the allusions carry a more pointed and rambunctious message hinting at Jonson's intention to surpass his

---

24. See Francis Meres, "A Comparative Discourse of Our English Poets with the Greeke, Latine, and Italian Poets" (from *Palladis Tamia* 1598), in *Elizabethan Critical Essays,* ed. G. Gregory Smith (London, 1904), pp. 314–24.

precursor. For example, we might compare "getting the hill" at Penshurst to an expostulation on hills and greatness in the *Arcadia:*

Great to thee my estate seems, thy estate is blest by my judgement:
And yet neither of us great or blest deemeth his owne selfe.
For yet (weigh this alas!) great is not great to a greater.
What judge you doth a hillocke shew, by the lofty *Olympus?*
Such this smale greatnes, doth seeme compar'd to the greatest.[25]

This speech appears in the First Eclogues, part of an exchange between Musidorus and Pyrocles, who are disguised at the time respectively as Dorus and Zelmane (Cleofila). Several aspects of the passage seem to echo in "To Penshurst." Sidney's contrast of a "hillocke" to the "lofty *Olympus*" seems to adumbrate Jonson's implicit contrast of the mount "to which the *Dryads* do resort" to Mount Helicon. Although the Muses might have met at Penshurst for Sidney's birth, possibly on their first trip to sixteenth-century England, their habitual abode is a far "greater" mountain than the hillock behind the country house. Presumably Jonson, as the later poet of this historic *locus amoenus,* has one foot on the high ground at Penshurst and one foot on Helicon for inspiration. While he may owe his leg-up to Sidney's hillock, his next step, we can surmise, will take him beyond Sidney, to a "lofty" classical height. As a poetic descendant, moreover, Jonson simultaneously moves backward to an originary poetic status and forward to the vanguard of English poetry. That he can indicate this genealogical maneuver by an allusion to Sidney's verse further emphasizes his intention to convert Sidney to his own use.

When Pyrocles (Zelmane) begins to make meaningful comparisons of great to greater, we are irresistibly reminded of Jonson's career-long obsession with the contradictory nuances of the word "great." While the word alone is not enough to confirm an intertextual link, nevertheless the hierarchical notion in Sidney's passage that "great is not great to a greater" suggests the opposing concepts of greatness that Jonson is so fond of highlighting. In "To Penshurst," where the word appears four times in very significant places, twice "great" suggests excellence and twice excess. The first and the last use seem to make a pair, describing first Philip and

---

25. *The Poems of Sir Philip Sidney,* ed. William A. Ringler, Jr. (Oxford: Clarendon Press, 1962), pp. 33–34. All further references to Sidney's poems are to this edition.

then Robert Sidney. There is in fact a suggestion of bona fide genealogy in Jonson's positive use of the word, a notion of the descent of greatness in that the older brother's "great birth" fore-shadows the legitimate births of Lord Lisle's children: "His children thy great lord may call his owne" (l. 91). Between these two descriptions Jonson uses the word to imply a sarcastic contempt for parvenu lords, echoing his earlier contrast of Penshurst Place with the likes of Wollaton or Knole. A comparable contrast is built into Jonson's use of the comparative word "taller" to describe Sidney's tree: and again the ambiguous value of tall trees to younger, shorter trees reminds us that Jonson perhaps resented Sidney's shadow and planned to convert the oak to fuel.

In the poem "To Sir Robert Wroth," which follows "To Penshurst" in *The Forrest,* Jonson explicitly describes the conversion of trees to home fires:

> The trees cut out in log; and those boughes made
> A fire now, that lent a shade! (8:98, ll. 45–46)

Lady Mary Wroth was Philip Sidney's niece. The convertible trees of her husband's estate, while providing one among many praise-worthy attributes of the Wroth hospitality, also establish a link with the origins of festivity and poetry:

> Thus PAN and SYLVANE, hauing had their rites
>   COMVS puts in, for new delights;
> And fills thy open hall with mirth, and cheere,
>   As if in SATVRNES raigne it were;
> APOLLO'S harpe, and HERMES lyre resound,
>   Nor are the *Muses* strangers found. (Ll. 47–52)

Just as in "To Penshurst" the Muses met round Sidney's tree "at his great birth," here they gather before the fire of trees that once "lent a shade." The flames in fact seem to summon the Muses, along with Apollo and Hermes, gods of poetry. And, moreover, Jonson emphasizes that Wroth's hospitable flames carry us back to the most ancient of times, to the originary epoch of "SATVRNES raigne." At one end of the temporal spectrum are Apollo, Hermes, and the Muses, and at the other end, presumably, is Jonson, the poet of the conversion. Mediating the span of poetic history are the trees of Wroth's estate, family trees, as it were, associated with (and perhaps descended from) Sidney's oak on the Penshurst estate.

The connection between the trees and between the estates is figured in the connection between the two poems in Jonson's forest.[26]

In converting Sidney's poetry to his own use in "To Penshurst" Jonson foreshadows the conversion of wood to flames in the poem. Alastair Fowler observes that "Penshurst may not have the elements of architecture, but it has the four elements Earth ('soil'), Air, Water, and Fire. The fourth resides potentially in the 'wood' used to make it: an association repeated in lines 15–16, where the 'writhed bark' of Sidney's Oak records the sylvans 'taken with his flames.'"[27] Although it is difficult to determine whether being "taken" with flames constitutes a worthwhile state of being, nevertheless Jonson leads us to infer the conversion of the wood of Sidney's tree to the fuel of the sylvans' passionate fire. Fowler suggests that "[s]uch tropic flames of love, zeal, and hospitality flicker over Penshurst like a benign St. Elmo's fire (p. 271)."

As Jonson proceeds in the poem from the Mount to the hearth, we detect an undertow pulling instead toward an earlier, perhaps more classical period. Just as Penshurst house recalls a prudent medieval architectural ethic, the flames of Sidney's sylvans eventually become the flames of the Penates, the tutelary deities of ancient classical Rome. The forward progress of the poet through the woods, walks, and halls is mirrored in a kind of regression to an indefinable antiquity. At the same time that Jonson's description of the grounds and woodland creatures surrounding Sidney's tree promises a descent to highly civilized order on the estate, it also implies a chorographical movement backward to a rustic, originary, pretechnological period—a time, in Erwin Panofsky's term, that is "*ante Vulcanum*," before fire, artifice, and the yoke of labor.

---

26. See also Jonson's ode to the young William Sidney, Sir Philip's nephew (*The Forrest*, no. 14). Referring to Sidney, Jonson urges the young man not to rest "on what's deceast" because they "that swell/With dust of ancestors, in graues but dwell." The sentiment echoes Jonson's concern about older, ancestral trees. The poem ends with an appreciation of bonfires, a call for the light that comes, not from mere logs, but from burning men:

> And with the flame
> Of love be bright,
> As with the light
> Of bone-fires. Then
> The Birthday shines, when logs not burne, but men.

27. Alastair Fowler, "The 'Better Marks' of Jonson's 'To Penshurst,'" *Review of English Studies* n.s., 24 (1973), p. 271.

In his superb discussion of Piero di Cosimo's representation of primeval culture, Panofsky points to the attraction of describing the phases of human history by connecting pagan myth and Christian symbolism:

The system on which Piero di Cosimo's evolutionistic compositions are based bears some resemblance to the theological division of human history in the era *ante legum,* the era *sub lege,* and the era *sub gratia.* Using the same prepositions, we could speak of an era *ante Vulcanum,* an era *sub Vulcano,* and an era *sub Prometheo;* the analogy of ideas holds good to the extent that in both cases the inaugurator of the third phase is crucified for those whom he was destined to save.[28]

Because of the coexistence of primitive and civilized states in Jonson's description of Penshurst, I find it provocative to analyze the poem with reference to Panofsky's three phases. We can certainly imagine both local Kentish history and English literary tradition divided into an era *ante Sidneium,* before the family tree and before the great son, and an era *sub Sidneo* in which the sylvans are "taken with his flames." The third phase, moreover, would have been inaugurated by Philip Sidney's death; though hardly crucified, Sidney was repeatedly praised by his elegists as a martyr to the Protestant cause. Perhaps the "great birth" is an oblique reference to Virgil's Messianic Eclogue in which Astrea and Saturn return to acknowledge the divine birth of a boy who will change the race from iron to golden.[29]

In any case, the third era is more difficult to name, chiefly because of Jonson's skepticism about Sidney's literary progenitorship and about the utility of Sidney's flames. Indeed it is possible to think of the third era either *sub arbore,* carefully guided by the

28. Erwin Panofsky, "The Early History of Man in Two Cycles of Paintings by Piero di Cosimo," in *Studies in Iconology,* pp. 55–56.

29. See Philip Sidney, *An Apology for Poetry,* ed. Geoffrey Shepherd (London: Thomas Nelson, 1965), p. 100. Shepherd's note on the passage (p. 156) is relevant: "In literary tradition the age of brass under the rule of Jove was considered the third age, between the age of silver and the present age of iron; see Ovid, *Metamorphoses,* I, 89ff. The golden age is the primal age, but also the hoped-for age of perfection and immortality; cp. Virgil, *Eclogues,* IV." In addition to perfection, the primal age restores the original monarchy of Saturn. Jonson may be acknowledging Sidney's golden birth under Elizabeth, but he clearly aligns himself with the orderly implementation at Penshurst of the new (or restored Stuart) monarch's values—he, more than Sidney, actually *delivers* the golden world.

ramifications of the Sidney family tree, or *sub ardore,* inflamed
and ruled by misguided Italianate passion, what Ralph S. Walker
once called "Petrarchian affectation."[30] The phenomenon of sylvans
"taken" with flames, a possible reference to the influence of Ario-
stan romance on Sidney and his followers, seems to favor a reading
of history *sub ardore.* On the other hand, the references to Barbara
Gamage's oak and to the Sidney copse indicate a continuation of
history *sub arbore,* a faith in bona fide genealogy.

The antagonistic relation of history *sub arbore* versus history *sub
ardore* is almost too obvious, particularly in a book entitled *The
Forrest:* the medium of passion, in this case Sidney's flames, would
be utterly destructive to his own tree, to his sister-in-law's oak, to
the family copse and, by analogy, to all the verse trees of Jonson's
book. Besides the self-consuming aspect of Sidney's inspirational
flames, we detect the implicit threat of extending a destructive
element from the past into the inflammable branches of the present
and the future. Yet the fire is also symbolic of discovery, a mixed
blessing of technological improvement and lost innocence. Para-
phrasing Boccaccio, Panofsky explains that "while Vulcan personifies the *ignis elementatus,* that is, the physical fire which enables
mankind to solve its practical problems, the torch of Prometheus . . . carries the 'celestial fire' which stands for the 'clarity of
knowledge infused into the heart of the ignorant,' and that this
very clarity can only be attained at the expense of happiness and
peace."[31]

Although our deductions depend, to a degree, on hypertroping,
we might nevertheless conclude that Jonson characterizes Sidney's
fire as being of the primitive rather than the Promethean kind.
Very deliberately he rusticates Sidney. Whereas Spenser criticizes
Astrophel (his Sidney character) for abandoning the bowers and
groves, Jonson implies that Sidney's remaining in the pastoral
landscape sums up his limitations. Jonson seems to cast him as the

30. Ralph S. Walker, "Ben Jonson's Lyric Poetry," in *The Criterion, 1922–1939,* ed.
T. S. Eliot (London: Faber and Faber, 1967), 13:447. Walker points out that "[t]he
Elizabethan renaissance writers, again, were essentially romantic, despite their superficial devotion to the classics. Only in Ben Jonson is there a complete absorption of the
abstract and indefinable spirit usually indicated by the epithet 'classical'" (p. 438);
Walker adds that Jonson "seeks to confound the mishandlers of the Petrarchian involu-
tion" (p. 445).
31. Panofsky, *Iconology,* p. 50. See his note 53.

Vulcan of English literary tradition, less as the author of a golden world than as a primal (and possibly incendiary) element of nature. Without absolutely denying Sidney's "celestial fire," Jonson emphasizes the more primitive and even destructive *ignis elementatus* of his flames. Rather than creatures of intellect, the sylvans who are inspired to carve their names in Sidney's tree call to mind savage, prehistoric, visceral beings—what Sidney himself described as "the wild untamed wits" of the benighted people who first listened to Orpheus and Linus (*Apology,* p. 96).

The sylvans' behavior is identifiably literary. Jonson probably could have expected his readers to recall several sources in the lines "There, in the writhed barke, are cut the names/Of many a SYL-VANE, taken with his flames" (ll. 15–16). Carving names on trees, as Rensselaer Lee points out, was "an already overworked topos in European pastoral literature."[32] Lee maintains that, although there are examples of tree-writing in Greek and Hellenistic poetry, the Renaissance poets were inspired chiefly by "the more sophisticated amatory context of Roman pastoral and elegiac poetry of the first century B.C." (p. 9). Virgil's tenth Eclogue is the *locus classicus* from which the tradition springs:

> certum est in siluis inter spelaea ferarum
> malle pati tenerisque meos incidere amores
> arboribus: crescent illae, crescetis, amores.

> The choice is made—to suffer in the woods among
> The wild beasts' dens, and carve my love into the bark
> Of tender trees: as they grow, so my love will grow.[33]

The poet Gallus is pining for his friend Lycoris. Although it is not clear exactly what words Gallus plans to carve into the bark, the important lesson is that whatever mark he inscribes in the tree today will increase in breadth in the future. This, Lee concludes, "will bestow a measure of immortality upon his passion" (p. 9). Similarly, in Ovid's *Heroides,* Paris carves Oenone's name in a tree and, though he abandons the nymph for Helen, she is pleased that

32. Rensselaer Lee, *Names on Trees: Ariosto into Art* (Princeton: Princeton University Press, 1977), p. 7.

33. Virgil, *Opera,* ed. R. A. B. Mynors (Oxford: Clarendon Press, 1969), p. 27, ll. 52–54. The translation is by Guy Lee, Virgil's *Eclogues* (Harmondsworth: Penguin Books, 1980), p. 105.

the more the trees grow, the greater her name becomes. In the sixteenth century the best-known occurrence of the motif is the Angelica and Medoro episode of the *Orlando Furioso*. For Ariosto and later poets the notion of such an inscription on the very face of nature would have had a powerful attraction. The carving of names in trees might have seemed a metaphor for poetic fame itself, a human inscription that becomes so much a part of the natural process that its renown increases as time passes. Uneasy as they often were about their interrupted genealogical relations to classical literature, Renaissance poets would have been more than content to imagine their inscriptions connected simultaneously to a rooted past and to a budding and outspread future.

Thus, not only do Jonson's sylvans call to mind Ariosto's inflamed lovers, but, more to the point, they are also attached to a long line of unrequited poet-lovers declaring their passion for all time in the bark of trees. Their bid for immortality involves a veritable scarring of Sidney's memorial oak, the symbol both of his earthly body and of his poetic fame, "where all the *Muses* met." Jonson's ambivalence toward the sylvans is manifest in the implication that, in seeking to be poets in the Sidneian tradition, they behave like impassioned and slavish imitators, letting their fame rely on the growth of their model rather than on their own literary achievements. But Jonson's ambivalence about Sidney, or at least his skepticism regarding Sidney's status as a precursor, is also evident in the sylvans. To some extent they are merely a generation of poet-apes, in their passion imitating an equally impassioned (and, therefore, less valuable) poetic antecedent. According to one of Lodowick Bryskett's elegies in the *Astrophel* collection, Sidney himself was given to carving in trees:

> Loe where engraued by his hand yet liues
> The name of *Stella,* in yonder bay tree.
> Happie name, happie tree; faire may you grow,
> And spred your sacred branch, which honor giues,
> To famous Emperours, and Poets crowne.[34]

Insofar as they imitate his impassioned tree-writing, Jonson's sylvans are direct descendants of Sidney. But, on closer examination,

34. Lodowick Bryskett, "A Pastorall Aeglogue vpon the death of Sir Phillip Sidney Knight," in *Spenser: Poetical Works,* ed. Smith and de Sélincourt, p. 555, ll. 125–29.

the sylvans' intentions are considerably different from the intention of their precursor in Bryskett's elegy. They do not write the
names of their unattainable loves in the bark. To the contrary,
Jonson finds that they have cut their own names into the tree,
inscribing themselves permanently into the very trunk of the
Sidney legend. As the legend grows so shall *their* names. In
Bryskett's elegy, Stella's name spreads as the bay tree grows and its
leaves are passed around to honor emperors and poets. The sylvans
apparently hope that, in a similar way, their own fame will grow as
Sidney's tree expands and flourishes. And, consequently, it would
be in their interest to promulgate the Sidney myth.

Harris Friedberg has suggested that Jonson's importation of
dryads, sylvans, and other pastoral figures into the landscape of
Penshurst is a means of defining his place and the place of his poem
in literary tradition.

Jonson uses pastoral in "Penshurst" to suggest the essential identity of
literary and real landscapes. Rather than separating the zone of the
human and historical, the realm of fact, from the zone of the literary and
symbolic as Martial does, Jonson superimposes them. The Sidneys share
their walks with the Dryads, participating in the same natural rhythms
of birth and feasting as these wood spirits. And through these pastoral
allusions Jonson is able to show the harmony with the natural world that
the middle section of the poem continues.[35]

The "essential identity of literary and real landscapes" includes the
identity of poets and the inhabitants of country estates—the identity, moreover, of literary and social genealogy. Presumably Jonson
superimposes the literary landscape on the actual one for the sake of
merging the Sidneys and the classical or historical past. But,
despite his efforts to flatter the Sidney family, he does not seem to
extend Philip Sidney's influence to the middle section of the poem.
Jonson, as the guest poet who is able to put to use the fire, lights,
and livery of the house, as if he "raigned here," is demonstrably not
"taken" with flames, not consumed so much as consuming. Like
King James, he is protected by the tutelary properties of the
converted wood, whose "fires/Shine bright on euery harth as the
desires/Of thy *Penates* had been set on flame" (ll. 77–79). And just

---

35. Harris Friedberg, "Ben Jonson's Poetry: Pastoral, Georgic, Epigram," *ELR* 4
(1974), p. 129.

as the family wood of the first part of the poem seems to become the fuel of the family fires in the later passage, the passion of the sylvans is transformed into the "desires" of the Penates. It is as if at Penshurst there were a continuity of classical figures, a progression from rustic to sheltered and dwelling, from the unproductive frenzy of the sylvans to the protective repose of the Penates "entertaining" the King and his son.[36]

The truth or persuasiveness of this model of cultivation and descent of course depends on adducing significant connotation to the tree inscribing. If, for the sake of argument, we agree to regard the sylvans as products of Sidney's *ignis elementatus,* then we must be struck by how inappropriate their inflammatory writing would be in a poem whose chief praise is of orderly function, ready hospitality, and fit proportion. They are messy creatures by this standard of praise, unfit for the job of reconciling the classical (or Sidneian) Arcadian wilderness with the modern Elizabethan country estate. Indeed, it seems unlikely that they would ever be invited into the house. In contrast to the sylvans, Jonson casts himself as the chronicler of and participant in an orderliness derived from social propriety and philosophical repose. He is clearly the post-Promethean poet, just as Penshurst Place is a pre-Palladian haven: together the poet and the estate achieve a balance between artifice and production, between modernity and grace.

Ernst Cassirer notes that, in imitating Prometheus, "[t]he wise man becomes his own creator and master; he acquires and possesses himself, whereas the merely 'natural' man always belongs to a foreign power and remains its eternal debtor."[37] If the sylvans are eternal debtors to Sidney's *ignis elementatus,* a "foreign" power that is feudal in its external control, then Jonson is an example of self-

36. See Martin Elsky, *Authorizing Words: Speech, Writing, and Print in the English Renaissance* (Ithaca: Cornell University Press, 1989), p. 97: noting that "[t]he way Jonson merges Penshurst's specifically English landscape with a classical literary setting is a critical commonplace," Elsky adds that "the point at which the estate becomes a prototypical emblem of quintessentially English values—when James visits—is also the moment when it realizes itself as a Roman household. On his approach to Penshurst, James sees the hearths aflame as if they were Penates, the Roman household gods that Aeneas carried with him from Troy and that informed him of his mission to found Rome—an apt emblem of both the domestic and the royal nature of James's visit."

37. Ernst Cassirer, *The Individual and the Cosmos in Renaissance Philosophy,* trans. Mario Domandi (Philadelphia: University of Pennsylvania Press, 1963), pp. 96–97.

possession in the poem, the enlightened humanist who carefully distinguishes himself from an ethic that requires social or literary indenture. His descent from Sidney, though undeniable, provides him with the means to surpass his origins. Cassirer concludes that "[a]s soon as we proceed to the order of *value,* we find a reversal of the temporal succession of the man of 'nature' and the man of 'art'—a reversal, that is, of the *primus homo* and the *secundus homo:* the second in time becomes the first in value" (p. 97). Such a reversal in the realm of poetic genealogy, where priority itself is one of the values, can only occur when the temporal succession is already in place. Not until Jonson does English literary tradition contain a fixed, and therefore reversible, genealogy. Consequently, not until Jonson does skepticism about precursors constitute a denial, however tentative, of those same poetic origins.[38]

THE QUESTION OF SHAKESPEARE

In terms of literary genealogy the question of Shakespeare and Jonson has been largely ignored. The long debate among critics, which is fueled by Jonson's few off-the-record remarks in *Timber* and the *Conversations,* has concentrated either on contrasting the writers as dramatists or on establishing Jonson's true feelings about the rival playwright.[39] As T. J. B. Spencer points out, Jonson himself began the "odious comparison" of the two poets: "the most

38. Harold Bloom's agonistic view of poetic genealogy perhaps begins to make sense with Jonson. See *Agon: Toward a Theory of Revisionism,* p. 23: "Deniers of genealogy . . . are lying against time, and to such lying I grant all honor." When Bloom speaks about the struggle against poetic belatedness, what he terms the "lying against time," he tends to describe a Miltonic or post-Miltonic frame of mind. Although, so far as I can determine, the Jonsonian belatedness itself is calculated to make Jonson appear part of a tradition that is not yet a tradition, nevertheless we find the seeds of the denial of genealogy in his work.

39. See, for example, John Freehafer, "Leonard Digges, Ben Jonson, and the Beginning of Shakespeare Idolatry," *Shakespeare Quarterly* 21 (1970), pp. 63–75; S. Schoenbaum, "Shakespeare and Jonson: Fact and Myth," in *Elizabethan Theatre II,* ed. David Galloway (Hamden, Conn.: Archon Books, 1970), pp. 1–19; L. J. Potts, "Ben Jonson and the Seventeenth Century," *Essays and Studies,* n.s., 2 (1949), pp. 7–24; J. Dover Wilson, "Ben Jonson and *Julius Caesar,*" *Shakespeare Survey* 2 (1947), pp. 36–43; Russ McDonald, *Shakespeare and Jonson, Jonson and Shakespeare* (Lincoln: University of Nebraska Press, 1988); and Ian Donaldson, ed., *Jonson and Shakespeare* (Atlantic Highlands, N.J.: Humanities Press, 1983).

articulate literary critic of the seventeenth century, [Jonson] found Shakespeare a convenient contrast to himself for the purposes of that rough-and-ready synthesis or miscellany of Renaissance literary theorizing which he compiled or 'conveyed.' "[40] Yet, despite Jonson's sharp private judgments of the elder poet's literary faults, one need not agree with Will Kempe's remark in *The Return from Parnassus* (1601) that Jonson was "a pestilent fellow."[41] To the contrary, we might speculate that Jonson's notorious negativity and contumely, like the contentious Jacobean literary climate in which he was such a visible target, were calculated partly to emulate the public critical battles of prior literary traditions. As Jonson and the other poets of the period undoubtedly understood, rivalry among near-contemporaries was a kind of imprimatur. Every ambitious English writer would have realized, perhaps enviously, that the renowned literary traditions, both classical and Continental, flourished and endured in an atmosphere of quibbling, sniping, and more serious critical disagreement. From Aristophanes' *Frogs* to Ovid's niggardly revision of the Aeneas story, from Petrarch's denial of Dante as a worthy precursor to the pitched battle over the *Orlando Furioso* in the latter half of the sixteenth century, wherever literary controversy existed, it seems, the national literature survived, echoing into future generations. In a way, Jonson learned this lesson best of his contemporaries. That he was conscious of his use of rivalry seems evident from the first lines of the elegy in memory of Shakespeare:

> To draw no enuy (*Shakespeare*) on thy name,
> Am I thus ample to thy Booke and Fame. (8:390, ll. 1–2)

Jonson brackets envy before beginning to praise a known rival, as if envy itself were the antecedent to the elegiac relationship. The question of competition between the two playwrights, in any case, furnishes only a background or an introduction to Jonson's public canonization of Shakespeare.

---

40. T. J. B. Spencer, "Ben Jonson on his beloved, The Author Mr. William Shakespeare," in *The Elizabethan Theatre IV*, ed. G. R. Hibbard (Hamden, Conn.: Archon Books, 1974), p. 22. In the same volume, see also S. Schoenbaum, "The Humorous Jonson," pp. 1–21; and E. B. Partridge, "Jonson's Large and Unique View of Life," pp. 143–67.

41. For discussion of this and many other references to the Jonson-Shakespeare relationship in English critical writing through the nineteenth century, see S. Schoenbaum, "Shakespeare and Jonson." Mention of Kempe appears on p. 4.

The two poems included in the 1623 Folio of Shakespeare's works, though of course intended as panegyrics, are nevertheless evidence of the extent to which Jonson wished to make his readers conscious of Shakespeare's position in the burgeoning family tree of English poetry. Several times Jonson refers to "gentle" Shakespeare. In the poem "To the Reader," for example, which accompanied a portrait of Shakespeare as the frontispiece to the Folio, Jonson begins:

> This Figure, that thou here seest put,
> It was for gentle Shakespeare cut. (8:390, ll. 1–2)

Jonson adds that the "Grauer" competed with Nature "to out-doo the life" (l. 4), but that the engraver's print cannot surpass Shakespeare's "Booke" as a representation of the poet's wit.[42] Elsewhere we also find Jonson hinting at a conflict between Shakespeare's public (or visual) and poetic personae, in effect between his social and literary genealogies. In the Folio elegy, which heads the verse tributes, Jonson caps a genealogy of Greek poets with reference again to "My gentle *Shakespeare*" (8:392, l. 56). And in *Timber*, when assessing Shakespeare's "*Phantsie*" and poetic facility, Jonson praises Shakespeare's "gentle expressions" (8:584).

More than merely a reference to Shakespeare's disposition, the term "gentle" denotes social standing. The familiar cognates *gentleman, gentility,* and *gentry* resonate in Jonson's phrase. Moreover, we might detect some irony in the appellation. As Jonson was doubtless aware, the Shakespeare family had only recently (in 1599) been awarded a coat of arms, "with no better claim," as S. Musgrove observed some time ago, "but also no worse, than many another rising Elizabethan house."[43] The Shakespeare gentility was somewhat parvenu, and, in Jonson's view, perhaps the result of fabrication. His well-known spoof on the Shakespeare family motto in *Every Man Out of His Humour* attests to his doubts about

---

42. Engravers, of course, also fashioned the shields that held coats of arms, and, extending Jonson's opinion on the limitations of the engraver's medium, we might conjecture that a mere heraldic device could not sufficiently represent Shakespeare's gentility.

43. S. Musgrove, *Shakespeare and Jonson* (Folcroft, Penn.: Folcroft Press, 1957), p. 4. In fact, in the early seventeenth century, Ralph Brooke, at the time Garter King of Arms, cast some doubt on the work of one of his predecessors, Richard Cooke (d. 1593), who presumably conducted the research into the granting of arms to John Shakespeare.

the heraldic creation of armigerous status in the case of his fellow playwright. As Musgrove explains:

[The Shakespeare family] had been allotted the slightly embarrassing motto "Non sanz Droict"—"Not without Right." In *Every Man Out* (which contains other references to Shakespeare), Jonson has to devise a comic coat of arms for a country bumpkin, and after a great deal of heraldic foolery about "boars' heads" and "puddings in a pewter field," hits upon the motto "Not without Mustard." This is a friendly pulling of the genteel leg, clear enough to those in the know, but sufficiently concealed by the technical coat itself, which bears no resemblance to Shakespeare's, not to be public mockery. (P. 4)

We can perhaps recognize Jonson's "friendly pulling of the genteel leg" as well in the references to "gentle Shakespeare." Whether we detect a satirical edge to the phrase or not, it seems undeniable that Jonson wished to remind "those in the know" of Shakespeare's arriviste claim to gentle status. Yet, in doing so, he reveals a powerful dialectical relationship between the Shakespeare family genealogy and Shakespeare's bona fide literary descent.

Jonson's long eulogy is taken up largely in comparing Shakespeare to other writers and to establishing him as a kind of avatar or culmination, "the Starre of *Poets*" (l. 77). At first, fitting Shakespeare into the hallowed English ground, Jonson affirms his subject's extraordinary credentials:

> I will not lodge thee by
> *Chaucer,* or *Spenser,* or bid *Beaumont* lye
> A little further, to make thee a roome. (Ll. 19–21)

Echoing William Basse's elegy in memory of Shakespeare, this brief catalogue is interesting for several reasons. To begin with, Chaucer and Spenser are the only nondramatic poets Jonson mentions in the entire poem. Presumably they are intended to represent English antiquity and its modern incarnation, a kind of genealogical progression. But, evidently, neither Chaucer nor Spenser is a compatible antecedent for Shakespeare. Although Jonson was known to acknowledge Spenser's poetic virtues, he complains in *Timber* that he "writ no language"; and he compares the abuse of what he calls "Custome of speech" among ancient poets such as Lucretius, who is "scabrous and rough" in some usages, to the contemporary use of "*Chaucerismes* with us, which were bet-

ter expung'd and banish'd" (8:622). Thus the contrast between
Shakespeare and the first two poets Jonson names seems predominantly to favor the modern over the antique. He implies that the
obsolete language of Chaucer has been handed down to Spenser and
that this particular line of literary descent is doomed, even though
at the time Spenserians like Drayton and the Fletchers were flourishing. But Jonson's intuition was accurate, if precocious (or pre-
mature). His revision of Basse's elegy, insofar as it repositions the
English poets while affecting *not* to reposition them, constitutes a
novel, prescient, and enduring literary history. But, in addition,
by suggesting that Shakespeare does not belong with Chaucer and
Spenser—in dismissing one of the only recognizable literary family trees in English poetry—Jonson effectively eliminates a legitimate English genealogy for Shakespeare.

Beaumont, who seems an odd choice for the third poet in the
list, most likely appears in Jonson because he appears in Basse.
But, although a catalogue consisting of Chaucer, Spenser, and
Beaumont is, at best, eclectic, Beaumont provides the link to the
stage as well as to dramatists of an earlier generation. Presumably Jonson leaves out the other prominent figures and conspicuous strains of English poetry, in particular Sidney and the turn-of-
the-century sonneteers, because their work is generically inappropriate to the Folio. Not surprisingly, Jonson ignores Shakespeare's sonnets in the eulogy; they were not printed in the Folio
and their reception in 1609 had been lukewarm. At the time it
would undoubtedly have seemed highly unlikely that the Shakespearean sonnets would have been remembered in the same way as,
say, *Astrophil and Stella*. Thus Jonson concentrates on considering
Shakespeare's dramatic poetry, and after promptly dropping Chaucer and the putatively misguided Spenser, his poem proceeds to a
careful list of modern and ancient dramatists.

Notably, the catalogue of Latin and Greek playwrights is sur-
rounded by English counterparts—Lyly, Marlowe, Kyd, and of
course Shakespeare—as if they were at once the origin and telos of
the ancient genealogy. Sara J. Van den Berg observes that this
catalogue omits English playwrights "who wrote in the more Jonsonian modes of satiric city comedy and neoclassical tragedy."[44]

44. Van den Berg, *The Action of Ben Jonson's Poetry*, p. 150.

The implication is that Jonson's list of dramatists is self-serving and tendentious in such a way as to protect his own literary genealogy from the advent of Shakespearean hegemony. Similarly, Evans warns that Jonson's "precisely calibrated praise, meant to reflect his careful judgment, also suggests the persistence of competitive feelings" (p. 212). But whether Jonson has in mind competition or self-preservation, his intention remains more or less ambiguous in the elegy. The most we can say is that, by casting a shade of doubt on Shakespeare's familial antecedents, Jonson perhaps hopes to cast similar doubt on the poet's literary bona fides.

To draw even such a tentative inference, however, requires the segregation of epideictic hyperbole from more truthful or substantiated appraisal. The hyperbole begins with the catalogue of ancient tragedians. Jonson summons them as if to testify to Shakespeare's comparable achievement:

> call forth thund'ring *Aeschilus,*
> *Euripides,* and *Sophocles* to vs,
> *Paccuuius, Accius,* him of *Cordoua* dead,
> To life again, to heare thy Buskin tread,
> And shake a Stage. (Ll. 33–37)

The halfhearted pun on the poet's name, "shake a Stage," is perhaps indicative of the sincerity of Jonson's appraisal of Shakespeare as a tragedian. Just as the pun improves by the end of the poem, becoming more aptly "shake a Lance" (l. 69), Shakespeare himself fares better as the catalogue of ancients progresses to comedy:

> when thy Sockes were on,
> Leaue thee alone, for the comparison
> Of all, that insolent *Greece,* or haughtie *Rome*
> Sent forth, or since did from their ashes come.
> Triumph, my *Britaine,* thou has one to showe,
> To whom all Scenes of *Europe* homage owe. (Ll. 37–42)

This praise has a more genuine ring than the list of tragedian-witnesses. In a way, the passage replaces hyperbole with a peculiarly Jonsonian kind of literary journalism. Shakespeare is credited as the leading comic light of the national literature, a fit opponent for the national literatures of Greece and Rome. This represents a high promotion for England; it is both a newsworthy report and a remarkably forceful accolade for Shakespeare. Yet all is

not precisely as it seems. If Shakespeare has brought English poetry to the forefront of international literary competition, then
Jonson is responsible for recognizing that fact. Indeed, Jonson
crowns Shakespeare with the poet's laurel. Calling for homage
from Europe for his rival, Jonson inverts what Richard Helgerson
has identified as his impulse to crown himself.[45] In a sense, and
despite his earlier claims not to be a herald, Jonson plays the role of
literary herald, the keeper of superior information by whose proc-
lamation Shakespeare is "created" the national poet.

The first seventeen lines of the poem contain an elaborate dep-
recatory justification of Jonson's own motives in writing the elegy,
a kind of vetting or credential check. The eighteenth line announces, "I, therefore will begin. Soule of the Age!" But, like the
pun on Shakespeare's name, this epithet improves as the poem
progresses. After Jonson's call for homage from "all Scenes of *Europe*," he declares that Shakespeare "was not of an age, but for all
time!" (l. 43). As though reassessing Shakespeare's value halfway
through the catalogue of ancient poets, Jonson awards the comedic
poet a new status: no longer merely the spirit of an age, Shakespeare now altogether transcends time. In proof of this, Jonson
thrusts Shakespeare into an originary scene of poetry, again with
the implication that especially in his socks Shakespeare transcends
literary genealogy.

> And all the *Muses* still were in their prime,
> When like *Apollo* he came forth to warme
> Our eares, or like a *Mercury* to charme!
> Nature her selfe was proud of his designes,
> And ioy'd to weare the dressing of his lines!
> Which were so richly spun, and wouen so fit,
> As, since, she will vouchsafe no other Wit. (Ll. 44–50)

Jonson invents an origin-fantasy for Shakespeare, casting him as a
prehistorical figure in the classical landscape of Helicon or Parnassus, during a period either before recorded time or before the
advent of the "drooping Stage" (l. 78). In this period "all the *Muses*
still were in their prime" (l. 44), and presumably Shakespeare had

---

45. See Helgerson, *Self-Crowned Laureates*, passim, but especially chapter 3. See also
Elsky, *Authorizing Words*, pp. 101–9, on Jonson's self-assigned role of "classical poet-
priest" who stands aside to judge the moral virtue of his subjects.

the advantage of their collaboration before their decline. He is, therefore, inseparable in Jonson's account from the source of age-less poetry. Moreover, just as Milton will later call Shakespeare "Nature's child," Jonson casts Nature as his proud parent and his exceedingly pleased audience. Amid the Muses, Apollo, Mercury, and Nature "her selfe"—a collocation of the elemental deities of poetic inspiration and design—Shakespeare makes his appearance as the earliest poet of the genre. But, in contrast, Jonson also suggests that Shakespeare is a culminating figure, the last word in comedy whose lines "richly spun" and "wouen so fit" have not been equaled in the time that has elapsed since that originary period on Parnassus. Ironically, of course, Shakespeare's time is the present moment of the Folio as well as that indefinable earlier time. One might think of his "lines" either as individual threads stitching epoch to epoch or as a direct linear connection from Jacobean England to the earliest period of poetic inspiration. Therefore, as source and ideal progeny rolled into one, Jonson's Shakespeare epitomizes a forged literary genealogy, at least insofar as he is a self-begotten original unconnected to the English family tree, a root that simultaneously tops its own upper branches.

Jonson emphasizes Shakespeare's unusual pedigree by discuss-ing his achievement in familial terms. He dismisses the Greek and Roman comedians because they do not belong to the correct family:

> The merry *Greeke*, tart *Aristophanes,*
> Neat *Terence,* witty *Plautus,* now not please;
> But antiquated, and deserted lye
> As they were not of Natures family. (Ll. 51–54)

If belonging to Nature's family provides the ideal pedigree, then Shakespeare, far beyond all earlier practitioners of the form, alone deserves the appropriate title of honor. But Jonson hastily notes that pedigree itself is not sufficient:

> Yet I must not giue Nature all: Thy Art,
> My gentle *Shakespeare,* must enioy a part,
> For though the *Poets* matter, Nature be,
> His Art doth giue the fashion. (Ll. 55–58)

At this pivotal juncture of praise, Jonson again refers to "gentle" Shakespeare, inevitably recalling the doubt surrounding his gentle status. There is the implication in Jonson's counterpoint that Shakespeare's gentility is derived from artifice rather than exclusively from nature. Moreover, if pedigree represents exceptional poetry in Jonson's metaphor of Nature's family, then the very notion of Shakespeare's literary pedigree is reversed and, perhaps, satirized in Jonson's well-known assertion that "a good *Poet's* made, as well as borne" (l. 64). Suddenly it seems that Jonson is "praising" Shakespeare's invented genealogy, in addition to his genuine and natural one.

The ambiguity of birth and merit continues. Although a good poet is made as well as born, Jonson chooses a metaphor of birth to describe poetic production itself:

> Looke how the fathers face
> Liues in his issue, euen so, the race
> Of *Shakespeares* minde, and manners brightly shines
> In his well torned, and true-filed lines. (Ll. 65–68)

The lines themselves, turned and filed, are transformed back into living "issue." As in a heraldic appreciation of a family, the final product of a forged genealogy is an identifiably noble "race" that extends from the past into the future. The emblem of that noble race is its coat of arms, or, more basically, the granting of the privilege to bear arms. Perhaps Jonson is alluding to the manufacture of arms in likening the poet to a blacksmith, a curiously rare image:

> he
> Who casts to write a liuing line, must sweat,
> . . . and strike the second heat
> Vpon the *Muses* anuile. (Ll. 58–61)[46]

---

46. There is a significant earlier use of a similar metaphor in Surrey's epitaph on Sir Thomas Wyatt:

> A head where wisdom mysteries did frame,
> Whose hammers beat still in that lively brain
> As on a stithy, where some work of fame
> Was daily wrought to turn to Britain's gain. (Ll. 5–8)

As will be recalled, Surrey also claims that Wyatt's poetry "reft Chaucer the glory of his wit." Both references, especially the stithy/anvil, encourage the speculation that Jonson consciously imitated Surrey's poem (and, perhaps, Surrey's literary relation to Wyatt). Possibly the image in both cases owes something to the story that Pythagoras invented music after listening to a blacksmith hammering on different anvils.

As Peterson observes, "[t]he muses have apparently lost their first freshness and acquired a workshop and tools" (p. 185). Vulcan and Minerva, as goddess of wisdom, have replaced Apollo and Mercury, just as labor seems to have supplanted, not leisure exactly, but the effortless inspiration of the aboriginal scene of poetry. Moreover, in considering Vulcan's forge, it is difficult to ignore that the divine smithy's most reknowned achievement, apart from the design of the trap for his wife and Mars, was the manufacture of splendid armor for epic heroes. Both Achilles and Aeneas had their arms from Vulcan, and Jonson's continual references to familial connection, to progeny, and to race seem to support the idea that, along with "true-filed lines," the "lance" that makes up half of Shakespeare's name in Jonson's pun might itself have been fashioned in the forge.

Extending the metaphor with a bit of critical *jeu d'esprit,* one can imagine that if the first heat of Vulcan's forge in classical literature produced Achilles' famous shield, then the second heat produced Aeneas's.[47] Perhaps Jonson intends to align the craftsmanship of the "made" poet with Virgil rather than with Homer, underscoring the superiority of imitation and patient skill in the production of a national literature. Indeed, Jonson might well have had Aeneas's shield in mind; as will be remembered, Vulcan depicts on Aeneas's shield the entire future of the Roman race. The shield contains the precise details of the success of Aeneas's issue, literally a true-filed line of descent.[48] Similarly, as Richard Peterson con-

47. In the "Ode to James, Earl of Desmond" (*Underwood,* 8:176), Jonson describes the forging of Aeneas's shield, naming the three cyclops responsible for the work:

> Let *Brontes,* and black *Steropes,*
> Sweat at the forge, their hammers beating;
> *Pyracmon's* houre will come to give them ease,
> Though but while mettal's heating:
> And, after all the *Aetnean* Ire,
> Gold, that is perfect, will out-live the fire.
> For fury wasteth,
> As patience lasteth,
> No Armour to the mind! (ll. 40–48)

48. See R. D. Williams, *The Aeneid of Virgil,* 2 vols. (New York: St. Martin's Press, 1972), 2:8, ll. 729–31: "Talia per clipeum Volcani, dona parentis,/miratur rerumque ignarus imagine gaudet/attollens umero famamque et fata nepotum." The phrase "second heat" might also be a more or less humorous reference to Vulcan himself. When Venus very seductively asks him to make armor for Aeneas, Vulcan becomes inflamed, as always, with an immortal passion that races like fire in the marrow of his bones: "ille repente/accepit solitam flammam, notusque medullas/intravit calor et labefacta per ossa

cludes, "in creating his 'living line' Shakespeare simultaneously creates a race of poetic children, *simulacra* of his own mental features, . . . and an array of tiny lances—appropriate progeny for Shake*speare,* alluding also to Vulcan's skill at making arms and Minerva's traditional attribute of warlike spear" (p. 189). That Shakespeare is at once the smith and the bearer of the arms adds a further twist to Jonson's metaphor, strongly implying that Shakespeare forges his own coat of arms in every poetic line of his that survives. We are inclined once more to call to mind the double sense of the verb "to forge," meaning either to manufacture or to counterfeit. Jonson's skepticism about the Shakespeare family descent seems to encourage this latitude of interpretation. Although Shakespeare himself may be a unique member of Nature's family, his poetic progeny can be only as "gentle" as a self-made, or "forged," genealogy permits.[49]

In conclusion, Jonson does not promote Shakespeare to parity with kings and queens, as he promotes himself in "To Penshurst." Rather, Shakespeare remains peripheral to the center of action, a source of entertainment like the Penates at Penshurst Place. After his death, the "Sweet Swan of *Auon*" continues to appear in London and still provides those flights of fancy "That so did take *Eliza,* and our *Iames*" (l. 74). But Shakespeare cannot be integrated into the social hierarchy; instead he becomes a part of the natural environment, a constellation in the "hemisphere" to be observed from a distance, as one observes the "heavens" of the stage. He may be "gentle Shakespeare" in the official documents, but, as we have seen, only Jonson can vouch for his poetic pedigree. Because Jonson is skeptical or ironical about Shakespeare's family genealogy, we tend to be suspicious of the literary genealogy he describes for his rival playwright. Shakespeare appears as both origin and telos in the line of comedic writing from the classical period up to the moment of the Folio. But his literary descent, in Jonson's rendering, has the aura of a forgery, as if it were an uneasy confection of natural sources and inflated, invented family ties.

---

cucurrit" (2:8, ll. 388–90). Presumably after satisfying this first heat of passion, Vulcan falls asleep. But he soon rouses himself and heads down from heaven to his workshop on Aetna, where he begins work on the armor; the "second heat" that night is the fire of the forge.

49. According to the OED, as early as the fourteenth century the verb "to forge" could mean to imitate fraudulently or to counterfeit. Shakespeare himself uses it in this sense in *Henry VI.* In addition, the phrase "to forge and file" is in use at the time.

FOUR

Repudiated Trees

Genealogy and Election in John Milton

What his breast forges, that his tongue must vent.
—*Coriolanus*, III. i

As I suggested earlier, Milton is the first great poet in the English tradition who is not a humanist in the conventional sense of that word. His project describes no urgency to rescue the classical literary past, whose existence intact Milton takes for granted. Milton betrays no lack of confidence about the literary genealogy he inherits. Rather, he sets out to overturn literary genealogy, to supplant his precursors, and to take his place as a full-fledged member of an indisputably bona fide family tree.

Milton's attitude toward literary genealogy should seem abundantly familiar to us, chiefly because we are all Miltonic in our perception of the literary past. Like Milton, but unlike Spenser or even Jonson, we have no doubt that there is something figuratively akin to a hereditary connection linking English poetry to the ancient *auctores* and English authors to each other. John Guillory has noted that Milton "often gravitates to the center of literary histories."[1] One of the reasons for this is that Milton was probably the first major author in the English tradition to treat the literary past as an historical entity. In contrast to his English vernacular predecessors, Milton exhibits negligible anxiety about the existence of a prior literary lineage. Rather, his most prevalent concern is whether, "long choosing, and beginning late," he will prove

1. J. Guillory, *Poetic Authority*, p. 68.

triumphant in an imaginative struggle with an extant literary past.

Harold Bloom suggests three levels of agon at work in *Paradise Lost:*

Milton's highly deliberate and knowingly ambitious program neces-sarily involved him in direct competition with Homer, Virgil, Lu-cretius, Ovid, Dante and Tasso, among other major precursors. More anxiously, it brought him very close to Spenser, whose actual influence on *Paradise Lost* is deeper, subtler and more extensive than scholarship so far has recognized. Most anxiously, the ultimate ambitions of *Paradise Lost* gave Milton the problem of expanding Scripture without distorting the Word of God.[2]

Bloom implies that Milton's success might be measured in his ability self-consciously to engage such an ambitious program. It is beside the point whether competitions of the Miltonic kind are ever won or lost. Poets transume their precursors, as Bloom and other critics have shown, although they may never conquer them. Similarly, it is irrelevant whether a literary genealogy actually existed for English poets before Milton or at the time Milton began writing in the 1630s. All that matters is that Milton treats the English literary family tree as an authentic extension of the classi-cal and Continental genealogies. Bloom emphasizes that "*Paradise Lost* distances itself from its most dangerous precursor, *The Faerie Queene,* for Spenser had achieved a national romance, of epic great-ness, in the vernacular, and in the service of moral and theological beliefs not far from Milton's own" (pp. 125–26). Although I do not entirely subscribe to the notion of a "dangerous precursor," nevertheless Milton's attitude toward Spenser proves that he re-garded the earlier poet as a legitimate member of a literary geneal-ogy stretching back to Virgil and Homer. When, in *Paradise Lost,* Milton out-descends or one-ups all previous poets by choosing an epic subject matter that antedates and produces the very notion of epic poetry, he works on the assumption of an existing literary genealogy that leads from Greek and Latin origins through the Continental languages up to and including the English vernacu-lar authors. This relatively untroubled assumption distinguishes

2. Harold Bloom, *A Map of Misreading* (New York: Oxford University Press, 1975), p. 125.

Milton inasmuch as his work does not struggle with literary descent as a subject matter. In contrast to Spenser and Jonson, he resists an equivocal attitude toward the English literary past and often seeks unblushingly to overcome his antecedents.

Thus, in a certain respect, Milton is the prize student of humanism, a member of a new generation imbued with pride in universal erudition as a cultural norm but spared the labor of reassembling the shredded textual history of the past. As a result, the concern of Milton's humanist predecessors with rescuing the past becomes, in Milton, a ruminative and often incensed concern with the future of the human family. William Kerrigan and Gordon Braden have pointed out that "[t]he ambition sanctified in *Paradise Lost* is the Renaissance fusion of parenthood with the humanist cult of literary immortality."[3] This fusion allows Milton to present his poetry as the embodiment of genealogy, or even its enactment, rather than as merely the vehicle of genealogical narrative.

Nevertheless, Milton repeatedly uses heraldic terminology as well as metaphors culled from blazonry. Apart from the actual appearance of heralds, such as the Herald of the Sea in *Lycidas,* we recall such complex and significant references as Satan's "ponderous shield," the "boastful argument" on the shields of the rebel host, the "glittering Tissues" of the angels that "bear imblaz'd/ Holy Memorials," and, as Satan descends toward the eastern Gate of Paradise in Book 4, the "Celestial Armory, Shields, Helms, and Spears." Despite the prevalence of heraldic terminology, however, in *Paradise Lost* Milton conspicuously rejects the traditional role of the herald. His rhetorical posture may seem reminiscent of Ben Jonson in Epigram 9, who declares "I a *Poet* here, no *Herald* am." But whereas Jonson intends to reject the use of poetry to praise particular genealogies, Milton repudiates the very notion of genealogical descent. For him, poetry—or at least the poetry of *Paradise Lost*—fulfills its appointed role only when it enacts the Protestant pattern of election and redemption.

For Milton, descent relations are less important than divine election. He is scornful of the heralds' duties as well as of their conclusions about aristocratic merit, but he does not offer his own alternative genealogies to replace theirs. In fact, Milton rejects the

3. William Kerrigan and Gordon Braden, *The Idea of the Renaissance* (Baltimore: Johns Hopkins University Press, 1989), p. 204.

notion of hereditary descent itself, regardless of whether it is literary descent, as in inherited heroic arguments, or social descent, as in heraldic description. Particularly in *Paradise Lost,* he makes continual reference to lines of descent that are corrupt, condemned, and in all ways fallen. For example, when Satan discovers his progeny, Sin and Death, Milton mocks both the rhetoric and the reality of descent. Sin exclaims:

> O Father, what intends thy hand, . . .
> Against thy only Son? What fury O Son,
> Possesses thee to bend that mortal Dart
> Against thy Father's head?[4]

The references to Father and Son, because they recall the divine relationship, seem to emphasize the incestuous corruption of this triad. Nevertheless, Satan's family remains intact even while the family members continue to fall away from God. Milton allows them to survive as a lineage, and, to a certain extent, it is as a lineage that they wreak destruction.

In contrast, Adam's line does not survive intact. In Book 11 of *Paradise Lost,* Michael begins his long narrative by telling Adam what might have been, specifically in terms of the Adamic genealogy:

> this had been
> Perhaps thy Capital Seat, from whence had spread
> All generations, and had hither come
> From all the ends of th'Earth, to celebrate
> And reverence thee thir great Progenitor.
> But this preeminence thou hast lost, brought down
> To dwell on even ground now with thy Sons. (Ll. 342–48)

By eating the forbidden fruit Adam has lost the chance to view the untroubled generations and to be revered as "thir great Progenitor." His eyes are closed as he views what might have been; when he opens them, the first thing that Michael shows him is the murder of Abel by Cain, proof of the corruption of Adam's line: "These two are Brethren, *Adam,* and to come/Out of thy loins" (ll. 454–55). The original sin corrupts Adam's offspring just as it condemns the

---

4. *John Milton: The Complete Poetry and Major Prose,* ed. Merritt Y. Hughes (New York: Odyssey Press, 1957), 2:727–30. All further quotations, except where noted, are from this edition.

notion of genealogy itself, leaving it to the family of Satan. As Michael will show, Adam's lineage can only be redeemed by the Son's sacrifice, which establishes an utterly new relationship between God and man. Genealogy is replaced by election and untroubled descent relations by a new combination of birthright with labor and merit.

The corrupted lines of descent are, for Milton, repudiated family trees. They often occur in literary contexts, cast as specious or even dangerous connections to the poetic genealogies of the past. But, ironically, Milton acknowledges these trees at the same time that he repudiates them. Indeed, with regard to literary descent, we might see Milton as a genealogist in the negative, simultaneously fixing and renouncing family trees in an effort to enclose and to overcome his literary antecedents.

TILTING FURNITURE

The proliferation of repudiated family trees is, perhaps, a measure of Milton's attempt to discredit the artifacts of genealogical descent. His poetry reveals an innovative, though now-familiar, ambivalence toward the conventional representations of descent and the traditional forms of description or praise of the elite. While heraldry is not entirely absent from his major poems, he nonetheless transforms the typical function of the literary herald. Because, for Milton, divine election is to replace descent relations, poetry cannot be merely a superior kind of heraldry. It must be more than the heraldic announcement of the relationship between God and man, no matter how exquisite that announcement might be.

Milton's resistance to heraldic description probably originates in his superseding of Spenser, who himself seeks to surpass heraldry with an exquisite and morally superior description of the courtly scene. In Book 5 of *The Faerie Queene*, Spenser acknowledges that his subject matter more properly concerns a herald than a poet:

> To tell the glorie of the feast that day,
>   The goodly service, the deuicefull sights,
>   The bridegromes state, the brides most rich array,
>   The pride of Ladies, and the worth of Knights,

> The royall banquets, and the rare delights
> Were worke fit for an Herauld, not for me. (5.3.3)

Apologizing for his usurpation of the herald's office, Spenser explains that his descriptive passages are necessary to the story he is bound to tell. So he borrows the "worke fit for a Herauld":

> But for so much as to my lot here lights,
> That with this present treatise doth agree,
> True vertue to aduance, shall here recounted bee. (5.3.3)

It is difficult to determine how much to read into Spenser's implicit contrast between the "True vertue" of *The Faerie Queene* and the kind of virtue typically narrated in heraldic treatises. Perhaps we are expected to recognize the familiar polarities of the Elizabethan debate over the competing values of merit and birth; or perhaps we should see in Spenser's usurpation of the herald's office a nascent doubt regarding the ultimate worth of genealogical determinism at court. In any case, Spenser demonstrates his superiority over the heralds, as well as over heraldic subject matter, by contrasting the moral intent of his narrative to the amoral content of typical heraldic treatises. He implies, therefore, that poetry is the better medium for the advancement of virtue.

C. S. Lewis claims that Spenser "dismisses the externals of a tournament as contemptuously as Milton."[5] In both poets the contempt for tournaments reflects a distrust of heraldry as an accurate representation of society, particularly insofar as heralds are ill-equipped to distinguish meritorious conduct. Spenser and Milton agree on the incompetence of heraldic narrative to establish a true list of virtuous nobles, but whereas Spenser simply takes the heraldic responsibilities upon himself and transforms for the better the herald's "worke," Milton overtly challenges the purpose of heraldic narrative. The clearest evidence of Milton's challenge appears in the introduction to Book 9 of *Paradise Lost:*

> If answerable style I can obtain
> Of my Celestial Patroness, who deigns
> Her nightly visitation unimplor'd,
> And dictates to me slumb'ring, or inspires
> Easy my unpremeditated Verse:

5. Lewis, *The Allegory of Love,* p. 329.

Since first the Subject for Heroic Song
Pleas'd me long choosing, and beginning late;
Not sedulous by Nature to indite
Wars, hitherto the only Argument
Heroic deem'd, chief maistry to dissect
With long and tedious havoc fabl'd Knights
In Battles feign'd; the better fortitude
Of Patience and Heroic Martyrdom
Unsung; to describe Races and Games,
Or tilting Furniture, emblazon'd Shields,
Impreses quaint, Caparisons and Steeds;
Bases and tinsel Trappings, gorgeous Knights
At Joust and Tournament; then marshall'd Feast
Serv'd up in Hall with Sewers, and Seneschals. (9.33–38)

Milton is emphasizing the contrast between the offices of poet and herald. Milton's criticism of previous epic poetry, one he will reiterate by condemning particular literary family trees throughout *Paradise Lost,* effectually casts as mere heralds those earlier poets who wrote "hitherto the only Argument/Heroic deem'd." The introduction aligns prior epics with heraldry, simultaneously repudiating the heroic poetry of the past as well as the heraldic occupation. Included in this repudiation would be Spenser, who, though he himself rejects heraldry as insufficient to recount "True vertue," nevertheless adapts his poetry to sing the praises of the men and women he considers to belong to the aristocracy.

To the contrary, Milton's poetry is itself part of the aristocracy he creates. In essence, Milton promises in the introduction to Book 9 that there will be no distinction between genealogy and the proper subject of heroic song. Just as the shift from rescuing the past to assuring the future transforms Milton into a different kind of humanist, it also makes him immeasurably more than a typical herald narrating a family history, even if that history, like Spenser's, is a revised and morally inspired narrative. Milton's poem is not meant "to dissect" or even to describe the past in a typical manner, whether epic or heraldic. And Milton does not arrogate a herald's power or privilege to himself, chiefly because a herald's power is descriptive. Throughout *Paradise Lost,* along with a good deal of scorn for the nostalgic conventions of chivalry associated with heraldry, lurks the suggestion that poetry is an embodiment or enactment of meritocracy (or election) rather than merely a description of supposedly heroic conduct.

On the surface, Milton intends his contempt for the traditional subjects of "Argument Heroic." But the introduction also serves as a job description (and a condemnation) of the herald's duties, which, beginning in the twelfth century, were primarily a means of distinguishing among the "gorgeous Knights" at tournaments and jousts. Heralds often provided prose and even verse narrative descriptions of "emblazon'd Shields,/Impreses quaint, Caparisons and Steeds," and their records eventually became not only a way of distinguishing among individual knights but also the official means of tracing aristocratic descent. But the early Tudor heralds, such as Thomas Wall and Sir Thomas Wriothesley, had a difficult time; the Heralds' Charter of Incorporation had been revoked by Henry VII and was not reestablished until 1555, though Henry VIII had instituted periodical Heraldic Visitations. Thus heraldry lay for more than half a century beyond the pale of officialdom, during what was arguably one of the most significant periods in the formation of English society. Without a sponsoring government, the Tudor heralds kept their books privately, apparently biding their time until the records they managed to protect would be recognized as unique and invaluable tools for entrenching an aristocracy. Their hour soon arrived. Under Elizabeth the legitimation of family lineage became exceedingly important, and the heralds gained professional prestige, power, and influence, and, probably, affluence in the form of bribes from aspiring gentry. Anthony Wagner suggests that it was "the Visitation work of the sixteenth and seventeenth centuries that made English heralds . . . professional genealogists. In the earlier stages much of their work was romantic and amateurish—some indeed fraudulent."[6] Despite continued accusations of fraudulence, even among succeeding heralds, by Milton's time heraldry had coalesced as the fully institutionalized source of information on the family trees of the Jacobean aristocracy.

6. Anthony Wagner, *Heralds and Ancestors* (British Museum Publications, 1978), p. 32. See also J. F. R. Day, "Primers of Honor: Heraldry, Heraldry Books, and English Renaissance Literature," *Sixteenth Century Journal* 21 (1990), p. 95; and Day's "Venal Heralds and Mushroom Gentleman: Seventeenth Century Character Books and the Sale of Honor" (Ph.D. dissertation, Duke University, 1985).

Presumably, as a revolutionary and a defender of regicide, Milton had contempt for titles of honor. His political posture, though not precisely egalitarian in our sense of the word, reflects antipathy to the prevalent seventeenth-century ideals of blooded aristocracy. In *The Readie and Easie Way to Establish a Free Commonwealth,* for instance, Milton strongly rebuts the notion of monarchy. His argument includes a contrast between the free commonwealth he envisions and the monarchical court he rejects.

And what government comes nearer to this precept of Christ than a free commonwealth, wherein they who are greatest, are perpetual servants and drudges to the public at their own cost and charges, neglect their own affairs, yet are not elevated above their brethren, live soberly in their families, walk the streets as other men, may be spoken to freely, familiarly, friendly, without adoration? Whereas a king must be adored like a demigod, with a dissolute and haughty court about him, of vast expense and luxury, masks and revels, to the debauching of our prime gentry, both male and female. (P. 885)

Although Milton clearly condemns the "dissolute and haughty court" attendant on a king, he seems to accept the existence, and even the value, of "prime gentry." His objection is that, in a monarchy, the gentry is transformed for the worse by the system itself; he expressly rejects "the multiplying of a servile crew, not of servants only, but of nobility and gentry, bred up then to the hopes not of public, but of court offices, to be stewards, chamberlains, ushers, grooms even of the close-stool" (p. 885). This statement is not a rejection of nobility per se, but instead a revaluation of the duties and privileges of nobles. Milton's example of how bad things can get is the French court of his day, "where enticements and preferments daily draw away and pervert the Protestant nobility" (p. 885).

Milton is particularly concerned to champion a policy that would prevent a restoration of the monarchy and, at the same time, would also avoid "a licentious and unbridled democracy" (p. 890). He recommends a "perpetual senate," a grand council chosen for life, and points out that this governing body would be "the whole aristocracy immovable" (p. 889). To some extent, his plan merely supplants the notoriously dissolute Caroline aristocracy with a public-minded Protestant elite. And the grand council is a tribute to the notion of *primus inter pares,* as Milton's proposed method of choosing this perpetual senate demonstrates:

Another way will be to well qualify and refine elections, not committing all to the noise and shouting of a rude multitude, but permitting only those of them who are rightly qualified to nominate as many as they will; and out of that number more judiciously, till after a third or fourth sifting and refining of exactest choice, they only be left chosen who are the due number and seem by most voices the worthiest. (P. 891)

This utopian plan brought criticism from contemporary critics who sought free elections and who had more faith in an enlarged Parliament than in Milton's senate. But, as Stanley Stewart has noted, "Milton appeals to history to disprove the notion that, in practice, oligarchies ('great men') were more inclined to excess than 'the common sort.' "[7] In all likelihood it would be impossible to implement such a judicious "sifting and refining of exactest choice" as Milton has in mind; Stewart remarks that "Milton's *'Utopia'* does not burden itself with too much thought of the practical world" (p. 216). Nevertheless, Milton's profoundly Platonic faith promises a just, if elitist, ruling few. He rejects popular rule, yet neither an episcopacy nor an aristocracy of blood satisfies his ideal of aristocratic government. In fact, the treatise later calls for "domestic suffrages" (p. 897) and other governmental policies more recognizable as modern democratic institutions.

Milton's idea of "exactest choice" in part grows out of the venerable debate regarding the value of merit over birth, a debate that Milton directly addresses in *Paradise Lost.* God's supreme flattery when the Son volunteers to sacrifice himself is to declare him more than merely well-born:

> Because thou hast, though Thron'd in highest bliss
> Equal to God, and equally enjoying
> God-like fruition, quitted all to save
> A world from utter loss, and hast been found
> By Merit more than Birthright Son of God,
> Found worthiest to be so by being Good,
> Far more than Great or High. (3.305–11)

7. Stanley Stewart, "Milton Revises *The Readie and Easie Way,*" *Milton Studies* 20 (1984), p. 216. See also Hugh M. Richmond, *The Christian Revolutionary: John Milton* (Berkeley and Los Angeles: University of California Press, 1974), as cited by Stewart.

Milton's God, and of course Milton's poem, here seem to fore-shadow the language of Milton's precursors. Milton revives the issue of merit and birth that was so popular in the Elizabethan and Jacobean courts, as if at once to challenge its origins and to surpass earlier English poets. One recalls, for instance, Ben Jonson's fas-cination with the meanings of the word "great," as in "To Pens-hurst," where the word twice implies excess and twice suggests a commendable condition. As Milton well knew, taking up the same contrast between goodness and greatness, the concept of "good" in the judgment of God far surpasses any such judgment among mere humans. Or we might hear in Milton's line "By Merit more than Birthright Son of God" an echo of Lear's intention to extend his largest bounty "Where nature doth with merit challenge" (I.i.55). But Milton's passage offers a superior, and anterior, model. Even if Lear were sane, his bounty could not hold a candle to God's, nor could his relatively paltry show of gratitude compare to God's willingness to spare the world his wrath. And neither Cordelia's merit nor her martyrdom is equal to the Son's originary merit and paradigmatic martyrdom. She dies without gaining the throne she deserves. The Son, on the other hand, dies precisely in order to inherit (or reinherit) the throne of heaven.

Milton's scene is also an abdication scene, though the Son is simultaneously a ruler and the courageous offspring of a ruler. As God explains, the Son was "Equal to God, and equally enjoy-ing/Godlike fruition," but he "quitted all" for the sake of human-ity. Yet his reward for this sacrifice seems to be almost exactly what he abdicates. In contrast to Cordelia, the Son is a successful martyr to royal prerogative, so that, as if in oblique challenge to Lear's pathetic impotence regarding Cordelia's fate, Milton's God can promise that "thy Humiliation shall exalt/With thee thy Manhood also to this Throne" (3.313–14). And, because Milton's story antedates all other stories, the Son is also the genealogical origi-nal from which later martyrs, including Cordelia, derive and devi-ate. Thus, typically, Milton surrounds his poetic predecessors, his poem appearing as the culmination of the debate over merit and birth and, at the same time, as the original inspiration of that debate.[8]

8. David F. Turk suggests that Milton's conception of the Son's merit reflects the radical viewpoint of the period: "The radicals also pointed out that Christ is a son of God

Yet, although Milton's presentation of the debate over merit and birth is progressive, his goal of selecting, rather than inheriting, an aristocracy is neither patently new nor especially insurrectionary. Even in the sixteenth century, when the urgency to prove noble lineage reached fanatical proportions, there was sufficient resistance to the hegemony of birth to produce a number of ingenious arguments on the origins of nobility. We need only adduce the proliferation of books and treatises on nobility and gentry to conclude that the previously unimpeachable status of noble birth undergoes some revision in Elizabethan England: among many others there are, for example, *The Boke of Noblenes* translated by John Larke (1550), Lawrence Humphreys's *The Nobles* (1563), John Heywood's *Of Gentlynes and Nobility,* and Richard Barkley's *Discourse on the felicitie of man* (1603). The popularity of translations from the Italian, such as Annibale Romei's *The Courtier's Academie* (trans. John Kepis, 1598) or Giovanni Battista Nenna's *Nennio, or a Treatise of Nobilitie* (trans. William Jones, 1595), perhaps indicates the Elizabethan attempt to find alternative criteria—that is, intellectual achievement as opposed to genealogy—with which to define nobility.[9] As William Jones phrases it in *Nennio:* "For we are not able to comprehend what aid this Nobilitie . . . may bring us: for as much as it neither bringeth wisdome, nor knowledge, incomparable gifts, which are sent from God, neither doth it make us more just, or more prudent, which are qualities that consist in the soule."[10] The contention that "wisdome" and knowledge rather than peerage are "sent from God" adumbrates Milton's political ambition to determine a peerage based on wisdom and knowledge. A form of *Nennio's* challenge, with Puritanism added, becomes the foundational social principle of *The Readie and Easie Way.*

---

through his own merit. . . . Thus Milton's Son is neither co-eternal nor co-essential with the Father; He is a created Son of God, but both merit (his obedience to the Father's will in redeeming mankind) and his birthright (he fully expresses the image of the Divine and thus is called 'the only begotten Son of God'; and as the word and effectual might of the Father, he created all things) entitle him to be anointed head of all the sons of God." See "Joint Heirs with Christ: John Milton and the Revolutionary Sons of God" (Ph.D. diss., New York University, 1989), p. 261.

9. For a learned contemporary discussion of genealogy, see John Selden's *Titles of Honour* (1614).

10. Giovanni Battista Nenna, *Nennio, or a Treatise on Nobility,* trans. William Jones (1595); introduction Alice Shalvi, Renaissance Facsimile edition (Jerusalem: Israel Universities Press; London: H. A. Humphrey Ltd., 1967), p. 66.

But, more than a theory of nobility, Milton's aim to establish an aristocracy based on merit is a reharnessing of the heraldic office in the service of election rather than blood descent. His opinions echo the wide-ranging political and social commentary found in sources as diverse as Shakespeare's *All's Well That Ends Well* and amateur heraldry books like John Ferne's *The Blazon of Gentrie* (1586) and Edmund Bolton's *The Elements of Armorie* (1610). Shakespeare's King of France defends the commoner Helena by declaring that "Honours thrive/When rather from our acts we them derive/Than our foregoers" (2.3.135–37). In a similar manner, John Ferne unambiguously dismisses blood as the sole criterion for determining a nobleman. The incredulous Torquatus (a Knight) interrogates Paradinus (the "Heerald") in Ferne's dialogue:

TORQ. Doth your Heraldrie preferre a new Gentleman, which by the industrie of his vertues, hath obteyned to be so called, before those of auncient bloud?
PARAD. Yea, certesse, as touching the verie essential substance of nobleness.[11]

Ferne continues in an even more definitive vein, asserting that "nobleness apprehended by proper merit, is far more excellent then the gentleness of linage and bloud, not beautifyed with vertue" (p. 20). A genealogy of lowborn but virtuous nobility follows, including Saul, David, Hostilius, Praemislaus, Tamburlaine, Theodosius, and Marius. Moreover, for Ferne, as for other amateur writers on heraldry, the notion of nobility as moral virtue garners considerable support from the story of Christ. As J. F. R. Day observes in a recent discussion of heraldry books, we are "frequently reminded that Our Lord was a gentleman, at least on one side of His family."[12] And, as I noted in the Introduction, Ferne's version of Christ's noble line contains the suggestive allegory of the Evangelists as heralds: "[O]ur Sauiour and King Jesus Christ: a Gentleman of bloud, according to his humanitie, Emperour of heauen and earth, according to his deitie, euen as his holy Herealdes, (the Euangelistes) haue out of the infallible recordes testified the same" (p. 3). There may be a bit of sarcasm in Ferne's reference to "infalli-

---

11. Ferne, *The Blazon of Gentrie*, p. 18.
12. Day, "Primers of Honor," p. 101. Day also notes the prevalence of "the medieval trope of Christ as Knight which the heraldry books adumbrate" (p. 102).

ble records," since it was well known even at the time, "holy Herealdes" apart, that the heraldic records were often inflated, forged, or inaccurate for other reasons. But the upshot of the lineage of Christ is that "his humanitie" and "his deitie" combine to make him a gentleman of blood.

Whether Milton ever saw *The Blazon of Gentrie,* he had probably come across examples of the rhetoric common to treatises on honor. The argued separation between nobility and high birth—in Shakespearean terms, between deeds and descent—would have served Milton in his diatribes against inherited monarchy. Further, Ferne's requirement that arms be awarded to the Doctor of Laws, specifically for the achievement of prudence and learning, would have suited Milton's agenda. Ferne asserts, "this spirituall Gentleman, hauing coat-armor deuised for him, I will place in the foremost rankes of gentleness, gotten by proper merit" (p. 32). This triumph of merit over birth, and indeed of bookish merit over soldierly achievement, echoes in Milton's plans to replace the haughty courts. As we noted above, Milton's solution to a monarchical government is an elite governing senate drawn from a select group of well-bred, educated Protestants. Their offices would, presumably, be "gotten by proper merit." Moreover, a meritorious aristocracy in the "foremost rankes of gentleness," a chosen gentry as permanent as the gentry of blood, would help to avert the dangers of a mobile democracy. Warning of the danger of rule by "the common sort," Milton recalls that Rome fell on bad times when the consuls—among them Marius, whom Ferne mentions as a lowborn "noble"—were "created plebeian, and the whole empire put into their hands" (p. 890). To "create" someone plebeian is heraldic terminology used in an unwonted, inverted way; usually the heralds, during their Visitations, created men nobles. Milton inverts the sense of the term to emphasize his resistance to "unbridled democracy": to create the once-elite consuls from the plebeian class, he is saying, is as dangerous as relying on a gentry of "new men" created by the heralds.[13] His use of the heraldic rhetoric is provocative. In a way, as his readers might have sensed, his

---

13. Again it is interesting to compare Ferne, who describes a Plebeian as one "whose byrth or condicion of life, is forbidden all honor, dignitie, or preheminence amongst us" (pp. 6–7).

intention seems to be to reassign the herald's role in the creation of an "immovable aristocracy."

Perhaps Milton's revised or corrected heraldry is clearest in his critique of chivalry and all that it entails in terms of the courtly ethic. As John Steadman suggests, all of Milton's major poems exhibit "the qualified rejection of the conventional heroic argument of warfare and its displacement (in whole or in part) by the ordeal of spiritual combat. This involves, with few exceptions, the substitution of dialectical process for the carnage of the battlefield or the dazzling farce of swordplay, and of right reason (or its specious counterfeit) for martial valor."[14] In *Paradise Lost* Milton rejects the typical values of the epic poet, heroic war and heroic love, values both the Elizabethan and the Stuart court clearly associated with aristocratic behavior. The displacement or substitution of the old epic valor not only transforms the notion of heroism but also prepares the way for a new panoply of epic heroes. According to Joan Malory Webber, "[p]atience and fortitude are the new epic virtues, and they are different, in Milton's mind, from self-control, because when well learned they do not require a holding back of unruly passion."[15] Thus the old martial heroes, all of whom might be characterized by their success or failure in controlling their excessive passions, become part of a rejected or renounced genealogy.[16] In effect, they disappear from Milton's account of true heroism in human history, as do the martial circumstances of their fame; in Webber's terms, "[t]he true heroism that is self-mastery and submission of oneself to life can be learned under any circumstances by a person who attends to inner rather than outer movements" (p. 127). The disappearance of battlefields and physical proving grounds signals the accompanying disappearance of tangible genealogical descent in the traditional sense. Rather than genealogy, Milton proposes election as the precipitating factor in the determination of true heroism.

We might say that *Paradise Lost* serves as the witness or even the enactment of divine election. Milton deliberately separates his epic

14. John M. Steadman, *Milton and the Paradoxes of Renaissance Heroism* (Baton Rouge: Louisiana State University Press, 1987), p. 173.

15. Joan Malory Webber, *Milton and His Epic Tradition* (Seattle: University of Washington Press, 1979), pp. 126–27.

16. On the heroic virtue, the active principle, *andreia* and *megalopsychia*, and particularly on the opposing principle of *sophrosyne*, see Helen North, *Sophrosyne*.

from past epics, thereby distinguishing his heroes and the new epic virtues they embody from the old martial patterns of passion, swordplay, and self-control. In a well-known passage describing the satanic forces, Milton recites a family tree of epic poetry from which *Paradise Lost* almost certainly does not stem:

> though all the Giant brood
> Of *Phlegra* with th' Heroic Race were join'd
> That fought at *Thebes* and *Ilium,* on each side
> Mixt with auxiliar Gods; and what resounds
> In fable or *Romance* of *Uther's* Son
> Begirt with *British* and *Armoric* Knights;
> And all who since, Baptiz'd or Infidel
> Jousted in *Aspramont* or *Montalban,*
> *Damasco,* or *Marocco,* or *Trebisond,*
> Or whom *Biserta* sent from *Afric* shore
> When *Charlemain* with all his Peerage fell
> By *Fontarabbia.* Thus far these beyond
> Compare of mortal prowess, yet observ'd
> Thir dread commander: he above the rest
> In shape and gesture proudly eminent
> Stood like a Tow'r. (Ll. 576–91)

The comparison of the heroes of these epics to Satan makes this a family tree to repudiate. Casting himself as a bit of a scolding literary genealogist, Milton implies that his epic belongs to another, unblemished lineage. According to Ferne, "Tully desired rather to be the first, then the last of his house" (p. 20), and Milton, too, seems to repudiate all that has gone before him. The twist, of course, is that Milton's epic, while refusing to be seen as a direct descendant of romance epics, is purportedly more ancient in subject matter than they are and therefore begets them. But Milton carefully dissociates his poem from the family tree of romance epic. His genealogy builds to an ominous literary crescendo with the image of Satan, who, in rising above his forces as high as a tower, promises to come crashing down and to bring Adam and Eve along with him. "[I]mplicit in the tower," Anthony Low notes, "is the threat of future disaster. Troy towers rise and fall; Babel is built and destroyed; cities reach their proud culminations and decay; Satan lifts himself up to be thrown down."[17] We might add to this

17. Anthony Low, "The Image of the Tower in *Paradise Lost,*" *SEL* 10 (1970), pp. 180–81.

list a particular kind of epic poetry. According to the inference we draw from Milton's literary genealogy, romance epic (including Homer, from which romances seem to descend in Milton's view) has raised itself to a proud literary eminence which, paradoxically, represents a decadence of Christian and heroic values.

Milton's genealogy of epics leaves out the *Aeneid,* which seems conspicuous by its absence. For some reason Virgil does not come under the same condemnation as the others in the passage in Book 1, though in the introduction to Book 9 Milton groups the subject matter of the *Aeneid* with those unfit for true heroic song:

> Sad task, yet argument
> Not less but more Heroic than the wrath
> Of stern *Achilles* on his Foe pursu'd
> Thrice Fugitive about *Troy* Wall; or rage
> Of *Turnus* for *Lavinia* disespous'd,
> Or *Neptune's* ire or *Juno's,* that so long
> Perplex'd the *Greek* and *Cytherea's* Son. (9.13–19)

In the contest of divine wrath, Milton trumps even Virgil. God's wrath is a more heroic subject matter than the wrath of Achilles, Turnus, Neptune, or Juno. But this direct comparison of the subject of *Paradise Lost* to that of the *Aeneid* only underscores the absence of Virgil's epic from the condemnatory list of epics in Book 1. It is difficult to explain Milton's apparent accommodation of the *Aeneid,* unless we can conjecture that his intention is to bracket Virgil as a worthy precursor, an "excepted Tree" in Milton's orchard of repudiated trees.[18]

In a sense, however, the idea of a worthy epic precursor to *Paradise Lost* is almost inconceivable. This is not to say that Milton does not acknowledge the greatness of past poets from Homer to Spenser nor that he is attempting to fashion an alternative family tree. To the contrary, Milton resists any explicit reference to the genealogy of *Paradise Lost,* presumably deeming that subject matter as well to be less heroic than the wrath of God and the fall of Adam. In a sense Milton transumes literary genealogy in the same way that, according to Bloom, "with *Paradise Lost,* Miltonic allusion is transformed into a mode of transumption, and poetic tradi-

18. Since "Th'excepted Tree" which Michael refers to in Book 11.426 is in fact the forbidden tree of Paradise, there is a certain irony in Milton's "excepting" Virgil from the genealogy of forbidden epics.

tion is radically altered in consequence" (p. 129). Whereas Spenser, especially in "Astrophel," takes literary descent to be a subject of his work, again and again Milton avoids the role of poet-as-herald or so singularly transforms it that heraldry is subsumed in poetry. And, just as Milton's transumptive allusion distances his later work from the "conspicuous allusion" of his early work, his references to heralds tend to underscore his distance from and his superiority to their conspicuous version of genealogy, both historical and literary.[19] For example, in Book 11, recalling the panoramic shields of Homer's and Virgil's heroes, Milton describes the martial conflicts of early civilization on earth. The passage is peppered with the rhetoric of chivalric encounters. Observing the scene, Adam sees "Concourse in Arms, fierce Faces threat'ning War" (11.641); the Giants "Part wield thir Arms, part curb the foaming Steed,/Single or in Array of Battle ranged" (643–44); the foraging bands take cattle and sheep as booty, and the shepherds flee when "With cruel Tournament the Squadrons join" (653). Milton's description emphasizes the needless slaughter, the pillaging, and the general strife of a military siege. Again the chivalric elements of conventional epic appear in a sharply negative light, retrogressive vestiges of "cruel Tournament."

At the center of his panorama, Milton places the heralds.

> In other part the scepter'd Heralds call
> To Council in the City Gates: anon
> Grey-headed men and grave, with Warriors mixt,
> Assemble, and Harangues are heard, but soon
> In factious opposition, till at last
> Of middle Age one rising, eminent
> In wise deport, spake much of Right and Wrong,
> Of Justice, of Religion, Truth and Peace,
> And Judgment from above. (Ll. 660–68)

The "scepter'd Heralds" convoke a meeting of worldly, warlike, and tyrannical enemies of God.[20] They represent prototypes of the

---

19. As cited by Bloom (p. 128), "conspicuous allusion" is Harry Berger's term for Spenser's allusionary practice: " 'the depiction of stock literary motifs, characters, and genres in a manner which emphasizes their conventionality, displaying at once their debt to and their existence in a conventional climate—Classical, medieval, romance, etc.— which is archaic when seen from Spenser's retrospective viewpoint.' "

20. In actuality God subverts the heralds' work. Unwittingly they announce the advent of Enoch, a type of Christ, who will represent peace rather than war. But the

royal heralds. It is possible to identify their "call" with a call to arms and to see them as harbingers of the "factious opposition" and of the hostility to Enoch. We recall that, in Milton's "On the Morning of Christ's Nativity," the absence of the call to arms betokens peace:

> No War, or Battle's sound
> Was heard the World around:
>> The idle spear and shield were high up hung;
> The hooked Chariot stood
> Unstain'd with hostile blood,
>> The Trumpet spake not to the armed throng. (Ll. 53–58)

If the trumpet spoke, it would announce war. But it is silent, and there is to be a "reign of peace" (l. 63). It is worth noting, moreover, that peace is signaled by the abatement of traditional heralds' work.

In *Paradise Lost,* Enoch is the one just man among the misguided councilors. Like Abdiel before him and Christ after him, he is denounced and set upon by a short-sighted throng. But Enoch is rescued from the "violent hands" by "a Cloud descending," an image reminiscent of Aphrodite's rescue of Paris on the Trojan battlefield. While the allusion constitutes an acknowledgment of Milton's epic predecessors, it also emphasizes the difference between Homer's heroes and Milton's. Paris effectively started the Trojan war; Enoch "spake" to end war. Enoch also antedates Paris, which makes Paris's entire battlefield adventure a copy of Enoch's, and Homer's account of it a later subject than Milton's. In fact, as elsewhere in *Paradise Lost,* Milton is scrambling his own literary genealogy so that his poem at times appears to be the origin of his precursor's. Arnold Stein has observed that "[o]ne of the great opportunities of the story is that it antedates all other stories, and therefore Milton's readers will find themselves often recognizing thoughts in a novel form, before they become original familiar quotations. Within the controlling perspective of time, not seldom the myth alluded to is still to be invented."[21]

---

connection of the trumpet and therefore the heralds to un-Godlike behavior is the main point of the passage.

21. Arnold Stein, *The Art of Presence: The Poet and 'Paradise Lost,'* (Berkeley and Los Angeles: University of California Press, 1977), p. 32.

Within the framework of *Paradise Lost,* Milton also alludes to and temporally scrambles the components of his own mythologies, as if eschewing a descriptive detachment of the poem from its subject matter. Thus, when Enoch stands up to speak, Milton deliberately echoes the end of the simile from Book 1 that compares Satan to the heroes of chivalric epics. Just as Satan "above the rest/In shape and gesture proudly eminent/Stood like a Tow'r" (ll. 289–91), so we find Enoch "rising, eminent." The rhetorical similarity appears to bring Enoch into uncomfortably close association with Satan, even though, in point of fact, Enoch is the type of Satan's resister and opposite. Milton's lesson in doubling the description—one of his favorite lessons on the subject of postlapsarian rhetoric—is that fallen language cannot even be trusted to remain fallen. Its negative connotations can be reversed or effaced or redeemed, just as the human family is redeemed by the intervention of the Son. Enoch presages Christ in history, yet if we recognize that Milton is polarizing identical language, then Enoch already embodies a restored humanity. The future (Christ) begets the past (Enoch), which, in addition to demonstrating the theory of Christian typological fruition, also constitutes a reappraisal of genealogical order. Thus the language of *Paradise Lost* does not announce or narrate a string of origins as conventional genealogical poetry or heraldry would. Instead, the language is itself a demonstration or embodiment of the architecture of a family tree that surrounds earthly time, revising our notions of order to suit the pattern of Christian redemption.

Once again we see that the key enabling fact is not descent in the traditional sense. Rather, divine election gives both the poem and its heroes—identifiable by their "new epic virtues" of self-mastery and submission to life—a place in providential history. The condemned family trees that Milton's heroes inherit, such as those whose roots are Satan-Sin-Death or Adam-Abel/Cain, are not replaced in *Paradise Lost* by redeemed trees or alternative lineages. We might recall, for instance, the difference between Racine's biblical tragedy, in which the hereditary line leading toward Christ is at stake, and the succession of chosen heroes. Both these traditions of descent (in the Old Testament to David) and election are present in the Bible, but Milton stresses only one. Indeed, for Milton, the relationship of father to son adumbrates and imitates (again, either authentically or speciously) the relationship of God to man. Man does not *descend* from God but is elected by Him, on the strength of merit as well as birthright, to the status of a son. And, because conventional heraldic versions of genealogy would be inappropriate to represent the relationship of God to the elect, Milton devises a poetry that is itself a rhetorical embodiment, rather than a mere description, of the enabling fact of divine election.

LYCIDAS AND ENGLISH ELEGIAC TRADITION

One of Milton's most famous repudiated genealogies occurs in *Lycidas,* in his denunciation of the bishops. Much of the poem is cast in genealogical terms, and, significantly, the swain's actual communication with figures of the classical and Christian past is set in motion by the "Herald of the Sea." While Triton conventionally proclaims Neptune's decrees on a conch shell, in *Lycidas* his presence seems also to herald the beginning of a genealogical panorama.[22] The family of nature includes "Sleek *Panope* with all her sisters" (l. 99) and "*Camus,* reverend Sire" (l. 103). Similarly, the family of the Church descends from the Pilot of the Galilean lake, whom Rosemond Tuve calls "the great symbolic father image."[23] Mary Christopher Pecheux has observed that this sternly patriarchal figure, often identified as Saint Peter, might be seen as a composite of Christ, Moses, the Prophets, and the Apostles.[24] The errancy of the bishops would then seem particularly egregious insofar as they are direct descendants of a divine, and diverse, ecclesiastical lineage. But there is more to the genealogical implications of *Lycidas,* and to the presence of a herald, than a diatribe against episcopacy and a corrupt clergy. There is, as well, a revision of English literary genealogy in the poem, perhaps the first such unambiguous revision in English poetic tradition.

In discussing *Lycidas* we often speak about the three kinds of pastoral to which the poem responds: classical, Hebraic, and New

22. On Triton, see Hughes, *John Milton,* p. 110, n. 873 to *Comus.*

23. Rosemond Tuve, *Images and Themes in Five Poems by Milton* (Cambridge, Mass.: Harvard University Press, 1962), p. 80.

24. Mary Christopher Pecheux, "The Dread Voice in *Lycidas,*" *Milton Studies* 9 (1976), p. 235. See also Stanley Fish, *"Lycidas:* A Poem Finally Anonymous," in *Milton's 'Lycidas': The Tradition and the Poem,* ed. C. A. Patrides (Columbia, Mo.: University of Missouri Press, 1983), p. 333.

Testament. We adduce a venerable poetic genealogy to the poem, "ranging it," as James Holly Hanford suggests Milton himself does, "with a long and not inglorious line of elegiac utterances, from Theocritus and Virgil to Edmund Spenser."[25] But the later English poets of that "not inglorious line" have received comparatively little attention, and Milton's conscious engagement of English poetic tradition and English literary genealogy is often neglected in discussions of *Lycidas*. This neglect is unfortunate, because Milton's relation to his English predecessors in the elegiac genre provides evidence of his urgent need to dissociate himself from poets who die young and unfulfilled, such as Philip Sidney and Edward King. Milton aligns himself with Spenser—and especially with the Spenser of "Astrophel"—who offers a disapproving opinion of the young knight whose death is caused by the subordination of poetic talent to the active life. And we learn from Milton's detachment of himself from those who die before fulfilling their promise that *Lycidas* not only embodies a finely spun synthesis of pastoral traditions, but also contains Milton's first tentative swerve away from the English canon as he perceived it.[26]

At the time of its publication *Lycidas* was something of a generic anachronism.[27] Pastoral poetry, as Milton well knew, invoked a literary relationship with Virgil and with Virgil's innumerable imitators. Among those imitators—indeed the most recent of them—were the Elizabethan and Jacobean elegists, the all but anonymous contributors to commemorative volumes for Philip

25. James Holly Hanford, "The Pastoral Elegy and Milton's *Lycidas,*" in Patrides, *Milton's 'Lycidas,'* p. 32.

26. Perhaps even the first words of *Lycidas* are a reference to its revisionary connection to modern English-language history. David S. Berkeley first noticed (*Notes and Queries* 201 [1961], p. 178) that the repetition of "Yet once more" and "and once more" recalls Hebrews 12:22–28. But the words "Yet once more" may also be intended to recall the most renowned (and notorious) Englishing in Protestant history. The phrase occurs prominently in William Tyndale's second preface to his 1534 translation of the New Testament: "William Tyndale, Yet Once More To the Christian Reader." See *Tyndale's New Testament*, ed. David Daniell (New Haven: Yale University Press, 1989), p. 13. The connection to Tyndale, and to Tyndale's mission, would have been attractive to Milton. Not unlike Tyndale's Bible, Milton's elegy ventures to rescue the message of Christ from a corrupt, exclusionary episcopacy and, at the same time, to renovate the English poet's relation to the recent literary past.

27. See, for example, Ellen Zetzel Lambert, *Placing Sorrow*, p. 145: "when Milton comes to the pastoral elegy in 1637 he comes to a form that is already passe, if not yet an anachronism."

Sidney, Elizabeth I, and Prince Henry. Critics have long acknowledged resonances of the English elegiac tradition in *Lycidas*. Few,
however, have ventured to characterize Milton's attitude toward
his national elegiac antecedents. Yet, I think that *Lycidas* contains
Milton's studied and selective rejection of the aims, ambitions,
and laudatory vision of prior English elegy writers. The poem
provides a measure of the effect of Milton's response to his English
predecessors on his sense of the literary past, and on ours as well.
Unlike his immediate predecessors, Milton does not seem at all
concerned about forging a believable English genealogy. For Milton, as for no other poet before him in England, there develops
instead an overt dialectic between poetry and poetic descent. He is
the first poet of the English tradition to regard his literary descent
with untroubled confidence and also the first poet actively (and
megalomaniacally) to try to overgo his predecessors. Our own
present sense of literary history tends to be Miltonic in this respect.
Rather than doubting the existence of a literary past, we, like
Milton, are more inclined to seek vulnerabilities in our supposedly
legitimate forebears and to engage those forebears in a kind of
dialectical renunciation.[28] Milton's swerve (if I may call it that)
should be of particular interest, especially insofar as swerving away
from the influences of the past has become so much a part of our
epistemological framework, whether we are analyzing the swerve
from precursor poets or, in Nietzsche's sense, from history itself.

Though Sidney and Milton are rarely mentioned in the same
breath, I would like to explore the extent to which *Lycidas* might
be seen, in part, as a rejection of Sidney's literary family tree.[29]

28. In his discussions of the poetic agon, Harold Bloom has articulated this notion
most extensively, though Bloom occasionally suggests that poets before Milton regarded
the past in a similar way to Milton. See, for example, his recent *Ruin the Sacred Truths*
(Cambridge, Mass.: Harvard University Press, 1989). My own sense is that English
writers before Milton were more concerned with rescuing their supposed genealogical
origins than with evading or repudiating them.

29. As I noted in the Introduction, I should add the disclaimer that I do not mean to
suggest that Milton would have rejected a specific lineage of poets by name (such as the
Sidney-Greville line or the Spenser-Drayton line), but that the posture of rejecting a
literary lineage grows out of his response to Sidney's elegists. Perhaps coincidentally, the
first words of the poem, in addition to recalling Tyndale, also echo an elegy on the death
of Sidney's sister, the Countess of Pembroke, which begins "Yet once more, my Muse."
The elegy appeared in *Songes and Sonnettes of Uncertain Auctours*. See Scott Elledge, *Milton's
"Lycidas": An Introduction to the Criticism* (New York: Harper & Row, 1966), p. 251.

Perhaps by looking at the poem with this rejection in mind we might begin to get a sense of Milton's version of the literary past as well as a sense of the source of our own version. More sustainedly than the earlier poems and academic exercises, *Lycidas* reveals strong evidence of Milton's astonishingly modern (and inevitably familiar) attitude toward the poetic past.

Milton's *Lycidas* appeared in an academic miscellany, *Justa Edouardo King,* published by Cambridge in 1638. The convention of publishing volumes on the occasion of important deaths had begun in England in the mid-sixteenth century with the elegies for Bucer and Brandon. But the practice had been entrenched chiefly by the elegies for Philip Sidney in 1587, in which year both Oxford and Cambridge produced volumes.[30] Alberta Turner claims that by Milton's time the appearance of elegiac volumes had become a familiar enough occurrence:

[B]eginning with the death of Elizabeth, both universities established a firm habit of publishing miscellanies to celebrate major events of joy or sorrow in the royal family. By 1625 Cambridge had also published miscellanies on the death of Sir Philip Sidney in 1587, and on the death of William Whitaker, Regius Professor and Master of St. John's, in 1596. But apparently no other Cambridge miscellanies on private persons were published before Milton entered college. Oxford, on the other hand, had published at least fourteen volumes on subjects ranging in importance from a Christ Church undergraduate to Bodley, Camden, and Saville.[31]

Participation in commemorative volumes had a twofold purpose: it was both an honor for young poets and an opportunity for them to advertise themselves—not as poets necessarily but as members of an elite group of putative mourners, which gave them visibility on the patronage market.

The volume for King does not seem to have been an exception. In format and editorial composition it is reminiscent of many of the volumes produced by Oxford and Cambridge between the

30. For discussion of the earliest volumes of English elegies, see Pigman, *Grief and the English Elegy;* also, particularly for the Sidney, Elizabeth, and Henry elegies, see Kay, *Melodious Tears.* Anne Prescott suggested to me that there was a French precedent or parallel with an English connection: the mid-century *Tombeau* for Marguerite de Navarre with poems by the Seymour sisters.

31. Turner, "Milton and the Convention of the Academic Miscellanies," pp. 86–87.

death of Sidney and the death of Edward King. But while one is hard-pressed to locate a concern in Milton about being seen among the correct mourners, he no doubt felt a certain collegiate piety. It is worth recalling, moreover, that as a young man he was still flirting with courtly patronage. Although Scott Elledge has suggested that "Milton's reputation as a poet in Christ's College was probably great enough to insure his being asked to contribute," we should not assume that Milton's contemporaries would have thought that he could do more for King than the King family connections could do for him (p. 165). Yet it is not necessary to be cynical about Milton's reasons for contributing to *Justa Edouardo King.* In the mid-1630s, he had already written *Arcades* and had managed, probably through the efforts of Henry Lawes, to receive the commission for *Comus* and to have the masque presented at Ludlow Castle. His literary career was beginning in a manner tried and proven in the courtly milieu. At the time, Ben Jonson, perhaps the most successful of the court poets, was the unofficial poet laureate of England, a prominent figure in London, and a likely example for a young *erudito*. (Jonson in fact died in the same month as King.) Milton's first literary successes remind us more of the fulfillment of Jonson's ambitions than of the ambitions we have come to associate with Milton. *Arcades, Comus,* and *Lycidas* were surprisingly indebted to the kinds of courtly patronage that seem incommensurate with the regicidal author of the antimonarchical tracts.

The model of Jonson notwithstanding, *Lycidas* more closely identifies Milton with his "original," Spenser. We might even say that *Lycidas* is Milton's "Astrophel." Although James Holly Hanford, in his important essay on the pastoral elegy and *Lycidas,* does not see much internal resemblance between the poems, there is at least a superficial comparison to be made.[32] As Joseph Anthony Wittreich suggests, "*Lycidas* asks to be viewed within the context of the whole pastoral tradition, but even more requires assessment in terms of Spenser's *The Shepheardes Calender* and *Astrophel.*"[33] Both

32. See Hanford, "The Pastoral Elegy and *Lycidas,*" in Patrides, *Milton's 'Lycidas,'* esp. p. 55.
33. Joseph Anthony Wittreich, "From Pastoral to Prophecy: The Genres of *Lycidas,*" *Milton Studies* 13 (1979), p. 60. Wittreich also points out that *Lycidas* would not be what

"Astrophel" and *Lycidas* lament the loss of a poet "untimely cropt"; and, for King as for Sidney, poetry was secondary to a Protestant mission. The *Astrophel* collection is not an academic volume, but it is nevertheless comparable to *Justa Edouardo King;* the *Astrophel* collection itself probably owes much to the academic volumes produced by Oxford and Cambridge to honor Sidney. Like Spenser, who evidently had a hand in the editing of *Astrophel*, Milton, as Michael Lloyd pointed out some time ago, responds to other poems in the King collection, "organizing not only his own themes but those of the book as a whole."[34] Milton's contemporaries would probably have identified pastoral poetry itself with Sidney and Spenser and with the antiquated Elizabethan versifying they represented. As Donald M. Friedman suggests, "Milton's choice of genre must have appeared to his contemporaries an act of conscious archaism, or an instance of his scholarly traditionalism, or even a kind of homage to his 'teacher,' Spenser."[35] In recalling, or engaging, the entire tradition of pastoral elegy, Milton would have been unlikely to overlook Spenser's pastoral lament for Sidney.

Related to the engagement of pastoral tradition is Milton's somewhat iconoclastic project in *Lycidas* to revise the hagiographic practices of the academic miscellanies. And, in this too, it made sense for him to look to the elegies for Philip Sidney. Besides Elizabeth, the only figure in England whose death produced an equivalent amount of public mourning was Prince Henry, for whom scores of elegies were published after his unexpected death in 1612. In fact, Sidney and Henry are often compared as patrons and soldiers, and both their deaths struck great sorrow into the heart of the nation. Henry's elegists implicitly compared their subject to Sidney, particularly in the conceit that Henry combined equal parts of wisdom and martial prowess. As Christopher Brooke puts it:

---

it is "without the model of generic confrontation provided by the juxtaposition of *Colin Clouts Come Home Againe* and *Astrophel* in a single volume" (p. 62), but he does not elaborate on this confrontation.

34. Michael Lloyd, *"Justa Eduoardo King," Notes and Queries,* n.s., 5 (October 1958), p. 434.

35. Donald M. Friedman, *"Lycidas:* The Swain's Paideia," *Milton Studies* 3 (1971), p. 20.

His time by equall portions he diuided
Between his bookes and th'exercise of warre:

. . . .

That Mars with wit's Minerua seem'd at iarre,
Which of them both should sway his princely hart,
Th'one with sterne armes; the other with milde art.[36]

The truth of the matter, however, was that Henry paid little attention to books, though he supported and encouraged a number of writers, not least among them Walter Ralegh. Rather, this picture of a young knight torn between Mars and Minerva has its roots in the verse tributes for Sidney. Even Anne Bradstreet in her elegy for Sidney (written incidentally in 1638, the same year *Lycidas* was published) says "*Mars* and *Minerva* did in one agree,/ Of Arms and Arts he should a pattern be."[37] As I noted in an earlier chapter, a common theme of the Sidney elegies is the combination of the Alexander-like figure and the figure of the poet, what Dominic Baker-Smith terms a "Scipionic resolution of conflicting talents."[38]

The analogy between Sidney and Henry made by Henry's elegists draws in part on religious and political connections between the two men with respect to their constituencies. Moreover, while the yoking of opposing qualities is not uncommon in elegiac writing, the model of Scipionic resolution is one that Milton can translate in *Lycidas* into his own peculiar cosmological terms. We can imagine no greater resolution of opposites than "*Lycidas,* sunk low, but mounted high" (l. 172). Of course, it is possible that, rather than a resolution, being sunk low but simultaneously mounted high constitutes an irresolvable Christian paradox, calling for faith instead of synthesis. But, nevertheless, King's strange state at the end of the poem suggests that the opposites have been reconciled, and that Milton, resolving nothing so mundane as war and wisdom, has exceeded such predecessors as Sidney's and Henry's elegists. Taking his cue from these less inspired predecessors, or less ambitious Christians, Milton further attempts to reconcile the

36. Quoted in Elkin Calhoun Wilson, *Prince Henry and English Literature* (Ithaca, N.Y.: Cornell University Press, 1946), p. 140.

37. *The Poems of Anne Bradstreet,* ed. Robert Hutchinson (New York: Dover, 1969).

38. We recall Ralegh's description of Sidney as "*Scipio, Cicero,* and *Petrarch* of our time," and John Palmer's neo-Latin elegy entitled "Martis et Mercurii Contentio."

inveterate elegiac conflict between untimely loss of life and the gain of a permanent afterlife.

That Milton knew a number of the elegies for Henry is well established.[39] It is unlikely, however, that he ever intends to acknowledge a poetic debt to Drummond or Sylvester or Wickham, as he might if he were alluding to Virgil, Ovid, or perhaps even Spenser. Rather, we are led to suspect that Milton's several echoes of the elegies for Henry are intended to lionize King as a royal prince, not to flatter Henry or his elegists. Is it going too far to conjecture that Milton is likening King to a prince of the blood? If not, then we have found another example of Milton's blazonry, a writerly means of promoting a Protestant minister to the highest imaginable social status. Indeed, he seems almost to emphasize the conjunction of King's attributes as a poet and a Protestant martyr with Henry's attributes of nobility and national importance, as if purposely to create a figure reminiscent of Sidney. Without stretching the resemblance too far, we might see *Lycidas* as, at once, Milton's memorial for a dead poetic contemporary and his farewell to a prominent poetic precursor.

The young Milton could not have avoided Sidney's literary presence. The *Arcadia* was the most popular book of the seventeenth century, and, while Sidney's militant Protestantism may have been consonant with the Good Old Cause and with the struggles against Laudianism, Milton nevertheless damns Sidney's writing with faint praise. His several mentions of the *Arcadia,* though respectful enough, leave little question as to his opinion of the literary tradition with which Sidney is identified. Castigating the dead Charles in *Eikonoklastes,* Milton notes that the king took his famous prayer in captivity from "no serious book, but the vain amatorious poem of Sir Philip Sidney's *Arcadia*—a book in that

---

39. E. C. Wilson suggested that "[a]s Milton worked at *Lycidas* his capacious memory surely embraced many verses from the 'various quills' that had sounded at Cambridge and everywhere else for lost Meliades [Prince Henry]. He would hardly have composed forgetful of the fullest elegiac chorus of his lifetime" (p. 151). Wilson particularly notes verbal echoes of William Drummond's "Mausoleum," in which we find a remembrance of flowers similar to Milton's; also, Joshua Sylvester's "A Funeral Elegie" includes a tirade against the corrupt clergy, and Henry Wickham's neo-Latin tribute contains a reference to "Chame pater," a possible source for "*Camus,* reverend Sire." Although these examples might be seen as relatively commonplace motifs, I am inclined to think, following Wilson, that Milton was familiar with the elegies for Henry.

kind full of worth and wit, but among religious thoughts and duties not worthy to be named, nor to be read at any time without good caution, much less in time of trouble and affliction to be a Christian's prayerbook" (p. 793). We should, of course, recall the occasion of this statement and recognize that Milton's polemic calls for his condemnation of Sidney's poem as inappropriate.

Yet it is inevitable that we should also consider Milton's opinion of Sidney apart from the pressures of religious conflict with the royalists. As a poet, Sidney was an icon of an aristocratic, chivalric tradition from which Milton hoped eventually to detach himself. We see evidence of his effort at detachment in his politicized sonnets (which overturn an amatory tradition), and we remember that in *Lycidas* Milton disparages those shepherds who would "sport with Amaryllis in the shade."[40] In addition, there is evidence in the famous catalogue of epic poems in Book 1 of *Paradise Lost*, where Milton charts his epic course away from previous romance epics, specifically the Italian strain. But before he can separate himself from chivalric Homer, the poets of the papist Continental tradition, or his English sonneteering ancestors, he must take an intermediate step, graduating himself from traditional pastoral to epic. As critics have all but suggested, the ending of *Lycidas* represents this intermediate step.

As if measuring a newly acquired distance from traditional funeral elegy, Milton invokes chivalric epic in the last eight lines of the elegy. It is ironic that Milton, who is otherwise intent on distancing himself from romance conventions, should choose romance epic as the form of his farewell to traditional pastoral. But, as will be remembered, he had not yet given up the idea of writing an Arthuriad, and, at this stage, he probably considered the romance format to be a morally acceptable choice. On the other

---

40. This is not to say that the lines about Amaryllis and Neaera refer to the composition of erotic poetry, as has in the past sometimes been asserted. In Edward Le Comte's explanation, "The context not only does not encourage, it does not permit so oblique an interpretation. . . . Amaryllis and Neaera stand for the natural pleasures. They are symbolic, but they are also girls" (*Yet Once More: Verbal and Psychological Pattern in Milton* [New York: Liberal Arts Press, 1953], p. 6). We might surmise, however, that Amaryllis and Neaera are symbolic of the nymphs and maidens Spenser describes in "Astrophel," where Sidney is the charismatic center of a pastoral court replete with the kind of amatory capriciousness that the Milton of *Lycidas*—as opposed, perhaps, to the Milton of the Italian sonnets or "Elegia Prima" and "Elegia Septima"—would definitely condemn.

hand, he may well have had doubts about the romance even at this
early stage. Nevertheless, he finds a formal reference to it helpful.
In the *coda* or *commiato,* we hear a distinctive change in perspective
that is probably meant to align Milton with Spenser, who also
skipped from pastoral to epic without stopping at georgic, as the
constraints of the Virgilian *rota* normally demanded:[41]

> Thus sang the uncouth Swain to th'Oaks and rills
> While the still morn went out with Sandals gray;
> He touch't the tender stops of various Quills,
> With eager thought warbling his *Doric* lay:
> And now the Sun had stretch't out all the hills,
> And now was dropt into the Western bay;
> At last he rose, and twitch't his Mantle blue:
> Tomorrow to fresh Woods, and Pastures new. (Ll. 186–93)

Peter Sacks points out that "[n]ot only is this coda written in *ottava
rima,* the form of Italian epic, but it reads precisely like those
moments in epic poetry when the narrator follows the speech of a
protagonist with 'Thus sang. . . .' It is as though Milton, in
ending and describing his elegy, has already entered an epic."[42] We
might add, moreover, that Doric music (as in the Doric lay that the
swain is warbling) was played to give courage for battle and would
be more appropriate for epic than for pastoral poetry.[43]

It is difficult to deny the rhetorical change, particularly the note
of farewell in the coda. Yet it is not a farewell only to Lycidas, now
planted as the "Genius of the shore" (l. 183). We hear as well a
farewell to *otium,* to tears, and to the foregoing elegiac strain.
During the apotheosis of the dead King, a few lines earlier while
the swain is still singing, Milton describes the newly rehabilitated
Lycidas entertained "by all the Saints above,/In solemn troops" (l.
179). Already there is a martial cast to the imagery, now that the
shepherds, told to "weep no more" (l. 165), have faded from the
poem (though they were probably never "in" the poem except as

---

41. There is considerable critical debate about the last eight lines of the poem. See
Stewart A. Baker, "Milton's Uncouth Swain," *Milton Studies* 3 (1971), pp. 35–53; and
also Stanley Fish, in Patrides, *Milton's 'Lycidas,'* p. 336ff., for a discussion of the controversy surrounding the so-called new voice at the end of the poem.

42. Sacks, *The English Elegy,* p. 115.

43. Cf. *Areopagitica:* "No music must be heard, no song be set or sung, but what is
grave and Doric" (Hughes, ed., *John Milton,* p. 732).

generic fixtures). Moreover, the troops of saints surrounding Lycidas proceed to "wipe the tears for ever from his eyes" (l. 181), a reference to the descent of the heavenly Jerusalem in Revelation (21:4): "And God shall wipe away all tears from their eyes. And there shall be no more death, neither sorrow neither crying, neither shall there be any more pain, for the old things are gone" (Tyndale, p. 388). Not only does this reference invoke Christ's triumph over death, justifying the command to the shepherds to stop their weeping, but the wiping away of the tears also foreshadows the change in perspective of the coda. It is well known that in the sixteenth and seventeenth centuries the word "tear," as in the "melodious tear" of line 14, could also mean song of mourning; collections of funeral elegies were often called *lacrymae*. In addition to wiping away the sorrow for his own death from King's eyes, the saints might also be wiping away the preceding commemorative elegies of *Justa Edouardo King,* the swain's pastoral verses, and even pastoral elegy itself as a rite of passage. Presumably, the saints are preparing the way for the incipient epic poet of the coda.

But the coda does not merely herald a new kind of poetry. I would like to suggest that it also deliberately responds to the closing lines of John Gifford's "Lycidas," a pastoral eclogue for Sidney that had appeared in *Peplus illustrissimi viri D. Philippi Sidnaei supremis honoribus dicatus,* the New College, Oxford, commemorative volume published in 1587. Milton could easily have had access to the volume, and although "Lycidas" is not such an unusual name for shepherds in Renaissance pastoral, it is rare enough that we might take a second look at the coincidence. For instance, the name "Lycidas" originally belonged to a Theocritan goatherd and was later used by Virgil in Eclogue IX.[44] But no-

44. In Theocritus VII, in a friendly singing match, Lycidas sings a propemtikon, a song for the safe arrival of his "beloved" Ageanax. In Theocritus XXVII, which is probably apocryphal, Daphnis claims that his father's name was Lycidas. And in the fragmentary Bion II, known as "Achilles among the Maidens" and probably also apocryphal, Lycidas sings the tale of how Achilles hid among the women, learning to spin and wearing a kerchief on his head, so as not to be recruited by the Achaeans to fight in the Trojan war. See *The Greek Bucolic Poets,* trans. J. M. Edmonds (Cambridge, Mass.: The Loeb Classical Library, Harvard University Press, 1938). For evidence of the use of the name Lycidas among later poets, including Virgil, Horace, Sannazaro, and Amalteo, see

where in Theocritus or Virgil does Lycidas die, and it is worth noting that both Milton and Gifford assign this particular name, not to their speaking persona, as Theocritus does, but to the deceased.[45] Gifford ends his poem in a conventional manner, with an apotheosis of his dead Lycidas:

> Nec te dum Eois lux aurea surgit ab oris,
> Hesperys nec dum Phoebus mergetur in undis,
> Effluere ex animis patiemur: te quoque nobis
> Arcadio dulcis resonabit fistula cantu.

Neither when the golden light of Eous [the morning star] rises on the shore, nor yet when Hesperus or Phoebus is sunk down in the waves, will you be allowed to slip from our minds: and everywhere in Arcadia the flute will resound with our sweet songs to you.[46]

The similarity between Milton's and Gifford's endings is noticeable. (Gifford's rhymed Latin, by the way, occurs only in these final lines and maybe should remind us that Milton also changes his rhyme scheme at the end of his poem.) Both poems close with descriptions of morning and evening to demonstrate the totality of the elegiac singer's preoccupation. Gifford's speaker—called Damoetas, another Theocritan name, like Milton's "old Damaetas"—promises not to forget his dead friend day or night, whether Hesperus (the evening star) or Phoebus (the sun) is visible. In the same way, Milton uses the sun and the advent of evening to emphasize the length of the swain's lament in the coda. But he goes

---

J. W. Hales, "The Name Lycidas," *Folia Literaria* (New York, 1893); and Sir John E. Sandys, "The Literary Sources of Milton's *Lycidas*," *Transactions of the Royal Society of Literature*, ser. 2, 32 (1914), pp. 233–64.

45. Warren B. Austin contends that the Latin elegies of Giles Fletcher the elder, in particular *Adonis* and the tribute to Walter Haddon, exerted a certain influence on *Lycidas*. See his "Milton's *Lycidas* and Two Latin Elegies By Giles Fletcher, the Elder," *Studies in Philology* 44 (1947), pp. 41–55. Fletcher's *Adonis* is an elegy for Clere Haddon, a promising young Cambridge student who drowned, like Edward King, on the threshold of his career; Fletcher's speaking persona takes the name Lycidas in *Adonis*, though Austin points out that "no significance attaches to Fletcher's use of the not uncommon pastoral name" (p. 44 n. 8). Both elegies were published in the same volume in 1571, and, given Milton's interest in the elder Fletcher's other writings, it does not seem unlikely that he would have been familiar with the elegies.

46. For Gifford, see *Peplus*, in Colaianne and Godshalk, *Elegies for Sir Philip Sidney*, p. 29. Where appropriate, I have tried to use the language of Milton's *Lycidas* in the translation.

further than Gifford and uses the cycle of day and night also to describe Lycidas's earthly demise and heavenly survival. This passage comes a few lines before the coda:

> So sinks the day-star in the Ocean bed
> And yet anon repairs his drooping head
> And tricks his beams, and with new-spangled Ore
> Flames in the forehead of the morning sky. (Ll. 168–71)

We should probably hear the echo of "tricks his beams" in the penultimate line "twitch'd his mantle blue."[47] The sun, rising and setting, sinking and "repairing" his drooping head, is meant to be a reflection of the dead Lycidas himself, "sunk low, but mounted high." Like Gifford, Milton can use the diurnal cycle to testify to the unbroken extension of sorrowful feeling. But he goes Gifford one better, adding to the image of permanent lamentation a superbly Miltonic conceit—the mirror image of permanent mourning, for Lycidas's "upright heart and pure," is an utterly comprehensive, and of course eternal, survival.

Ultimately, then, Milton's coda diverges from Gifford's more traditional farewell. In heightened elegiac voice, Gifford's Damoetas vows that, from dawn to dawn, all Arcadia will resound with songs to Lycidas. We can expect from Gifford's shepherds a continual celebration of the past and of their love for their dead peer. In striking contrast, Milton's swain (assuming it still is the swain) promises nothing whatever to his dead friend in the future. His song had done its duty: it has celebrated the resurrection of Edward King on the shore, and tomorrow the shepherd-poet will employ his pipe in "fresh Woods, and Pastures new." This disengagement from the elegiac subject is a generic rarity. Set beside Gifford's ending, Milton's separation of his swain from the swain's elegiac subject must strike us as deliberately revisionary, either explicitly of Gifford or of the traditional ending.

At first, as an academic elegist, Milton identifies himself with the generation of elegists who, in canonizing Sidney, so influenced

---

47. Discussing the pronoun of the penultimate line, Edward Tayler makes the point that "'Sun' is in fact the nearest grammatical antecedent of the 'he' in 'he rose,' and of course we know that the sun drops into the western bay only to arise at last attired in its blue mantle." See "*Lycidas* in Christian Time," in Patrides, *Milton's Lycidas*, pp. 317–18. Tayler also notes that, in the early seventeenth century, *its* was still considered "rather colloquial or newfangled" as the genitive neuter.

both English elegiac tradition and English literary history. Milton's *Lycidas,* especially considering its anachronistic genre, seems a prime example of Sidney's literary heritage. But in the closing lines of *Lycidas,* Milton disentangles his poem from the genealogy that leads from Gifford's pastoral to the elegies for Prince Henry. He prepares to diverge not only from pastoral poetry in general but also from his hereditary link to English literary descent.

Milton's reason for severing or attempting to sever his link with the past is telling. If we acknowledge the similarity among Sidney, Prince Henry, and Edward King, in particular their untimely deaths as poets (Sidney and King) and noblemen (Sidney and the Prince), then we must also recognize why Milton would want to dissociate himself from them as they appear in their elegies. Anthony Low calls attention to the resemblance between Milton's Lycidas and Virgil's Marcellus, the last of the shades that Anchises shows Aeneas in the underworld. Marcellus, Low reminds us, is the "nephew and son-in-law of the Emperor Augustus, who will show great promise as a youth but will unhappily die young. . . . Like Lycidas, Marcellus is a young man whom fate cuts off just as he is about to fulfill his promise, thus depriving his country of his goodness and his abilities. Unlike Lycidas, a potential poet and priest, Marcellus would have led the Romans in government and war; otherwise the two are similar in their unfulfilled promise."[48] Marcellus resembles an earlier version of Prince Henry, who also would have led his country in government and war. The combination of the two, Lycidas and Marcellus, once again produces a figure irresistibly reminiscent of Sidney, a poet and Protestant activist who, had he lived and thrived, might also have led the country from a high government post.

But the salient unifying factor among these elegiac subjects is their unfulfilled promise. As poets, priests, and soldiers, each of them failed to consummate his hopes and to fulfill the hopes of others for his success. Because of this failure, Marcellus, Sidney, Henry, and King could have represented to Milton a doomed line of descent, an abhorrent heredity of failure which a poet as conscious of his own promise as Milton—and as ambitious both as a

48. Anthony Low, "Some Notes on *Lycidas* and the *Aeneid,*" *English Language Notes* 13 (March 1976), p. 175.

poet and as a man—could not help but avoid. Of particular interest to Milton would have been the failures of poets to fulfill the promise of their talent. He would have recognized in the two examples to hand, King and Sidney, that a species of activism scuttled both men's careers, though, certainly, Sidney's campaign in the Netherlands is not the equivalent of King's journey to Ireland. Later in his life Milton articulated the sentiment we sense in his genealogical dissociation from those who squander their gifts in dangerously active pursuits. As will be recalled, in Sonnet 19 Milton meditates uneasily on "that one Talent which is death to hide," finally concluding that his talent will be more productively realized with patience than with the haste of those who "post o'er Land and Ocean without rest." (Perhaps in this context one could more fittingly compare Sidney in the Netherlands and King on the Irish Sea.) Milton was already blind and approaching fifty when he wrote Sonnet 19, so the question of unfulfilled promise, though it may resonate with the same question in *Lycidas,* has a somewhat different force. Nevertheless, one senses a continuity of sentiment between the two poems. The memorable statement that "They also serve who only stand and wait" might be seen as a deliberate repudiation of those servants of God, poets especially, who fail to serve through poetry because they refuse to wait, as Milton waits, for poetic talent to reach maturity.[49]

Not surprisingly, Spenser's "Astrophel" contains a precedent for Milton's dissociation from poets who are too impatient to wait for the fruition of their poetic gifts. This precedent is important because it allows Milton actually to imitate Spenser in rejecting the hereditary line that descends from Sidney. At Sidney's expense, Spenser directly addresses the question of activism and the poet's responsibility to his verse. It will be recalled that "Astrophel" is divided roughly into four stages: Astrophel's early life in "bowre and hall"; his falling in love with Stella; his foreign military exploits and consequent death in battle; and the mourning of Stella, her death, and the general lament. Although Spenser is superficially complimentary to Stella—"A fairer star saw neuer liuing eie" (l. 57)—she should probably be seen as the instigator of Astrophel's reckless adventurism. Stella's unresponsiveness to As-

---

49. Le Comte, in *Yet Once More,* points out that Milton's anxiety about beginning late appears in very similar form in *Eikonoklastes* and *Paradise Lost* (p. 102).

trophel's poetic piping, which had already won him the hearts of "Full many Maydens" (l. 37), drives Astrophel to attempt other means to impress her:

> To her he vowd the seruice of his daies,
> On her he spent the riches of his wit:
> For her he made hymnes of immortall praise,
> Of onely her he sung, he thought, he writ.
> Her, and but her, of loue he worthie deemed,
> For all the rest but little he esteemed. (Ll. 61–66)

In the relentlessness of this list we detect Spenser's contempt for Astrophel's obsession. And, in addition to the implicit condemnation of Stella's hard-heartedness, there is the hint of Spenser's disgust with the young shepherd-poet (and maybe with Sidney himself) who transforms "the riches of his wit" into baubles to impress his mistress.

As will be remembered, the crux of the poem is Astrophel's abandonment of poetry, which, for all intents and purposes, gets him killed. His active deeds, denigrated merely as performances meant to catch Stella's eye, replace his verses. The implication is that Astrophel should not have been so hasty; his verses, Spenser insists, were not vain, because verses in general are not vain. Astrophel simply should have had more faith in his abilities. His patience presumably would have been recompensed, if not by Stella's devotion (which seems to be of dubious value to Spenser), then by the appropriate development of his poetic talent.

Although Spenser blames Astrophel's impatience on unrequited love, there is enough meditation on timeliness and untimeliness in the elegy to provide Milton with a powerful argument for standing and waiting. Spenser is not recommending a cessation of all active pursuits, nor does he suggest that poetry flourishes in a social vacuum. Rather, he demonstrates, albeit somewhat heavy-handedly, that a lack of faith in one's own verses might lead to the tragedy of unfulfilled promise. The dilemma, which Spenser does not resolve in "Astrophel," is how to distinguish patience form paralysis, and, moreover, how to determine when to stop waiting. This dilemma of course reflects the Renaissance debate surrounding the virtues of the *vita contemplativa* versus the *vita activa,* a debate that Milton seems uniquely competent to resolve.

Indeed, despite Milton's concern about his too-slowly-fulfilled promise, which is added to his anxiety regarding productivity, we nevertheless find an exceptionally mature rhetorical self-possession already taking shape in *Lycidas*. For example, Milton's poem does not dissolve into permanent and universal lamentation, as is conventional in funeral elegies of the period. Instead, the lamentation ends (a rare enough occurrence in elegiac verse), and, moreover, the mournful speaker is replaced by a speaker who seems both self-possessed and full of a sense of promise rather than burdened by loss and permanent sorrow. Of course, there is a confusion in the last eight lines between the new voice of the coda and Milton himself. Although I do not wish to suggest that the coda is precisely autobiographical, there is some benefit derived from recognizing Milton's deliberate confusion—or, perhaps, fusion—of voices at the end of the poem. We discover that the uncouth swain has been singing only after he stops; the question of who is singing, or narrating, the coda remains open, to some extent, though the need to identify the speaker is made more urgent by the precedent of the "Thus sang."

The temptation is strong to replace the self-possessed speaker with Milton himself and to inflate his abandonment of the locale to include Milton's poetic ambitions. Thus the very reason for the elegiac mood, Lycidas's unfulfilled promise, is overturned or co-opted by Milton's implied move toward epic poetry and his abandonment both of the swain's song and of the bucolic setting. The connection between the two passages on the morning and the evening stars emphasizes the lack of sorrow. And Milton's implied dissociation from Lycidas might be seen as a kind of protection against the eventuality that Milton's own slow beginning could be interpreted, whether he lives or dies, as "yet once more" an example of unfulfilled promise.

For the most part, Milton's anxiety grows out of his preoccupation with the proper moment to begin, to leave the cloister, and to join the fray. The conflict between unripeness and ripeness, between readiness and prematurity resounds especially in the early poetry. Significantly, one of Milton's first efforts to address the subject of ripeness, Sonnet 7, has an English precursor in Sidney's *Astrophil and Stella,* Number 23. Sidney, too, expresses concern about his own delay, identifying the gap between ambition and fruition:

The curious wits, seeing dull pensivenesse
   Bewray it selfe in my long setled eyes,
   Whence those same fumes of melancholy rose,
With idle paines, and missing ayme, do guesse.
Some that know how my spring I did addresse,
   Deeme that my Muse some fruit of Knowledge plies:
   Others, because the Prince my service tries,
Thinke that I thinke state errours to redresse.
   But harder Judges judge ambition's rage,
Scourge of it selfe, still climing slipprie place,
Holds my young braine captiv'd in golden cage.
O fooles, or over-wise, also the race
   Of all my thoughts hath neither stop nor start,
   But only *Stella's* eyes and *Stella's* hart.[50]

Sidney touches on all the endeavors in politics and poetry for which he eventually becomes so famous. The speaker attempts to justify the time he is now squandering in contemplation after a very active and scholastically productive youth. Pretending to identify the source of his pensiveness, he denies that his muse is occupying his mind with "some fruit of Knowledge." Similarly, he feigns indifference to serving the Prince, claiming, in playful contradiction to his well-known courtly ambitions, that he has no interest in redressing "state errours." Only Stella is on his mind, and her eyes and heart are both his ambition and his judge.

Although Sidney does not address ripeness precisely, his defense of inactivity adumbrates Milton's anxious reflections on lost time in Sonnet 7. But whereas Sidney looks to Stella's eye for his inspiration and his final recompense, Milton looks to God's:

How soon hath Time, the subtle thief of youth,
   Stol'n on his wing my three and twentieth year!
   My hasting days fly on with full career,
   But my late spring no bud or blossom show'th.
Perhaps my semblance might deceive the truth,
   That I to manhood am arriv'd so near,
   And inward ripeness doth much less appear,
   That some more timely-happy spirits endu'th.
Yet be it less or more, or soon or slow,
   It shall be still in strictest measure ev'n

50. *The Poems of Philip Sidney,* ed. William Ringler, p. 176.

> To that same lot, however mean or high,
> Toward which Time leads me, and the will of Heav'n;
> All is, if I have the grace to use it so,
> As ever in my great task-Master's eye.

While Sidney implies that his spring is over, Milton speaks of his "late spring," still full of the promise of bud and blossom. Both poets protest that their appearances to the outer world are not reliable measures of their inner thoughts and potential. The difference between the poems, however, lies in the difference between the kinds of things hidden from view. Astrophil's apparent pensiveness conceals a secret love, which, according to the strictures of the Petrarchan tradition, is successful and pure precisely because it will not come to fruition. In contrast, Milton's late spring conceals growth toward an "inward ripeness," an already-blossoming fruition that waits only for the right time to be revealed. The unattainable Stella holds Astrophil's "young braine captiv'd in golden cage." But Milton holds himself back, putting his faith in "Time" as an extension of his "great task-Master." Milton revises the notion of love, in the conventional genre of love poetry, from a posture of frustrated paralysis to one of patience and prudent attendance on God, who is a more appropriate source of inspiration and judgment than a coy lover.

Just as in the sonnets Milton revises the Petrarchan, or Elizabethan, notions of love and delay, in *Lycidas* he revises the notion of poetic genealogy as it had until then appeared in elegiac pastoral. Milton's poem is itself a literary genealogy. We are conscious of a generational progression when the swain's song is replaced at the end of the elegy by a third-person observation. That this observation also implies generic progress increases our sense that Milton is writing a genealogical descent into the literary relations of the poem.

Unlike many pastoral elegies, *Lycidas* contains no shepherd-peers. The swain sings to no one in particular, as if he were alone in the field; his command to the shepherds to "weep no more" is directed to the abstract notion of Lycidas's weeping comrades, wherever and whoever they might be. There is no sense of a face-to-face encounter or even of a specific audience in *Lycidas*—except, of course, the intended audience of readers at Christ's College. In contrast, we recall that Spenser's shepherd deliberately identifies his audience in the introductory verses of "Astrophel":

> Hearken ye gentle shepheards to my song,
> And place my dolefull plaint your plaints emong.
>
> To you alone I sing this mournfull verse,
> The mournfulst verse that euer man heard tell. (Ll. 5–8)

In addition, Spenser concludes his elegy with an openness and comradely suffering contrary to the isolation of Milton's swain. The shepherd's description of his personal grief becomes a description of the grief of the bucolic population:

> And euery one did make exceeding mone,
> With inward anguish and great griefe opprest:
> And euery one did weep and waile, and mone,
> And meanes deviz'd to show his sorrow best. (Ll. 205–8)

We can only guess at the "meanes deviz'd" to show sorrow. But even the idea that the mourners behaved in certain unusual ways, that they acted out idiosyncratic demonstrations of grief, underscores the poem's movement from internal, private suffering to external, communal (and perhaps conventional) mourning. Paradoxically, at the moment that Spenser calls attention to "inward anguish" he describes outward and public displays of grief.

Milton concludes his poem in exactly the opposite mood. It is true, of course, that Spenser's "Astrophel" is the first poem in a commemorative collection and therefore might be seen to introduce the various "meanes deviz'd" of the following poems. *Lycidas*, on the other hand, is the last poem in the King collection, and there is evidence that Milton knew it would be the last. Thus it would perhaps have been appropriate for the swain to finish alone, to sign off, as it were, from the preceding elegies. But there is more to the swain's isolation than merely the ending of *Justa Edouardo King*. Milton emphasizes the sense of ending first with the narrator's detachment from the swain, the "Thus sang" perspective, and then with the swain's intended abandonment of the bucolic site. The result is that we are left with Milton himself as the heir of the poetic descent in the poem.

It is worth considering the import of recognizing Milton as the poetic heir-apparent of the poem. Such a recognition adumbrates the tendency of modern literary generations to repudiate the old, a tendency observed by critics as different as Walter Jackson Bate, Paul de Man, and Harold Bloom. This tendency begins in English literature most convincingly in *Lycidas*. Milton's genealogical dissociation of himself from a family tree of unfulfilled promise, a tree that grows upward from Sidney to King, marks a turning point in the notion of literary descent. On some level, all English poets before Milton were threatened by the possible lack of a poetic genealogy and were therefore necessarily reluctant to repudiate their precursors—indeed, before Milton English poets were much more eager to find and to possess a genealogy than to evade one. Milton, on the other hand, manages to regard the English elegiac tradition—particularly as it is manifested in the line of poems about unfulfilled promise—and the fledgling English poetic genealogy as fixed and intact, a kind of early canon from which he might profitably swerve. He does not struggle to establish a literary past in the same way that his humanist forebears struggled on the Continent or in England. Instead (and in this respect little has changed since that last stanza published in 1638), Milton struggles against his literary past. The result of his struggle was, and always will be, paradoxical: Milton's pretense that he is swerving away from a fixed and intact genealogy serves to establish that genealogy's bona fides. His much-heralded triumphs over his poetic antecedents only more solidly fix those same antecedents as the roots of his, and our, family tree.

Conclusion

We might be justified in saying that, after Milton, English literary genealogy becomes authentic. In the eighteenth century, the dubious roots of the English family tree no longer inspire skepticism or self-repudiation, as they did among poets of the late Elizabethan and the Jacobean periods. After Milton, and in large measure because of Milton's influential acceptance of the poetic genealogy he inherits, English poets get on with the business of overthrowing their predecessors. To a certain extent, the memory of Philip Sidney fades. Important as Sidney's precursor status was to the formation of an English literary tradition that might compete with the Continental traditions, his conceived presence as an originary force is soon forgotten in the official poetic lineage.

In fact, while forging a genealogy of influential precursors, Milton tends to suppress the very concerns that troubled and inspired those same precursors. For example, Milton's Spenser is, in *Paradise Lost* and elsewhere, the legitimate heir of Italian chivalric romance. But the inferences we can draw from Milton's treatment of Spenser, and even from his obvious indebtedness to *The Faerie Queene,* do not include a particularly realistic conception of Spenser's ambivalence concerning the relation of an English Protestant poet to a pagan or popish past. In the late sixteenth century, as we noted earlier, Ascham's warnings against Italianate writing still rang in the ears of aspiring Elizabethan poets, who, given the dearth of a homegrown tradition, turned to Petrarch, Bembo, Castiglione, Ariosto, Tasso, and the Pleiade poets for models of imitation. Founding a comparable English tradition, as worthy of imitation as the Italian that so irritated Ascham, required the establishment of a national literary genealogy from which English poets could legitimately descend. Sidney's death provided an opportunity to canonize an English original. Spenser's effort to establish Sidney as the first precursor of English poetry reflects the peculiarly Elizabethan attitude to national precursors. Poets of that early period could neither reject nor entirely accept their predecessors. They do not enter into what we would now see as a post-Miltonic agon with antecedents. Rather, as we recognize especially in Spenser's "Astrophel," the act of poetic revival is just as important as the act of surpassing or of transumption.

This ambiguous relation to the past is an inheritance of humanism, or even of Dante's proto-humanistic relation to his *latinitas*. We recall that in Canto 1 of the *Inferno* Dante rescues Virgil from the "lungo silenzio" of medieval misreading at the same moment that Virgil rescues Dante from the Beast. That double rescue is characteristic of the major efforts of humanism during the next three hundred years. The humanists' efforts to revive or reassemble the shredded texts of the classical past not only preserved the lost books but also gave the humanists themselves a kind of wholeness by furnishing a lingual, philosophical, and moral continuity with the classical past.

Beginning with Boccaccio, humanist scholars strove to mitigate their imitation of pagan models. They defended their sources in a number of ways, asserting, for instance, that the pagan poets were the first theologians or that the early Hebrews first spoke in formal verse. They sought to prove that the first poetry came into being to praise the gods, and that, therefore, poetry itself was divine. Family trees of poets proliferated during the fifteenth and sixteenth centuries, often charting a literary descent from the fabulous Orpheus or Amphion as conceived precursors (whose writing, like the painting of the ancients, did not exist) through Hesiod, Homer, and Virgil to the Continental vernacular literatures.

In England, because there was no direct lingual connection to Latin, the defense of the vernacular required a particularly imaginative effort to establish a literary genealogy. Moreover, although they were considerably belated, the poets and humanists of the English Renaissance felt the urgency of the double rescue of the classical past as keenly as the Italians or the French. As Spenser's translation of du Bellay in the "Ruines of Rome" shows, a sense of rescue and revival prevailed:

Rome is no more: but if the shade of *Rome*
May of the bodie yeeld a seeming sight,
It's like a corse drawne forth out of the tombe
By Magicke skill out of eternall night:
    The corpes of *Rome* in ashes is entombed,
And her great spirite reioyned to the spirite
Of this great masse, is in the same enwombed;
But her braue writings, which her famous merite
    In spight of time, out of the dust doth reare,
    Doo make her Idole through the world appeare. (Ll. 61–70)

The idolization of Rome, as Spenser here describes it, adumbrates the establishment of Sidney's precursor status. Sidney too is "like a corse drawne forth out of the tombe/By Magicke skill," and Spenser is the chief magician. The "braue writings" of Rome are rescued from the ashes of the tomb and "reioyned" to the spirit of the living population. And, in a similar way, Sidney's writings are rescued and published, and Sidney is established as a genealogical original just as Rome had been revived as the meritorious patriarch of Renaissance civilization.

But, while "the shade of *Rome*" might yield a great spirit, Sidney's shadow was a mixed blessing to later poets. As we saw in the work of Ben Jonson, Sidney was a necessary precursor, an enabling genealogical original, but, like wide trees in a forest, his shadow tended to hinder the growth of the younger trees growing up near him. Jonson begins the swerve from Sidney that Milton is able to complete. But he still needs the conceived presence of Sidney as a poetic original. In "To Penshurst" we encounter Sidney's Arcadian wilderness at the instant of its transformation to ordered society. Placing himself in the scene, Jonson emphasizes the importance of his kind of poetry—and, perhaps, of the professional poet in contrast to the courtly amateur—as a civilizing influence. The Arcadian scene, moreover, reveals a familiar generational conflict, a further example of Jonson's ambivalent relationship to Sidney. The lost world of leisure, like the Elizabethan literary past, is simultaneously the focus of Jonson's nostalgia and the object of his condemnation.

Milton, on the other hand, clearly dissociates himself from the genealogical strain with which Sidney is identified. At the end of *Lycidas,* Milton turns away from the forbidden family tree of unfulfilled promise. The poem's coda seems to foreshadow a new genre and a new poetic resolve, and we might detect in the shaking-off of the swain's sorrow the abandonment of an elegiac strain that leads from Sidney to Prince Henry to Edward King. While Milton may regret the untimely death of King, he seems to celebrate his freedom from the literary line of descent that the pastoral tradition represents in England. Yet, Milton's agonistic posture toward the English literary past somehow provides an imprimatur for the family tree he rejects.

Nevertheless, it is difficult to judge whether English literary genealogy is, finally, bogus or bona fide—or to choose which meaning of the verb *to forge* we should apply. The Elizabethans' swift invention of a national literature was accomplished partly by fraudulence. English literature was parvenu, and like many of the "new men" created by the Heraldic Visitations, it relied on the establishment of the conceived presence of family connections, a poetic father and poetic offspring and even offspring of the off-spring. Although at first the English poetic lineage caused notice-able skepticism even among those who propagated it, Milton's deliberate swerve from that lineage makes its existence difficult to deny. And, as we have seen throughout this study, any literary genealogy that supplies an antecedent from which later poets can either descend or publicly evade descent befuddles even the most assiduous attempts to question bona fides.

SELECTED BIBLIOGRAPHY

Alpers, Paul J. *The Poetry of "The Faerie Queene."* Princeton: Princeton University Press, 1967.
————, ed. *Elizabethan Poetry: Modern Essays in Criticism.* New York: Oxford University Press, 1967.
Ascham, Roger. *The Scholemaster.* Ed. Edward Arber. Boston, 1989.
Attridge, Derek. *Well-Weigh'd Syllables: Elizabethan Verse in Classical Metres.* London: Cambridge University Press, 1974.
Augustine. *On Christian Doctrine.* Trans. D. W. Robertson. New York: Macmillan, 1958.
Austin, Warren B. "Milton's *Lycidas* and Two Latin Elegies by Giles Fletcher, the Elder." *Studies in Philology* 44 (1944), pp. 41–55.
Baker, Stewart A. "Milton's Uncouth Swain." *Milton Studies* 3 (1971), pp. 35–53.
Baker-Smith, Dominic. "Great Expectation: Sidney's Death and the Poets." In Van Dorsten et al., eds., *Sir Philip Sidney: 1586 and the Creation of a Legend,* pp. 83–103.
Barnes, Catherine. "The Hidden Persuader: The Complex Speaking Voice of Sidney's *Defence of Poetry.*" *PMLA* 86 (1971), pp. 422–27.
Barroway, Israel. "The Accentual Theory of Hebrew Prosody: A Further Study in Renaissance Interpretation of Biblical Form." *ELH* 17 (1950), pp. 115–35.
————. "The Bible as Poetry in the English Renaissance: An Introduction." *JEGP* 32 (1933), pp. 447–80.
————. " 'The Lyre of David': A Further Study in Renaissance Interpretation of Biblical Form." *ELH* 8 (1941), pp. 119–42.
Bate, W. J. *The Burden of the Past and the English Poet.* Cambridge, Mass.: Harvard University Press, 1970.
Berger, Harry. "Orpheus, Pan, and the Poetics of Misogyny: Spenser's Critique of Pastoral Love and Art." *ELH* 50 (1985), pp. 27–60.
————. "The Prospect of the Imagination: Spenser and the Limits of Poetry." *SEL* 1 (1961), pp. 93–120.
————. *Revisionary Play: Studies in Spenserian Dynamics.* Berkeley and Los Angeles: University of California Press, 1988.
Berry, Edward. "The Poet as Warrior in Sidney's *Defence of Poetry.*" *SEL* 29 (1989), pp. 21–34.
Binns, J. W. *Intellectual Culture in Elizabethan England: The Latin Writings of the Age.* University of Leeds, England: Francis Cairns, Ltd., 1990.

————, ed. *The Latin Poetry of English Poets*. London: Routledge & Kegan Paul, 1974.

Bloom, Harold. *Agon: Toward a Theory of Revisionism*. New York: Oxford University Press, 1982.

————. *The Anxiety of Influence*. New York: Oxford University Press, 1973.

————. *A Map of Misreading*. New York: Oxford University Press, 1975.

————. *Ruin the Sacred Truths*. Cambridge: Harvard University Press, 1989.

————, ed. *Edmund Spenser*. New York: Chelsea House Publishers, 1986.

Boccaccio, Giovanni. *Boccaccio on Poetry*. Trans. Charles Osgood. Princeton: Princeton University Press, 1930.

————. *Genealogie Deorum Gentilium Libri*. Ed. Vincenzo Romano. Bari: Gius. Laterza & Figli, 1951.

Bond, William H. "The Epitaph of Sir Philip Sidney." *MLN* 58 (1943), pp. 253–57.

Bradshaw, Graham. "Three Poems Ben Jonson Did Not Write: A Note on Jonson's Christian Humanism." *ELH* 47 (1980), pp. 484–99.

Brennan, Michael. *Literary Patronage in the English Renaissance: The Pembroke Family*. London and New York: Routledge, 1988.

Butler, Samuel. *Hudibras, with Dr. Grey's Annotations*. London, 1819.

Buxton, John. "The Mourning for Sidney." *Renaissance Studies* 3 (1989), pp. 46–56.

————. *Sir Philip Sidney and the English Renaissance*. New York: St. Martin's Press, 1965.

Calderisi, Raffaele. *Antonio Sebastiano Minturno: Poeta e Trattatista de Cinquecento Dimenticato*. Aversa, 1921.

Cassirer, Ernst. *The Individual and the Cosmos in Renaissance Philosophy*. Trans. Mario Domandi. Philadelphia: University of Pennsylvania Press, 1977.

Cheney, Donald. *Spenser's Image of Nature: Wild Man and Shepherd in 'The Faerie Queene.'* New Haven and London: Yale University Press, 1966.

Colaianne, A. J., and W. L. Godshalk, eds. *Elegies for Sir Philip Sidney*. Delmar, N.Y.: Scholars' Facsimiles and Reprints, 1980.

Colie, Rosalie. *The Resources of Kind: Genre Theory in the Renaissance*. Ed. Barbara K. Lewalski. Berkeley: University of California Press, 1973.

Davies, John. *The Poems of Sir John Davies*. Ed. Robert Krueger. Oxford: Clarendon Press, 1975.

Davison, Francis. *A Poetical Rhapsody*. Ed. H. E. Rollins. 2 vols. Cambridge, Mass.: Harvard University Press, 1931.

Day, J. F. R. "Primers of Honor: Heraldry, Heraldry Books, and English Renaissance Literature." *Sixteenth Century Journal* 21 (1990), pp. 93–103.

————. "Venal Heralds and Mushroom Gentlemen: Seventeenth Century Character Books and the Sale of Honor." Ph.D. diss., Duke University, 1985.

de Man, Paul. *Blindness and Insight*. Minneapolis: University of Minnesota Press, 1983.

Donaldson, Ian. "Jonson and Anger." In Rawson, ed., *English Satire and the Satiric Tradition*, pp. 56–71.

————, ed. *Jonson and Shakespeare*. Atlantic Highlands, N.J.: Humanities Press, 1983.

Donoghue, Denis. "Attitudes Toward History: A Preface to *The Sense of the Past.*" *Salmagundi* 68–69 (1985–86), pp. 107–24.

Dryden, John. *Of Dramatic Poesy and Other Critical Essays*. 2 vols. Ed. George Watson. London: J. M. Dent & Sons, 1962.

Du Bartas, Guillaume de Salluste Sieur. *The Works*. 3 vols. Ed. Urban Tigner Holmes, Jr., John Coriden Lyons, and Robert White Linker. Chapel Hill: University of North Carolina Press, 1940.

Duncan-Jones, Katherine. *Sir Philip Sidney, Courtier Poet*. New Haven: Yale University Press, 1991.

Edmonds, J. M., trans. *The Greek Bucolic Poets*. Cambridge, Mass.: The Loeb Classical Library, Harvard University Press, 1938.

Eliot, T. S. *Selected Prose of T. S. Eliot*. Ed. Frank Kermode. New York: Harcourt Brace Jovanovich, 1975.

Elledge, Scott. *Milton's 'Lycidas': An Introduction to Criticism*. New York: Harper & Row, 1966.

Elsky, Martin. *Authorizing Words: Speech, Writing, and Print in the English Renaissance*. Ithaca, N.Y.: Cornell University Press, 1989.

Elyot, Thomas. *The Book Named the Governor*. Ed. S. E. Lehmberg. New York: Dutton, 1962.

Esplin, Ross Stolworthy. "The Emerging Legend of Sir Philip Sidney, 1586–1652." Ph.D. diss., University of Utah, 1970.

Ettin, Andrew V. "The Georgics in *The Faerie Queene*." *Spenser Studies* 3 (1982), pp. 57–71.

Evans, Robert C. *Ben Jonson and the Poetics of Patronage*. Lewisburg, Penn.: Bucknell University Press, 1989.

Ferne, John. *The Blazon of Gentrie*. London, 1586.

Fish, Stanley. "Authors-Readers: Jonson's Community of the Same." *Representations* 7 (1984), pp. 26–58.

————. "*Lycidas:* A Poem Finally Anonymous." In C. A. Patrides, ed., *Milton's 'Lycidas': The Tradition and the Poem*, pp. 319–40.

Foucault, Michel. *Language, Counter-Memory, Practice: Selected Essays and Interviews*. Ed. Donald F. Bouchard. Trans. Donald F. Bouchard and Sherry Simon. Ithaca, N.Y.: Cornell University Press, 1977.

Fowler, Alastair. "The 'Better Marks' of Jonson's 'To Penshurst.'" *Review of English Studies*, n.s., 24 (1973), pp. 266–82.

————. "Spenser's Names." In Logan and Teskey, eds., *Unfolded Tales: Essays on Renaissance Romance*, pp. 32–48.

Fraser, Russell. *The War against Poetry*. Princeton: Princeton University Press, 1970.

Freehafer, John. "Leonard Digges, Ben Jonson, and the Beginning of Shakespeare Idolatry." *Shakespeare Quarterly* 21 (1970), pp. 63–75.

Freud, Sigmund. *Totem and Taboo*. Trans. James Strachey. New York: W. W. Norton, 1950.

SELECTED BIBLIOGRAPHY

Friedberg, Harris. "Ben Jonson's Poetry: Pastoral, Georgic, Epigram." *ELR* 4 (1974), pp. 111–36.
Friedman, Donald M. *"Lycidas:* The Swain's Paideia." *Milton Studies* 3 (1971), pp. 3–34.
Galloway, David, ed. *Elizabethan Theatre II.* Hamden, Conn.: Archon Books, 1970.
Golding, Arthur. *Shakespeare's Ovid: Being Arthur Golding's Translation of the Metamorphoses.* Ed. W. H. D. Rouse. Carbondale: Southern Illinois University Press, 1961.
Gosson, Stephen. *The Schoole of Abuse.* In Arthur F. Kinney, ed., *Markets of Bawdrie.*
Greenblatt, Stephen. *Renaissance Self-Fashioning: More to Shakespeare.* Chicago: University of Chicago Press, 1980.
Greene, Thomas. "Ben Jonson and the Centered Self." *SEL* 10 (1970), pp. 325–48.
———. *The Light in Troy: Imitation and Discovery in Renaissance Poetry.* New Haven: Yale University Press, 1982.
Greenslade, S. L., ed. *The Cambridge History of the Bible: The West from the Reformation to the Present Day.* Cambridge: Cambridge University Press, 1963.
Gregory, E. R. *Milton and the Muses.* Tuscaloosa: University of Alabama Press, 1989.
Greville, Fulke. *The Life of the Renowned Sr Philip Sidney.* Delmar, N.Y.: Scholars' Facsimiles and Reprints, 1984.
Guillory, John. *Poetic Authority: Spenser, Milton, and Literary History.* New York: Columbia University Press, 1983.
Hager, Alan. "The Exemplary Mirage: Fabrication of Sir Philip Sidney's Biographical Image and the Sidney Reader." *ELH* 48 (1981), pp. 1–16.
Hales, J. W. "The Name Lycidas." *Folia Literaria.* New York, 1893.
Hamilton, A. C. *Sir Philip Sidney: A Study of His Life and Works.* Cambridge: Cambridge University Press, 1977.
Hanford, James Holly. "The Pastoral Elegy and *Lycidas.*" In C. A. Patrides, ed., *Milton's 'Lycidas': The Tradition and the Poem,* pp. 31–59.
Hardison, O. B. *Prosody and Purpose in the English Renaissance.* Baltimore and London: Johns Hopkins University Press, 1989.
———. "Two Voices of Sidney's *Apology.*" In Arthur F. Kinney, ed., *Sidney in Retrospect,* pp. 45–61.
Harrison, T. P. "Spenser, Ronsard, and Bion." *Modern Language Notes* 49 (1934), pp. 139–45.
Helgerson, Richard. *The Elizabethan Prodigals.* Berkeley: University of California Press, 1976.
———. *Self-Crowned Laureates: Spenser, Jonson, Milton and the Literary System.* Berkeley: University of California Press, 1983.
Herodotus. *The Histories.* Trans. Aubrey de Sélincourt. Harmondsworth, England: Penguin Books, 1987.
Herrick, Marvin T. *The Fusion of Horation and Aristotelian Literary Criticism, 1531–1555.* Illinois Studies in Language and Literature. Champaign: University of Illinois Press, 1946.

214

Hibbard, G. R. "The Country House Poem of the Seventeenth Century." *JWCI* 19 (1956), pp. 159–74.

———, ed. *Elizabethan Theatre IV.* Hamden, Conn.: Archon Books, 1974.

Hollander, John. *The Untuning of the Sky.* Princeton: Princeton University Press, 1961. Reprint. New York: W. W. Norton, 1971.

Holstun, James. "Ranting at the New Historicism." *ELR* 19 (1989), pp. 189–225.

Horace. *Ars Poetica.* Trans. H. Rushton Fairclough. Loeb Classical Library. Cambridge, Mass.: Harvard University Press; London: William Heinemann, 1978.

Hunt, Edmund. "*Laudatores Temporis Acti.*" *Classical Journal* 40 (1945), pp. 221–33.

Javitch, Daniel. "The Impure Motives of Elizabethan Poetry." *Genre* 15 (1982), pp. 225–38.

———. *Poetry and Courtliness in Renaissance England.* Princeton: Princeton University Press, 1978.

Jonson, Ben. *Ben Jonson.* 11 vols. Ed. C. H. Herford, Percy Simpson, and Evelyn Simpson. Oxford: Clarendon Press, 1947.

Junius, Franciscus. *The Painting of the Ancients.* Westmead, England: Gregg International Publishers, 1972.

Kay, Dennis. *Melodious Tears: The English Funeral Elegy from Spenser to Milton.* Oxford: Clarendon Press, 1990.

Kerrigan, William, and Gordon Braden. *The Idea of the Renaissance.* Baltimore: Johns Hopkins University Press, 1989.

King, John N. *English Reformation Literature: The Tudor Origins of the Protestant Tradition.* Princeton: Princeton University Press, 1982.

Kinney, Arthur F. *Markets of Bawdrie: The Dramatic Criticism of Stephen Gosson.* Salzburg, Austria: Institut für Englische Sprache un Literatur, Universität Salzburg, 1974.

———, ed. *Essential Essays for the Study of Sir Philip Sidney.* Hamden, Conn.: Archon Books, 1986.

———, ed. *Sidney in Retrospect.* Amherst: University of Massachusetts Press, 1988.

Lambert, Ellen Zetzel. *Placing Sorrow: A Study of the Pastoral Elegy Convention from Theocritus to Milton.* Chapel Hill: University of North Carolina Press, 1976.

Lanham, Richard A. *A Handlist of Rhetorical Terms.* Berkeley: University of California Press, 1969.

———. "Sidney: The Ornament of His Age." *Southern Review* (Australia) 2:4(1967), pp. 319–40.

Le Comte, Edward. *Yet Once More: Verbal and Psychological Pattern in Milton.* New York: Liberal Arts Press, 1953.

Lee, Rensselaer. *Names on Trees: Ariosto into Art.* Princeton: Princeton University Press, 1977.

Lewis, C. S. *The Allegory of Love: A Study in Medieval Tradition.* New York: Oxford University Press, 1958.

———. *English Literature in the Sixteenth Century, Excluding Drama.* Oxford: Clarendon Press, 1954.

———. *Spenser's Images of Life.* Edited by Alastair Fowler. Cambridge: Cambridge University Press, 1967.

Lloyd, Michael. "*Justa Edouardo King.*" *Notes and Queries* (October 1958), pp. 432–34.

Loades, David. *The Tudor Court.* Totowa, N.J.: Barnes and Noble Books, 1987.

Logan, George, and Gordon Teskey, eds. *Unfolded Tales: Essays on Renaissance Romance.* Ithaca, N.Y.: Cornell University Press, 1989.

Lotspeich, Henry G. *Classical Mythology in the Poetry of Edmund Spenser.* Princeton: Princeton University Press, 1932.

Low, Anthony. *The Georgic Revolution.* Princeton: Princeton University Press, 1985.

———. "The Image of the Tower in *Paradise Lost.*" *SEL* 10 (1970), pp. 171–81.

———. "Some Notes on *Lycidas* and the *Aeneid.*" *English Language Notes* 13 (March 1976), pp. 175–77.

McClung, William. *The Country House in English Renaissance Poetry.* Berkeley: University of California Press, 1977.

———. "Jonson's 'To Penshurst,' 1–5, 99–102." *Explicator* 33 (May 1975), Item 78.

McCoy, Richard. *Sir Philip Sidney: Rebellion in Arcadia.* New Brunswick, N.J.: Rutgers University Press, 1979.

McDonald, Russ. *Shakespeare and Jonson, Jonson and Shakespeare.* Lincoln: University of Nebraska Press, 1988.

Major, John M. *Sir Thomas Elyot and Renaissance Humanism.* Lincoln: University of Nebraska Press, 1964.

Marotti, Arthur F. " 'Love is not love': Elizabethan Sonnet Sequences and the Social Order." *ELH* 49 (1982), pp. 396–428.

Miller, Edwin Haviland. *The Professional Writer in Elizabethan England.* Cambridge, Mass.: Harvard University Press, 1959.

Milton, John. *John Milton: The Complete Poetry and Major Prose.* Ed. Merritt Y. Hughes. New York: Odyssey Press, 1957.

Minturno, Antonio. *L'Arte Poetica.* Muzio: Naples, 1725.

Miskimin, Alice. *The Renaissance Chaucer.* New Haven: Yale University Press, 1975.

Moffett, Thomas. *Nobilis.* Ed. and trans. Virgil B. Heltzel and Hoyt H. Hudson. San Marino, Calif.: The Huntington Library, 1940.

Montrose, Louis Adrian. "Celebration and Insinuation: Sir Philip Sidney and the Motives of Elizabethan Courtship." *Renaissance Drama,* n.s., 8 (1977), pp. 3–35.

———. "The Elizabethan Subject and the Spenserian Text." In Parker and Quint, eds., *Literary Theory/Renaissance Texts,* pp. 303–40.

———. "Of Gentlemen and Shepherds: The Politics of Elizabethan Pastoral Form." *ELH* 50 (1983), pp. 415–59.

———. " 'The perfecte patterne of a Poete': The Poetics of Courtship in *The Shepheardes Calender.*" *TSLL* 21 (1979), pp. 34–67.

Musgrove, S. *Shakespeare and Jonson*. Folcroft, Penn.: Folcroft Press, 1957.

Nenna, Giovanni Battista. *Nennio, or a Treatise on Nobility*. Trans. William Jones (1595). Introduction Alice Shalvi. Jerusalem: Israel Universities Press; London: H. A. Humphrey Ltd., 1967.

Norbrook, David. *Poetry and Politics in the English Renaissance*. London: Routledge, Kegan Paul, 1984.

Norlin. G. "The Conventions of the Pastoral Elegy." *American Journal of Philology* 32 (1911), pp. 294–312.

North, Helen. *Sophrosyne: Self-Knowledge and Self-Restraint in Greek Literature*. Ithaca, N.Y.: Cornell University Press, 1966.

Ovid. *Metamorphoses*. 2 vols. Trans. Frank Justus Miller. Loeb Classical Library. Cambridge, Mass.: Harvard University Press, 1916. Reprint 1984.

Panofsky, Erwin. *Meaning in the Visual Arts*. Garden City, N.Y.: Doubleday, 1955.

———. *Studies in Iconology*. 1939. Reprint. New York: Harper, Row, 1962.

Parker, Patricia. *Inescapable Romance: Studies in the Poetics of a Mode*. Princeton: Princeton University Press, 1978.

Parker, Patricia, and David Quint, eds. *Literary Theory/Renaissance Texts*. Baltimore: Johns Hopkins University Press, 1986.

Parry, Graham. *The Golden Age Restor'd: The Culture of the Stuart Court, 1603–42*. Manchester, England: Manchester University Press, 1981.

Partridge, E. B. "Jonson's Large and Unique View of Life." In G. R. Hibbard, ed., *Elizabethan Theatre IV*, pp. 143–67.

Patrides, C. A., ed. *Milton's 'Lycidas': The Tradition and the Poem*. Columbia: University of Missouri Press, 1983.

Patterson, Annabel. *Pastoral and Ideology: Virgil to Valéry*. Berkeley: University of California Press, 1987.

Patterson, Lee. "On the Margin: Postmodernism, Ironic History, and Medieval Studies." *Speculum* 65 (1990), pp. 87–108.

Pears, S. A., trans. *The Correspondence of Sir Philip Sidney and Hubert Languet*. London, 1845. Reprint Westmead, England,: Gregg International, 1971.

Pecheux, Mother Mary Christopher. "The Dread Voice in *Lycidas*." *Milton Studies* 9 (1976), pp. 221–41.

Peterson, Richard S. *Imitation and Praise in the Poems of Ben Jonson*. New Haven: Yale University Press, 1981.

Pigman, G. W., III. *Grief and English Renaissance Elegy*. Cambridge: Cambridge University Press, 1985.

———. "Versions of Imitation in the Renaissance." *Renaissance Quarterly* 33 (1980), pp. 1–32.

Potts, L. J. "Ben Jonson and the Seventeenth Century." *Essays and Studies*, n.s., 2 (1949), pp. 7–24.

Prescott, Anne Lake. *French Poets and the English Renaissance: Studies in Fame and Transformation*. New Haven and London: Yale University Press, 1978.

Puttenham, George. *The Arte of English Poesie*. Menston, England: The Scolar Press Limited, 1968.

Quint, David. *Origin and Originality in Renaissance Literature: Versions of the Source*. New Haven: Yale University Press, 1983.

Rainolds, John. *Oratio in laudem artis poeticae*. Trans. Walter Allen, Jr. Princeton: Princeton University Press, 1940.

Rathmell, J. C. A. "Jonson, Lord Lisle, and Penshurst." *ELR* 1 (1971), pp. 250–60.

Rawson, Claude, ed. *English Satire and the Satiric Tradition*. Oxford: Basil Blackwell, 1984.

Richmond, Hugh M. *The Christian Revolutionary: John Milton*. Berkeley and Los Angeles: University of California Press, 1974.

Riggs, David. *Ben Jonson: A Life*. Cambridge, Mass.: Harvard University Press, 1989.

Ringler, W. A. "Sir Philip Sidney: The Myth and the Man." In Van Dorsten et al., eds., *Sir Philip Sidney: 1586 and the Creation of a Legend*, pp. 3–15.

Robey, D. J. B. "Virgil's Statue at Mantua and the Defense of Poetry: An Unpublished Letter of 1397." *Rinascimento* 9 (1969), pp. 183–203.

Rollins, Hyder Edward, ed. *Brittons Bowre of Delights*. New York: Russell & Russell, 1968.

Ronsard, Pierre de. *Abbrege de L'Art Poetique François*. Geneva: Slatkine Reprints, 1972.

Rose, Mark. *Heroic Love: Studies in Sidney and Spenser*. Cambridge, Mass.: Harvard University Press, 1968.

Sacks, Peter. *The English Elegy: Studies in the Genre from Spenser to Yeats*. Baltimore: Johns Hopkins University Press, 1985.

Salutati, Coluccio. *Letter to Peregrino Zambeccari*. Trans. Ronald G. Witt. Ed. Benjamin G. Kohl and Ronald G. Witt, with Elizabeth B. Welles. Philadelphia: University of Pennsylvania Press, 1978.

Sandys, Sir John E. "The Literary Sources of Milton's *Lycidas*." *Transactions of the Royal Society of Literature*, ser. 2, 32 (1914), pp. 233–64.

Schoell, Franck L. "Les Mythologistes Italiens de la Renaissance et la Poesie Elisabethaine." *Revue de Litterature Comparative* (1924), pp. 1–24.

Schoenbaum, S. "The Humorous Jonson." In G. R. Hibbard, ed., *Elizabethan Theatre IV*, pp. 1–21.

———. "Shakespeare and Jonson: Fact and Myth." In David Galloway, ed., *Elizabethan Theatre II*, pp. 1–19.

Scodel, Joshua. *The English Poetic Epitaph: Commemoration and Conflict from Jonson to Wordsworth*. Ithaca and London: Cornell University Press, 1991.

Sessions, William. "Spenser's Georgic." *ELR* 10 (1980), pp. 202–38.

Shafer, Robert. "Spenser's *Astrophel*." *Modern Language Notes* 28 (1913), pp. 224–26.

Sidney, Sir Philip. *An Apology for Poetry*. Ed. Geoffrey Shepherd. London: Nelson, 1965.

———. *Miscellaneous Prose of Sir Philip Sidney*. Ed. Katherine Duncan-Jones and Jan Van Dorsten. Oxford: Clarendon Press, 1973.

———. *The Poems of Sir Philip Sidney*. Ed. William A. Ringler, Jr. Oxford: Clarendon Press, 1962.

Skelton, John. *The Complete English Poems*. Ed. John Scattergood. New Haven: Yale University Press, 1983.

Smith, G. Gregory, ed. *Elizabethan Critical Essays.* 2 vols. London: Oxford University Press, 1904.

Sollors, Werner. *Beyond Ethnicity: Consent and Descent in American Culture.* New York: Oxford University Press, 1986.

Spaeth, Sigmund. *Milton's Knowledge of Music.* Princeton: Princeton University Library, 1913.

Spencer, T. J. B. "Ben Jonson on his beloved, The Author Mr. William Shakespeare." In G. R. Hibbard, ed., *Elizabethan Theatre IV,* pp. 22–40.

Spenser, Edmund. *Poetical Works.* Ed. J. C. Smith and E. de Sélincourt. Oxford: Oxford University Press, 1912.

———. *The Works of Edmund Spenser.* Ed. Edwin Greenlaw, C. G. Osgood, F. M. Padelford, and Ray Heffner. A Variorum edition, 9 vols. Baltimore: Johns Hopkins University Press, 1932–49.

Steadman, John M. *Milton and the Paradoxes of Renaissance Heroism.* Baton Rouge: Louisiana State University Press, 1987.

Stein, Arnold. *The Art of Presence: The Poet and 'Paradise Lost.'* Berkeley and Los Angeles: University of California Press, 1977.

Stewart, Stanley. "Milton Revises *The Readie and Easie Way.*" *Milton Studies* 20 (1984), pp. 205–24.

Stone, Lawrence. *The Crisis of the Aristocracy.* Oxford: Clarendon Press, 1965.

Stubbes, Phillip. *The Anatomie of Abuses.* New York: Garland Publishing, 1973.

Swift, Carolyn Ruth. "Feminine Self-Definition in Lady Mary Wroth's *Love's Victorie* (c. 1621)." *ELR* 19 (1989), pp. 171–88.

Sylvester, Joshua, trans. *The Divine Weeks and Works of Guillaume de Saluste Sieur Du Bartas.* Ed. Susan Snyder. Oxford: Clarendon Press, 1979.

Tasso, Torquato. *Prose.* Ed. Ettore Mazzali. Milan: Riccardo Ricciardi, 1959.

Tayler, Edward W. "*Lycidas* in Christian Time." In C. A. Patrides, ed., *Milton's 'Lycidas': The Tradition and the Poem,* pp. 303–18.

———. *Nature and Art in Renaissance Literature.* New York: Columbia University Press, 1961.

Thompson, John. *The Founding of English Meter.* New York: Columbia University Press, 1961.

Thynne, Francis. *Animadversions uppon the Annotacions and Corrections of some Imperfections of Impressiones of Chaucers Workes (sett downe before tyme and nowe) reprinted in the yere of oure Lorde 1598.* Ed. F. J. Furnivall. London: Kegan Paul, Trench, Trübner and Co., 1875.

Turk, David F. "Joint Heirs of Christ: John Milton and the Revolutionary Sons of God." Ph.D. diss., New York University, 1989.

Turner, Alberta T. "Milton and the Convention of the Academic Miscellanies." *Yearbook of English Studies* 5 (1975), pp. 86–93.

Tuve, Rosemond. *Images and Themes in Five Poems by Milton.* Cambridge, Mass.: Harvard University Press, 1962.

Tylus, Jane. "Spenser, Virgil, and the Politics of Poetic Labor." *ELH* 55 (1988), pp. 53–77.

Tyndale, William. *The Work of William Tyndale.* Ed. G. E. Duffield. Appleford, England: The Sutton Courtenay Press, 1964.

Van den Berg, Sara. *The Action of Ben Jonson's Poetry.* Newark: University of Delaware Press, 1987.

Van Dorsten, Jan, Dominic Baker-Smith, Arthur F. Kinney, eds. *Sir Philip Sidney: 1586 and the Creation of a Legend.* Leiden: E. J. Brill/Leiden University Press, 1986.

Virgil. *The Aeneid of Virgil.* Ed. R. D. Williams. 2 vols. New York: St. Martin's Press, 1972

———. *Eclogues.* Trans. Guy Lee. Harmondsworth, England: Penguin Books, 1980.

———. *Opera.* Ed. R. A. B. Mynors. Oxford: Clarendon Press, 1969.

Wagner, Anthony. *Heralds and Ancestors.* British Museum Publications, 1978.

———. *Pedigree and Progress: Essays in the Genealogical Interpretation of History.* London: Phillimore, 1975.

Walker, D. P. *The Ancient Theology: Studies in Christian Platonism from the Fifteenth to the Eighteenth Century.* Ithaca, N.Y.: Cornell University Press, 1972.

Walker, Ralph S. "Ben Jonson's Lyric Poetry." In *The Criterion, 1922–1939,* edited by T. S. Eliot. Vol. 13, pp. 431–48. London: Faber and Faber, 1967.

Wallerstein, Ruth. *Studies in Seventeenth-Century Poetic.* Madison: University of Wisconsin Press, 1950.

Wayne, Don E. "Jonson's Sidney: Legacy and Legitimation in *The Forrest.*" In *Sir Philip Sidney's Achievements,* ed. M. J. B. Allen, Dominic Baker-Smith, and Arthur F. Kinney, with Margaret M. Sullivan. New York: AMS Press, 1990.

———. *Penshurst: The Semiotics of Place and the Poetics of History.* Madison: University of Wisconsin Press, 1984.

Webber, Joan Malory. *Milton and His Epic Tradition.* Seattle: University of Washington Press, 1979.

Weinberg, Bernard. *A History of Literary Criticism in the Italian Renaissance.* 2 vols. Chicago: University of Chicago Press, 1961.

———. "The Poetic Theories of Minturno." *Studies in Honor of Frederick W. Shipley.* St. Louis: Washington University Studies in Language and Literature, n.s., 14, 1942.

———, ed. *Trattati di Poetica e Retorica del Cinque-cento.* 4 vols. Bari: Gius. Latuza + Figli, 1970.

Weisinger, Herbert. "The Renaissance Theory of the Reaction against the Middle Ages as a Cause of the Renaissance." *Speculum* 20 (1945), pp. 461–67.

———. "The Self-Awareness of the Renaissance as a Criterion of the Renaissance." *Papers of the Michigan Academy of Science, Arts, and Letters* 29 (1943), pp. 561–67.

Wiggins, Peter DeSa. "Spenser's Anxiety." *Modern Language Notes* 103 (January 1988), pp. 75–86.

Wilson, Elkin Calhoun. *Prince Henry and English Literature.* Ithaca. N.Y.: Cornell University Press, 1946.

Wilson, Gayle Edward. "Jonson's Use of the Bible and the Great Chain of Being in 'To Penshurst.'" *SEL* 8 (1968), pp. 77–89.

Wilson, J. Dover. "Ben Jonson and *Julius Caesar.*" *Shakespeare Survey* 2 (1947), pp. 36–43.

Wittreich, Joseph Anthony. "From Pastoral to Prophecy: The Genres of *Lycidas.*" *Milton Studies* 13 (1979), pp. 59–81.

Wright, Herbert G. *Boccaccio in England, from Chaucer to Tennyson.* London: University of London, 1957.

INDEX